The Rise of Christianity

Recent Titles in Crossroads in World History

The Enlightenment: History, Documents, and Key Questions
William E. Burns

The Rise of Christianity

HISTORY, DOCUMENTS, AND KEY QUESTIONS

Kevin W. Kaatz

Crossroads in World History

An Imprint of ABC-CLIO, LLC
Santa Barbara, California • Denver, Colorado

Library of Congress Cataloging-in-Publication Data

Kaatz, Kevin.
    The rise of Christianity : history, documents, and key questions / Kevin W. Kaatz.
        pages cm.—(Crossroads in world history)
    Includes bibliographical references and index.
    ISBN 978-1-61069-807-8 (alk. paper)—ISBN 978-1-61069-808-5 (ebook) 1. Church history. I. Title.
    BR150.R57 2016
    270.1—dc23   2015029343

ISBN: 978-1-61069-807-8
EISBN: 978-1-61069-808-5

20 19 18 17 16   1 2 3 4 5

This book is also available on the World Wide Web as an eBook.
Visit www.abc-clio.com for details.

ABC-CLIO
An Imprint of ABC-CLIO, LLC

ABC-CLIO, LLC
130 Cremona Drive, P.O. Box 1911
Santa Barbara, California 93116-1911

This book is printed on acid-free paper ∞
Manufactured in the United States of America

To Doug and Elizabeth,
And to my Dad, Warren.

Contents

Alphabetical List of Entries

Topical List of Entries

OBJECTS

Catacombs
Earliest Fragment of the New Testament
The Pilate Inscription

PLACES

Jerusalem
Qumran

IDEAS

Apostolic Succession
Christology
Dating
Ecclesiology

INDIVIDUALS

Ambrose
Athanasius
Augustine
Constantine I
Diocletian
Eusebius of Caesarea

How to Use This Book

Throughout the course of history various events have forever changed the world. Some, like the assassination of Julius Caesar, happened centuries ago and took place quickly. Others, such as the rise of Christianity or the Enlightenment, occurred over an extended period of time and reshaped worldviews. These pivotal events, or crossroads, were departures from the established social order and pointed to new directions and opportunities. The paths leading to these crossroads in world history were often circuitous, and the routes branching off from them led to developments both anticipated and unexpected. This series helps students understand the causes and consequences of these historical turning points.

Each book in this series explores a particular crossroad in world history. Some of these events are from the ancient world and continue to reverberate today through our various political, cultural, and social institutions; others are from the modern era and have markedly changed society through their immediacy and the force of technology. While the books help students discover what happened, they also help readers understand the causes and effects linked to each event.

Each volume in the series begins with a timeline charting the essential elements of the event in capsule form. An overview essay comes next, providing a narrative history of what happened. This is followed by approximately 50 alphabetically arranged reference entries on people, places, themes, movements, and other topics central to an understanding of the historical crossroad. These entries provide essential information about their topics and close with cross-references and suggestions for further reading. A selection of 10 to 15 primary source documents follows the reference entries. Each document is accompanied by an introductory paragraph discussing the background and significance of the text. Because of their critical nature, the events covered in these volumes have generated a wide range of opinions and arguments. A section of original essays presents responses to key questions concerning the events, with each essay writer offering a different perspective on a particular topic. An annotated bibliography of print and electronic resources concludes the volume. Users can locate specific information through an alphabetical list of entries and a list of entries grouped in topical categories, as well as through a detailed index.

The various elements of each book are designed to work together to promote greater understanding of a crossroad in world history. The timeline and introductory essay overview the event, the reference entries offer easy access to essential information about key topics, the primary source documents give students firsthand accounts of the historical event, and the original argumentative essays encourage students to consider different views related to the events and to appreciate the complex nature of world history. Through its combination of background material, primary source documents, and argumentative essays, the series helps students gain insight into historical causation as they learn about the pivotal events that changed the course of history.

Preface

This book is about the history of Christianity, directed towards high school, first/second-year college students, or really anyone interested in this important historical period. It is designed to be a reference book highlighting some of the important events, people, ideas, and writings from early Christianity. It covers many topics from Jesus, some of the Roman emperors who were somehow involved in Christianity, up through some of the important Christian theologians and teachers in the 300s. The scope of the book stretches from before Christianity became a religion up until the end of the fourth century. This is considered to be the time period called "Early Christianity" (at least the period after Jesus was born). It is a pivotal epoch in Christianity since this is when many of its writings (especially the New Testament) and theology were set for future generations. It is also the time when Christianity began to spread through the Roman Empire and beyond. Finally, it is a time when Christians went from being a persecuted minority to becoming the leading political and ecclesiastical power in the 300s with the rise of Constantine I, the first Christian emperor.

The book is organized into seven major parts. The first is a timeline that highlights some of the important periods and people in early Christianity. The second part is a historical overview of Christianity, from its beginnings in Judea up through the end of the fourth century with the cementing of Christianity as the only legally recognized religion of the Roman Empire. The third part consists of a number of different topics, arranged alphabetically, on subjects related to early Christianity. These entries range from "Dating" to "Women in Early Christianity," "Pharisees," "Diocletian," and so on. While this book cannot cover every single aspect and person involved in early Christianity, it is hoped that these topics will guide readers to a better understanding of what happened 2,000 years ago.

The fourth part of the book consists of excerpts of 12 primary texts or documents written in early Christianity. Each primary text comes with a short introduction, followed by the document itself. They were chosen to highlight important periods in the development of Christianity, and once again they stretch from the New Testament up through the end of the fourth century. The fifth part of the book contains six essays written by scholars in the field of early Christianity or by scholars who have an active interest in the topic. Two scholars wrote about why Christians were persecuted; two scholars wrote about how Christianity spread so quickly; and the last two scholars wrote about why Christianity was so popular. Each author has a particular viewpoint on the question. The sixth part consists of a select annotated bibliography of books, journal articles, and a few Web sites that allow the reader to get more information on the topic of early Christianity. The last section of the book is a general subject index.

You will find a number of quotes from primary texts (the original writing from the early Christians), including quotes from the New Testament. These are taken from the New Revised Standard Version Bible (NRSV, copyright 1989, Division of Christian Education of the National Council of the Churches of Christ in the United States of America. Used by permission. All rights reserved).

Timeline

587 BCE	The Neo-Babylonian king Nebuchadnezzar II destroys the First Jewish Temple and takes many high-ranking Jewish families to Babylon.
332 BCE	Alexander the Great, the Macedonian king, arrives in Syria and the Levant, conquers it, and adds it to his growing kingdom. He then conquers Egypt.
167 BCE to 160 BCE	During this period the Jewish population revolts against its Greek king Antiochus IV Epiphanes when he tried to prevent them from practicing their religion.
150 BCE to 68 CE	The caves at Qumran begin to be used for storage and safe-keeping of religious material.
73 BCE to 4 BCE	Herod is born in 73 BCE and is appointed king of Judea in 39 BCE. King Herod is most famous for the story found in the Bible about him ordering the killing of all Jewish children younger than two years old in the hope of murdering the infant Jesus.
63 BCE	Judea becomes a Roman province when the Roman military leader Pompey the Great besieges Jerusalem.
30 BCE to 14 CE	Augustus, the first Roman emperor, is the sole ruler of Roman territory, starting in 30 BCE. Augustus is known for ending the numerous civil wars that took place in the first century BCE.
4 BCE	We aren't sure of the exact date of the birth of Jesus, but he was alive during the time of Herod the Great, who died in 4 BCE. Tradition has it that he was born in year 1 CE.

26 CE to 36 CE	Pontius Pilate is appointed the governor of Judea during this period. He is most famous for ordering the crucifixion of Jesus.
30 CE to 33 CE	Like the date of his death, we aren't sure when Jesus was crucified, but it probably happened sometime between 30 and 33 CE, during the governorship of Pontius Pilate.
50 CE	Paul writes 1 Thessalonians, the very first text of the New Testament.
60s CE	The birth year of Paul the apostle is not known, nor is the date of his death. Tradition places his death during the middle of the 60s CE.
60s CE	The first Gospel, Mark, is written at some point in the 60s CE.
64 CE	A large fire in Rome destroys many of its precincts. Emperor Nero blames the Christians for starting the fire and proceeds to torture many of them to death.
66 CE to 73 CE	The Jewish War begins. The Jewish population rises up against its Roman overlords. The Romans fight back and eventually win, kicking out the Jewish and Christian population from the city of Jerusalem.
69 CE to 79 CE	Vespasian rules as the Roman emperor. Roman troops under the command of Vespasian in 67 CE are sent to control Judea when the Jewish War breaks out.
70 CE	When Vespasian becomes emperor, he sends in his son Titus to finish the work of subduing Judea. In the process Titus is responsible for destroying the Jewish Second Temple.
73 or 74 CE	The Jewish fortress of Masada is taken by the Romans. It is the last Jewish stronghold in the Jewish War.
79 CE to 81 CE	General Titus becomes Emperor Titus when his father Vespasian dies. The Romans build a triumphal arch in honor of him conquering Judea.
81 CE to 96 CE	Domitian is crowned emperor. It is believed that the Christians were persecuted during this period.
Early 100s CE	Ignatius, the bishop of Antioch, is arrested and taken from Antioch to Rome because he is a Christian. Ignatius is famous because he wrote a series of letters to various Christian communities on his forced trip to Rome.

98 CE to 117 CE	Emperor Trajan rules. Trajan is famous because he exchanged letters with Pliny the Younger, who was a Roman governor. In these letters Pliny asks about punishing the Christians.
125 CE to 150 CE	The earliest fragment of the New Testament is dated between 125 to 150 CE. It is called the Rylands Fragment and consists of a few lines from the Gospel of John.
154 CE	It is in this year that Marcion is thought to have died. Marcion had very different ideas about what Christianity was supposed to be like. He settled in Rome but was kicked out of the church because of his ideas.
156 CE	Polycarp, the bishop of Smyrna, was thought to be killed in this year. He was a martyr because of his Christian beliefs.
160 CE to early 200s CE	Tertullian was born sometime in the 160s and died in the early 200s CE. He was a Christian who lived in Carthage, North Africa. He wrote Christian works in both Latin and Greek and is considered to be an early church father.
185 CE to 251 CE	Origen is born about 185 CE and becomes one of the most prolific Christian writers. He is extremely educated. He is persecuted during the Decian Persecution (250 CE) and, although he didn't die in the persecution, he dies from his wounds suffered during that period.
200s CE to 300s CE	It is during this time that numerous Christian texts are written and eventually hidden. These texts are called the Nag Hammadi collection and were discovered in the 1940s when they were found in a jar. They revolutionized our understanding of early Christianity.
200 CE to 258 CE	Cyprian is bishop of Carthage from 248 to 258. In his early bishopric he is caught up in the Decian Persecution. He is later martyred for his belief in Christ.
203 CE	Many Christians, including Perpetua and her friend Felicity, are martyred for their belief in Christ. This happens in the Roman city of Carthage, located in North Africa.
216 CE to 276 CE	Mani, the founder of a Jewish/Christian religion called Manichaeism, is born. The religion starts in Persia and soon moves west into the Roman Empire and east into central Asia. He is martyred in 276 by one of the Persian kings.

240 CE to 316 CE	Diocletian, a solder in the Roman army, eventually makes his way up to being emperor. His policies help to stabilize the Roman Empire at a time when it could have easily collapsed. He is best known for the Great Persecution.
250 CE	The Roman emperor Decius orders a general persecution of the Christians called the Decian Persecution.
260 CE to 336 CE	Arius is born around 260 CE. He has different beliefs than many of his Christian colleagues and begins to argue with his bishop. This argument spreads throughout the eastern part of the Roman Empire, leading to his exile by Emperor Constantine I. Arius is eventually allowed back, only to die in 336 CE.
260 CE to 339 CE	Eusebius is born about 260 CE and becomes the bishop of the eastern Roman city of Caesarea. Eusebius is famous for writing one of the earliest Christian histories. Eusebius of Caesarea is also involved in the Arian controversy and the Council of Nicea in 325.
285 CE to 337 CE	Constantine I is born to Constantius and Helen. Constantine becomes emperor in the west in 306 CE after the death of his father. He is most famous for his conversion to Christianity and then allowing Christians to practice their faith without fear of persecution.
300 CE to 373 CE	Athanasius is at first a deacon and secretary to Alexander, the bishop of Alexandria, Egypt. Athanasius is at the Council of Nicea and later becomes the bishop of Alexandria. Athanasius is Catholic and has many fights with Arius and the Arians. He spends much of his time as bishop in exile because of his arguments with Emperor Constantius II.
300 CE to the early 400s CE	The Donatists are a group of North African Christians who follow a priest named Donatus. During the Great Persecution many bishops and priests curse Christ to avoid being martyred. When the Great Persecution finishes, these same people want their church positions back. Donatus and his followers refuse to let them have their jobs back, and this leads to a fight that lasts over a century.
303 CE	The Great Persecution of Christians begins. It is organized by Emperor Diocletian and his Caesar (almost like a vice president) Galerius. The persecution has a much stronger effect in the eastern part of the empire.

313 CE	After Constantine I becomes the sole ruler of the Romans in the western side of the empire, he joins with Licinius, the Roman emperor in the east in the city of Milan, Italy. It is believed that in 313 both emperors issue the Edict of Milan, which gives Christians the freedom to practice their religion without being harassed or killed.
325 CE	Emperor Constantine I calls the first large church council in 325 to deal with the arguments between the Arians, or those who follow the beliefs of Arius, and the Nicenes, or those who would eventually become the Catholics. At this council the Arians are condemned and the bishops create the Nicene Creed, or the statement of beliefs that all Christians are to follow.
331 CE to 363 CE	Julian is born in 331. He was part of the Constantinian family but when he was little, his father was killed when Emperor Constantine I died. Julian is raised as a Christian outside of the court but is brought back in the late 350s. Julian becomes emperor in 361 with the death of Constantius II. Julian is most famous for his anti-Christian laws, and dies in battle in Persia.
339 CE to 397 CE	Ambrose was probably born in 339 CE. His father was a Roman governor, and when Ambrose comes of age he becomes a governor of northern Italy as well. When the Arian bishop of Milan dies, Ambrose is chosen as bishop in 374 CE. He remains bishop of Milan until 397 CE.
346 CE to 395 CE	Theodosius becomes the Roman emperor of the East and then eventually the sole emperor. He is famous for his arguments with Ambrose, the bishop of Milan, and for setting up the second ecumenical council in 381, held in Constantinople.
347 CE to 419/420 CE	Jerome is born sometime around 347 CE. He is a prolific writer and sets up a monastery for both men and women in Bethlehem.

354 CE to 430 CE	Augustine is born in North Africa to a Christian mother and a pagan father. He is highly educated and eventually joins the Manichaeans. Augustine leaves North Africa for Italy, where he meets Ambrose. Augustine converts to Catholic Christianity and is also a prolific writer. He dies in 430 just as the barbarian group named the Vandals are invading North Africa.
384 CE	Ambrose argues with Emperor Valentinian II over putting the pagan statue of Victory in the Roman Senate. Ambrose writes a series of letters to the emperor, and the emperor writes back. In the end the Altar of Victory is not allowed back into the Senate.

Historical Overview

THE FIRST CENTURY

Christianity started off, not as a Christian movement, but as a Jewish movement in a very multicultural area. Jesus was born into a Jewish family, and all of his disciples were Jewish. They lived in Judea, which was then a Roman province (also called Judea). They were bi- and sometimes trilingual: many could speak Hebrew, Aramaic, and Greek. Many read the main religious text, the Hebrew Scripture, in Greek (titled the *Septuagint*). They were heavily influenced by both Jewish and the Hellenistic (Greek) culture, which was brought to the area when Alexander the Great (a Macedonian king) conquered Judea in the late 300s BCE. They were also influenced, positively and negatively, by Roman culture when the Romans claimed Judea as a client kingdom and then totally took it over in 6 CE when it became a Roman province. The Romans spoke Latin and Greek, and it is possible that some of the early followers of Jesus also spoke Latin.

Why is all of this important to understanding the rise of Christianity? The main answer is that this multicultural environment that it grew up in allowed Christians to spread to other areas with relative ease, primarily within already-established Hellenized, Romanized, and Jewish communities spread throughout the Mediterranean. Christianity started off as a small movement in Judea in the first century CE, and by the early fourth century CE (the early 300s), it had become the preferred religion in the Roman Empire. By the end of the fourth century, it became the only legally recognized religion of the Roman Empire and essentially triumphed over the polytheistic religion of the Romans and the Greeks.

The early history of Christianity is a fascinating mix of multicultural communities that at the same time contained small, inward-looking communities that resisted this multicultural movement. What do we know about Jesus? We really know only what the New Testament texts tell us since Jesus never wrote anything, at least as far as we know. As stated above, Jesus was born into a Jewish family. We don't know the year of his birth; it is sometime between 4 BCE and 6 CE. Unfortunately we don't know much about the period between his childhood and adulthood except what later stories tell us. These include Jesus cleansing the Temple of money changers and holding his Last Supper with his disciples. According to the New Testament Jesus was a carpenter. There are certainly lots of stories about the life of Jesus, but these come in writings much later than his lifetime.

Jesus picked his 12 followers (or disciples) from his community, and they were a mix of people with varying jobs. If we can take the New Testament texts as giving accurate history, they left their employment to follow Jesus and to spread this new message, especially after being given directions from Jesus himself. By all accounts the message of Christ spread quickly through Judea, at least fast enough to come to the attention of the Jewish population who did not believe that Jesus was the messiah. We will go further into this in the book, but for right now we know that he was seen as a criminal and was crucified under the governorship of Pilate sometime between 30 and 33 CE. It is fairly certain that the early followers were persecuted and that this persecution continued right up through the early 300s CE when Emperor Constantine I made the religion legal.

Despite its quick growth, Christianity had problems other than persecution. One of the earliest controversies to occur in this early movement was who exactly should become followers of Jesus: the Jewish or the Gentile population? The Gentiles consisted of everyone who was not Jewish. James, the brother of Jesus, became one of the main leaders of the early Christians after the death of Jesus. James wanted Jewish people to convert to their belief in Jesus as the Messiah. Other members, like Peter and especially Saul (later Paul), wanted to have all people join, both Jewish and Gentile. One clue to why Paul wanted this was his multicultural background. He belonged to a Jewish sect called Pharisees. He spoke Hebrew, Aramaic, and Greek. He grew up in Tarsus, a city in southeastern Turkey, far outside of Judea, and finally, his parents were apparently Roman citizens. Paul was certainly a Roman citizen, and being recognized as a citizen at this early stage was rare for someone who lived on the far eastern border of Roman control.

Unlike James, Paul was not satisfied that only Jewish people should be able to join Christianity. Paul, along with Peter, convinced James that Gentiles should be allowed to join, under three conditions: that they not eat anything with blood or anything that had been strangled, abstain from idols, and abstain from fornication. Paul got his wish and opened up the new religion to everyone who would accept Jesus as the Messiah. It is primarily because of Paul that Christianity spread as it did—all people could now join, regardless of their religious background. As will be discussed, Paul wrote the earliest part of what is now call The New Testament. He traveled outside of Judea and up through his native land of Turkey to spread his new faith. Many times he went to the Jewish synagogues first to try and sway the Jewish population to believe in Jesus, and many times the Jewish population rejected him. He then tried to convert the Gentile population.

Paul, while a Pharisee, was apparently involved in persecuting Christians. He had a conversion to Christianity when he was on the road from Jerusalem to Damascus. After his conversion he was convinced that he was a true disciple of Jesus even though he had never met Jesus in person. It was then that he started to convert people to Christianity. Paul had some successes, but it wasn't easy for him and there were many problems that Paul had to overcome in order to get people to believe that he was really part of the early Christian movement. The first was, as mentioned above, that he was well known in Jewish circles and had more than likely taken part in persecuting Christians before he himself converted. Many Christians remembered Paul's history and didn't totally trust him. The second was that many Gentiles believed they needed to become Jewish in order to follow Jesus. This meant, at least for men, that they needed to be circumcised. This was a painful procedure for adult men, and it is clear that many did not want to do this. The third is that many Gentiles did not want to follow the food restrictions that the Jewish population followed. Paul tried to satisfy the potential followers by stating that men did not need to be circumcised nor did they have to follow the Jewish diet except for the rules we have already mentioned. This seemed to work, and many more people joined the new religion.

Paul's writings form the earliest part of the New Testament. His writings take the form of letters that Paul wrote to the various communities he had founded while traveling through modern-day Turkey and Greece or to Christians he knew in other cities like Rome. It was not an easy time for Paul. He suffered because people did not believe his message, and he suffered because people did not believe he was a true disciple. He had many conflicts with people he met, both in the Jewish and the Gentile population, and usually he argued with Christians he met who were already in Turkey/Greece before he arrived. Christianity was a religion based on proselytizing, and Paul was not the first to travel around trying to get people to convert. But it is Paul's version of Christianity that became the mainstream, mostly because it is his letters that survive. We have to keep in mind two things here. The first is that we know there were other Christians with differing beliefs in the first century. Unfortunately it isn't clear what they believed. Second, we have to remember that we do not have any of the original texts from early Christianity. The earliest part of a manuscript we have comes from the middle of the 100s CE, or over 120 years after the death of Jesus. The modern New Testament is a best guess what the originals looked like (and that is why there are so many different translations of this text).

It isn't clear what happened to Paul and to Peter. It is thought that they met their death in Rome by the Roman government during the time of Emperor Nero. Today, St. Peter's Basilica in Rome is the center of the Catholic world, with the church being a monument to Peter and his faith. Other stories have Paul going on to Spain. Regardless, the first half century of the Christian period was spent converting the Jewish and Gentile population to Christianity. The second half of the first century was spent solidifying the set of beliefs, creating a church hierarchy, and dealing with problems brought on by the Roman control of Judea. This control led directly to the Jewish Wars. During this period the Romans destroyed the main Jewish temple, now named the Second Temple (the First Temple had been destroyed by a Neo-Babylonian king named Nebuchadnezzar II in 586 BCE) and forced the Jewish and Christian population out of Jerusalem. This only led to a further spread of Christianity and also led to a distinct separation between the Christians and those who followed Judaism. The Christians now saw themselves as being different from their mother religion.

SECOND CENTURY

The evidence for what was happening in Christianity in the early part of the second century (the 100s CE) is sketchy, mostly because of the lack of primary sources. There are a few very important writings that give small glimpses at Christian communities throughout the Mediterranean. But it should be remembered that these texts, like those from the first century, cannot tell us everything that happened to Christianity. Despite this, some educated guesses can be made about what happened in some geographical areas.

Let's first look at what was happening in northern Turkey towards the beginning of the second century. We are very fortunate to have a series of letters that were exchanged between the governor of Bithynia-Pontus (in northern Turkey) named Pliny the Younger (this is to distinguish him from his famous uncle, Pliny the Elder, who was killed in the eruption of Mt. Vesuvius). While governor, Pliny the Younger wrote to Emperor Trajan about some Christians who were living in his controlled territory. They were being officially persecuted, but Pliny was concerned about the circumstances of their persecution.

Some people were being accused of being Christian anonymously. He wasn't sure what to do with them—should they still be persecuted? Emperor Trajan wrote back and told Pliny that people who admit to being Christian should be persecuted, meaning they should be put to death. Those, however, who were accused anonymously should not be harmed unless they openly confess. This series of letters are extremely important in understanding the official position on Christianity in the Roman Empire during this formative stage.

Just as there were divisions in Christianity in the first century (especially between Paul and those who believed differently than him), there were divisions in the second century. These differences, however, were extremely important in terms of developing theology, or the study of God. A good example of this is a man named Marcion. Marcion was from Sinope, a city in the northern part of Turkey. He was a Christian but had very different ideas about what Christians should believe. For example, he thought that Christians should not be using the Hebrew Scriptures/Old Testament. The reason for this is that he believed that there were two gods—one of the Old (who was evil) and one from the New (who was good). It is also thought that Marcion was one of the earliest people to put together a list of writings that would eventually become the New Testament. So why is he important? Because it forced other Christians to think about why the Old Testament was important and it more than likely forced them to create their own list of texts that Christians should be reading. This list would eventually become the New Testament.

The second century was also the period when Christians tried to solidify their beliefs, especially on the nature of the church in general (called ecclesiology—the study of the church). At the end of the first century and into the beginning of the second it was accepted that there were three main types of leaders in Christian communities: teachers, prophets, and apostles, along with bishops and deacons. However, by the middle of the second century the importance of the teacher and prophet was gradually reduced while the office of the bishop became more important. The main reason for this is that the teachers and prophets were wanderers, going into various established Christian communities and teaching their own ideas about what Christians should be doing and thinking. They would eventually leave and the community would be in an uproar about what to believe and who to follow. The clash between the bishop and the teachers/prophets was eventually won by the bishops.

Another important movement in theology during the second century was Christology, or the study of Christ. Jesus had been dead for nearly 100 years, but the question of who he actually was continued for centuries. Was he truly God when he was a little boy? Was he truly God when he was a grown man?

If so, how could he be God and man at the same time? And if he was God and man all in one, when did this happen? At conception? At his baptism? Before his physical birth? Was he just a regular man upon whom God bestowed special gifts? The arguments were important ones and caused a lot of controversy, because the New Testament writings have different ideas of the nature of Christ. The questions also caused many people to write about these issues.

By the middle of the second century there were other Christians writing about Christianity, and instead of arguing with other Christians, they began to argue with the Roman government. One of the most important was Justyn Martyr. He wrote the *First and Second Apology* (here "apology" means a defense). These are important works because Justyn writes directly to the Romans, including the emperor himself. Justyn states that Christians are not criminals and, in fact, following Christianity made them better Romans. The writings are important as well because Justyn discusses some of the charges against the Christians—that they met secretly to overthrow the Roman government, drank human blood and ate flesh, killed children, and were atheists because they did not believe in the Roman gods and goddesses. Justyn Martyr examines all of these charges and finds the Christians innocent of all of these "crimes."

THIRD CENTURY

As Christianity moved into the third century (the 200s CE) the battles over who Christ was and who should be leading Christians continued. But it was also in this century that Christianity officially came to the attention of the Roman government. This is especially the case during the time of Emperor Decius and later under Emperor Diocletian. Decius started a persecution of the Christians, and this episode is called the Decian Persecution. As discussed above, the Christians had been accused of many crimes, including cannibalism. This accusation was widely believed because many Christians took the Eucharist (in the form of a wafer and wine) during their religious ceremonies. The Eucharist was (and still is) believed to literally be the body and blood of Christ. The ingestion of the Eucharistic wine and wafer was therefore thought to be cannibalism. Christians were also accused of killing children and having sexual orgies when they had their so-called secret meetings. Another charge was that they were atheists. The reason for this particular charge was because the Christians rejected the Roman polytheistic religion as a form of devil worship. Christians refused to pray to these gods, and they especially refused to pray to the emperor who was seen as a living god. To the Romans it meant that Christians were antisocial at the least and traitors at worst. This last charge was the ultimate cause for persecution.

Luckily for Christians, Emperor Decius did not live very long. After his death there were a few outbreaks of persecution until the very end of the 200s under the rule of Emperor Diocletian. Diocletian seemed not to have noticed the Christians very much in the first part of his reign, but he certainly noticed them later. The story is that Diocletian and his caesar (like a vice president), Galerius, were sacrificing some animals to tell the future. For some reason, the priests could not read the signs in the sheep livers. It was then that Galerius noticed that some Christians were making the sign of the cross every time a sheep was sacrificed. This ultimately led to an episode called the Great Persecution. Most of the persecutions took place in the eastern half of the Roman Empire. We are lucky to have firsthand accounts from Eusebius, the first Christian historian. He describes the conditions for the Christians in his book *Ecclesiastical History*.

These persecutions probably led some Christians in Egypt to hide their religious writings. The collection, called the Nag Hammadi Codices or Books, wasn't discovered until 1945 at Nag Hammadi. This collection was one of the most important textual finds of the 20th century. There were 52 texts found in this collection, and many of them are religious texts. These, however, were not the usual Christian texts like the New Testament but were from groups called the Gnostics. This title comes from the Greek word *gnosis*, which means knowledge. Gnostics believed that the knowledge found in their texts and teachings would help people get to heaven. These texts have changed the way that scholars look at early Christianity. Most importantly, it is very clear that there were many different types of Christianity and thus many types of Christian beliefs.

FOURTH CENTURY

The fourth century, which started with Emperor Diocletian and the Great Persecution of Christians, ended with the domination of Christians and Christianity over the Roman Empire. As discussed in the section for the third century, the Great Persecution affected Christians mostly on the eastern side of the Roman Empire. There were sporadic cases of persecution in the West, but in general, the Christians in the west were left alone. Emperor Diocletian retired in 305, and this left Galerius in charge. Towards the end of his rule Galerius became very ill. It isn't clear what he had, but it was more than likely bowel cancer. He ended up rescinding the Great Persecution and even asked the Christians to pray for his health and his soul. This did not save his life, however, and soon after, the emperor in the west, Constantine I, met with the emperor in the east, Licinius, to issue an official document named the Edict of Milan that gave Christians the freedom to openly practice their religion without fear of persecution. This was the first time in Christian history where Christians would be treated as religious equals.

Emperor Constantine was really the key factor here. Constantine was raised to emperor by troops in Britain in 306. There were, however, two other people who claimed to be emperors in the west: Severus (the official emperor) and Maxentius. Severus fought against Maxentius first and lost. Constantine decided to take his troops to Rome to fight with Maxentius. On the eve of battle, we are told by two sources, that Constantine saw the image of the cross in the sky and heard a voice tell him, "With this sign you will conquer." Constantine decided to take this advice and promised to become a Christian if he won his battle with Maxentius. And this is exactly what happened—Constantine won and started to seriously support the Christians in his empire. It isn't totally clear when Constantine became an official Christian, but it is clear that his rise to power was followed closely by the rise of Christianity.

While Constantine was solidifying his power, Christians were beginning to fight among themselves. There were two main groups of Christians: those called Arians and those we can call Nicenes (who are the forerunners of the Catholic Church). The main difference between the two was over Christology—or who Christ was. The Nicenes believed that the Father, Son, and Holy Spirit were one in power and were together since the beginning, while the Arians believed that God was always in existence and at some point later Jesus comes from the Father. After all, the Arians said, who comes first, the Father or the Son? For them the answer was clearly the Father. This basic difference set off numerous fights, both physical and theological, for nearly the rest of the fourth century. To end the fighting, Constantine called for the first ecumenical council, the Council of Nicea in 325. During this council many bishops in the east met to resolve the problem. Hardly any from the west attended, including the bishop of Rome, although he did send his representatives. At the end of the conference it was decided that the Nicene belief would be the only officially recognized form of Christianity, and one of the most important documents in Christian history, the Nicene Creed, was written. Some of the Arians were sent into exile, and this was meant to put an end to the division. But it did nothing of the sort. In a few years all of the exiled Arians were called back and Constantine himself was baptized by an Arian bishop before he died.

The Roman Empire was now divided between Constantine's three sons, Constantius II, Constans, and Constantine II. Like royal brothers, these sons fought, and in the end Constantius II became the sole emperor. Constantius just so happened to support the Arian cause, bringing to the fore again all of the theological problems that the Council of Nicea and the Nicene Creed were supposed to have taken care of. This of course led to more difficulties for

Christians throughout the Empire who were caught between the arguing bishops and emperors.

The important part of this battle, however, was not necessarily who was winning, but what was happening in terms of theology. People on both sides of the aisle were trying to understand what the Nicene Creed actually meant, especially the key term *homoousious* ("one nature"). Out of these arguments came the foundation of the current Catholic Church. By the end of the fourth century Arianism had run its course in the Roman Empire, at least for the time being (it would soon reenter with the coming of the so-called barbarians who were for the most part Arian Christian—but their history lies outside of the timeframe for this volume). Many Christians were involved in the battle to design Nicene/Catholic theology. Some of the important ones were the Cappadocian fathers in the east and Augustine in the West.

Towards the end of the fourth century, with the coming of Emperor Theodosius, Catholicism was clearly cemented in place as the only form of Christianity that was officially tolerated by the Roman government. This did not mean that other forms of Christianity had disappeared. On the contrary, many flourished, albeit outside of the main centers of Catholic Christianity, including the Donatists, the Manichaeans, and the Gnostics. However, by the fifth century, the Donatists and the Manichaeans would be suppressed by the Roman government and Catholic Church, while the Gnostics would eventually become enfolded into other Christian groups or die out completely. This is, however, beyond the timeframe for this book.

The Rise of Christianity: A–Z

AMBROSE   Ambrose, born around 340 and died in 397 CE, was the bishop of Milan, Italy, from 374 to 397 CE and was one of the most influential bishops at the end of the fourth century. He is known primarily for his interactions with Emperor Valentinian II and Emperor Theodosius I. He was a prolific writer, and luckily many of his books and letters have survived so we can get a good glimpse at his life and his theology. There were also people who wrote about Ambrose, so we can also add those to our list of knowledge about this bishop.

Ambrose came from a very wealthy family. His father was a praetorian prefect (a high-level administrator) in the Roman province of Gaul (modern-day France). Like most sons of Roman political leaders, Ambrose followed in his father's footsteps, first becoming a lawyer, and then in 370 CE he was appointed governor of northern Italy. During this period Ambrose was a member of the Catholic Church, but not in any official capacity. At the time that he was governor, the bishop of Milan, named Auxentius, was an Arian. When Auxentius died in 374, there were debates on who should be the next bishop—should the bishop be Arian, or Catholic? The local people were very interested in this question, and this soon led to rioting between the two groups. Ambrose, as the governor, stepped in to stop this. To his surprise, the people wanted him to be bishop, even though he was not baptized, nor was he even a priest. Paulinus, the biographer of Ambrose, stated that when Ambrose was trying to settle the issue, the voice of a girl could be heard saying, "Ambrose for bishop, Ambrose for bishop," and that was all it took to convince the people that they wanted him. Within a week he was baptized and then became the next bishop of Milan.

Once the bishop, Ambrose became involved with imperial affairs, including acting as ambassador for Emperor Valentinian II, who ruled from 375 to 392 CE. Valentinian II and his wife, Empress Justina, were both Arians, while Ambrose was a Catholic. Despite their theological differences, the three of them were able to work together until Justina wanted to take some Catholic Church buildings and make them available to the Arians. Ambrose refused to do this, which led to a standoff between the imperial troops and those in the church. After a tense week, Valentinian II and Justina backed down and allowed Ambrose to retain his churches.

After the death of Valentinian II, Theodosius I took control of the western part of the Roman Empire. Theodosius was a Catholic, which of course made Ambrose very happy. However, the two did not always get along. One example of this happened in 388 when some Christians in the eastern city of Callinicum destroyed a Jewish synagogue and a Christian Gnostic church. Theodosius decided that the bishop of this city should have to pay, and then he later decided that the Christian congregation should also be held liable for damages that were done to both buildings. Ambrose, however, did not like this decision and was very vocal with his opposition. He sent a letter to the emperor saying that since the Roman Empire was now Christian, it would not look very good for the emperor to be helping those who were not Christian and forcing Christians to pay. Theodosius ignored this request. Theodosius would attend the church in Milan with Ambrose as the bishop. One Sunday Ambrose was giving his sermon and was about to hand out the communion wafer, but stopped and made the announcement that he would not do communion until Theodosius ended the investigation into what had happened at Callinicum. Theodosius then promised to stop all proceedings against the Christians and that they would not have to pay for the damages to the synagogue or the Gnostic church. Ambrose then gave out communion.

Another episode shows how powerful Ambrose the bishop really was. In 390 there was a riot in Thessalonika (in northern Greece). The riot started when soldiers were abusing the local population. The local population rose up and killed a number of soldiers, including some high-ranking commanders. When the news reached Theodosius, he was furious and he sent a message telling the soldiers to protect themselves with any means available. After he sent this message he became worried that the soldiers would attack the local people, and then sent another message asking for restraint. However, his first message arrived and the soldiers did exactly what Theodosius had feared—they attacked the civilian population and thousands of people were murdered. When Ambrose heard about the slaughter, he was furious and sent a letter to the emperor demanding that the emperor apologize. The letter is known as *Letter 51*. Here is part of that letter (section 12):

> I advise, I entreat, I exhort, I admonish; for I am grieved that you who were an example of singular piety, who stood so high for clemency, who would not suffer even single offenders to be put in jeopardy, should not mourn over the death of so many innocent persons. Successful as you have been in battle, and great in other respects, yet mercy was ever the crown of your actions. The devil has envied you your chief excellence: overcome him, while you still have the means. Add not sin to sin by acting in a manner which has injured so many. (Schaff, n.d.)

After sending the letter, Ambrose then took the step of excommunicating the emperor. The emperor had no choice in the matter. After this, Theodosius made a public apology and was not allowed to wear the purple robes that royalty normally wore. After a period of time, Theodosius was allowed back into the Catholic Church and was given communion.

Ambrose died in 397, at the peak of his ecclesiastical power. He had argued with two emperors and almost always got his way. He was very popular with his congregation, so much so that they would protect him with their own bodies when imperial troops were sent in to force Ambrose into doing something he did not want to do. He began his life as an imperial servant and then spent the rest of his life as a servant of the church. Today his church in the Italian city of Milan is still visited by thousands of people.

Further Reading

Kaatz, K. W. *Early Controversies and the Growth of Christianity*. Santa Barbara: ABC-CLIO, 2012.

McLynn, Neil B. *Ambrose of Milan: Church and Court in a Christian Capital*. Berkeley: University of California Press, 1994.

Moorhead, John. *Ambrose: Church and State in the Late Roman World*. New York: Routledge, 1999.

Schaff, Philip. "Ambrose, Letter 51." *Ambrose: Selected Works and Letters*. T&T Clark: Edinburgh, n.d. Available online at http://www.ccel.org/ccel/schaff/npnf210.

APOSTOLIC SUCCESSION Apostolic succession is none other than a list of people who have church offices and who can trace their lineage back to Jesus and the original disciples. The doctrine of apostolic succession became very important in early Christianity when people started to believe different things. The question became: who is teaching the original doctrine of Christ? This was partially solved through the use of laying on of hands (one person consecrating another, all in a line) and more importantly, keeping a written list of bishops from each city, proving that their consecration as bishop could lead all the way back to Jesus and the disciples.

The doctrine of apostolic succession was an important tool in the church's control of its teachings and of its congregations. As soon as the original disciples started to spread outwards from Israel, it was natural that some of the teachings of Jesus began to change over time. The teacher was in many cases a bishop or a traveling teacher. Some early Christians did not like the fact that some of the teachings were beginning to change into what they would call heresy. A way to prevent heresy from spreading or to make it illegitimate was to keep track of the line of teachers or bishops, starting from Christ, then to the disciples, and then to their disciples and so on. If you were a bishop/teacher who could not prove you were in that line of true disciples, then you were considered to be a heretic and your teachings could be seen as invalid.

Many cities began to keep lists of their bishops in order to make sure that heretics would not take over the church. One early Christian who really pushed for the idea of apostolic succession was Irenaeus, the bishop of Lyon. Irenaeus wrote an influential book titled *Against Heresies* sometime in the 180s CE. Irenaeus wrote this in order to control what he perceived as the true teachings of Christ against all of those who taught something different (the heretics). Part of his method of control was to state where in the list of previous bishops someone could be found. A good example from his *Against Heresies* can be found in Book 1, chapter 27:

> Cerdo was one who took his system from the followers of Simon, and came to live at Rome in the time of Hyginus, who held the ninth place in the episcopal succession from the apostles downwards. He taught that the God proclaimed by the law and the prophets was not the Father of our Lord Jesus Christ. For the former was known, but the latter unknown; while the one also was righteous, but the other benevolent. (Schaff, n.d.)

Hyginus, the bishop of Rome, was listed as the ninth bishop, starting from the apostles. Irenaeus mentions Hyginus for two reasons here: the first is that he is the legitimate bishop, and the second is that because he is the legitimate bishop, his teaching is the correct one. This teaching is sometimes referred to as "tradition." Later in his *Against Heresies* (Book 3, chapter 2), Irenaeus gives a very clear statement on why the doctrine of apostolic succession was vital to the church:

> But, again, when we refer them to that tradition which originates from the apostles which is preserved by means of the succession of presbyters in the Churches, they object to tradition, saying that they themselves are wiser not merely than the presbyters, but even than the apostles, because they have

discovered the unadulterated truth . . . It comes to this, therefore, that these men do now consent neither to Scripture nor to tradition. (Schaff, n.d.)

Later Christians, especially Augustine, bishop of Hippo (North Africa), also understood the importance of apostolic succession when it came to protecting what he saw as the true Catholic doctrine. Augustine wrote a book in 395 or 396 titled *Against the Letter of Mani called The Foundation*. In it Augustine writes:

> There are many other things which most properly can keep me in the Catholic Church's bosom. The unanimity of peoples and nations keeps me here. Her authority, inaugurated in miracles, nourished by hope, augmented by love, and confirmed by her age, keeps me here. The succession of priests, from the very see of the apostle Peter, to whom the Lord, after his resurrection, gave the charge of feeding his sheep [John 21:15–17], up to the present episcopate, keeps me here. And last, the very name Catholic, which, not without reason, belongs to this Church alone, in the face of so many heretics, so much so that, although all heretics want to be called "Catholic," when a stranger inquires where the Catholic Church meets, none of the heretics would dare to point out his own basilica or house. (Schaff, n.d.)

There were many things that kept Augustine in the Catholic Church, and the doctrine of apostolic succession was one of the most important ones. The idea that the legitimate bishops were only those who had direct ties to the original apostles is also still a very important one in the Catholic Church today. The pope can trace his line back to the original disciples of Christ. As it states on the Vatican website, "The Roman Pontiff, as the successor of Peter, is the perpetual and visible principle and foundation of unity of both the bishops and of the faithful" (http://www.vatican.va/holy_father/index.htm). The idea of apostolic succession is a long one going back to the earliest times in the history of Christianity. It was used to control the hierarchy and the teachings of the church.

Further Reading

Ehrhardt, Arnold. *The Apostolic Succession: In the First Two Centuries of the Church*, reprint. Eugene, OR: Wipf & Stock, 2009.

Rogers, Gregory. *Apostolic Succession*, 2nd ed. Chesterton, IN: Conciliar Press, 1997.

Schaff, Philip. "Against the Epistle of Manichaeus, called Fundamental." *Augustine: The Writings against the Manichaeans and against the Donatists*. T&T Clark: Edinburgh, n.d. Available online at http://www.ccel.org/ccel/schaff/npnf104.html.

Schaff, Philip. "Against Heresies." *The Apostolic Fathers with Justin Martyr and Irenaeus*. Edinburgh: T&T Clark, n.d. Available online at http://www.ccel.org/ccel/schaff/anf01.html.

Sullivan, Francis Aloysius. *From Apostles to Bishops: The Development of the Episcopacy in the Early Church.* New York: Paulist Press, 2001.

ARIANS   Like today, in the 300s Christianity was still really "Christianities." There were a number of Christian groups all trying to become the main form of the religion. One group is what we could call Catholic (although it is better to call this group Nicene at this early stage), and the other, Arian. These two groups fought it out for theological supremacy through a good part of the fourth century, with the Nicene/Catholic side eventually winning after a very long struggle. We can examine the history of the Arians by looking at how they got started, the major differences between the Nicene/Catholics and the Arians, the events at the Council of Nicea, and the history of Arianism at the end of the 300s.

Arianism is named after its founder, Arius. Arius was an Egyptian Christian priest living in the Delta of Egypt (in the north). By all accounts Arius was a well-loved priest. He seemed to be very active in his community and was very good at what he did. However, he started to have some very public arguments with his bishop, Alexander. Alexander was equating God with Jesus, making them exactly equal. Arius, however, did not like this idea because it created two gods (God and Jesus). Arius also believed that God the Father must have been in existence first, and then the Son came into existence sometime after the Father. His reasoning was that if God was called the Father, then he had to exist before His Son. The Nicene/Catholics believed that God, the Son, and the Holy Spirit all were in existence at the same time, forever.

Both sides could turn to the Bible to support their views. The Arians (or those who followed the beliefs of Arius) turned to Proverbs 8:22–25: "The Lord created me at the beginning of his work, the first of his acts of long ago." For Arius and the Arians, this verse proved that God had to come first and the Son after. The Arians could also point to passages in the New Testament, especially to Romans 11:36 and John 16:28. Romans 11:36 reads: "For from him and through him and to him are all things. To him be the glory forever. Amen." John 16:28 reads: "I came from the Father and have come into the world; again, I am leaving the world and am going to the Father." Both of these verses show, at least to the Arians, that the Son came second.

The Nicene/Catholic side also used the Bible to back up their ideas. They used (among others): John 14:1, which states: "I am in the Father, and the Father in me"; and John 10:30, "I and the Father are one." They also used John 1:1 ("In the beginning was the Word") and John 14:9 ("He who has seen Me has seen the Father"). Here, to the Nicene/Catholics, it was pretty clear that there was no difference between God and The Son, and therefore they must have been in existence together from the very beginning.

Arius was then condemned and excommunicated by his own bishop and a number of other bishops from Egypt. Arius refused to accept this and wanted back in. He then proceeded to write to a number of bishops he thought could help him. The fight for who was correct soon left Egypt and went to modern-day Turkey and directly to the emperor. These bishops included Eusebius of Nicomedia and Eusebius of Caesarea. Once the letters reached these men, they then began their own letter campaign to reinstate Arius. They even held their own church council and decided that Arius should be reinstated to his home church, regardless of the position of his own bishop. This infighting led directly up to Emperor Constantine I. Constantine met with multiple people on both sides. He ultimately decided to hold the first large gathering of bishops since he made Christianity legal in 313 CE. This meeting took place in 325 CE, in Nicea, southeast of Constantinople. His hope was that they would decide which type of belief Christians should follow—the Nicene kind or the Arian kind. This is the first ecumenical council, meaning all the bishops were supposed to show up from all over the Roman Empire. However, only a few from the western part of the empire made the journey to Nicea. The exact number of bishops who attended is not known, but many think it was around 300.

Another thing that is not known is what exactly happened in the Council of Nicea. Luckily the bishops wrote down some material, including the most famous document from early Christianity: the Nicene Creed. This creed or statement was created to ensure that all Christians followed the same practice and beliefs wherever they might be living. Here is the first part of the Nicene Creed:

> We believe in one God, the Father Almighty, Creator of all things seen and not seen, and in one Lord Jesus Christ, the Son of God, begotten from the Father, the Only Begotten, that is to say, from the nature of the Father, God from God, Light from light, True God from true God, begotten, not made, one nature [*homoousius*] with God, through whom all things were made, things in heaven and on earth, who because of us men, and because of our salvation, came down and became flesh, and took human form, suffered, and rose on the third day, went up into the heavens, will come to judge the living and the dead, and in the Holy Spirit.

The most important part, however, for our purposes, is the end of the Nicene Creed. Since one of the main reasons for calling the bishops together was to deal with the Arians, they decided to put a warning to all Christians who believed in the Arian version of Christianity:

Those saying that there was a time when he was not, and before he was born he was not in existence, and that he came to be out of nothing, or who claim that the Son of God is of another hypostasis or nature, or is created, or is changeable or alterable, these the Holy Catholic and Apostolic church anathematizes.

As discussed above, the Arians liked to use Proverbs to show that God came first, and then the Son. The Nicene Creed directly discusses this when it states, "Those saying that there was a time when he was not, and before he was born he was not in existence." Its ruling was crystal clear—the Catholic Church cursed everyone who believed anything the Arians believed. The Nicene Creed and the council itself couldn't stop the spread of Arianism, even with the curse, but it did slow it down a bit. Soon after the council finished, Arius and Eusebius of Nicomedia were sent into exile. Eusebius was also removed from being the bishop of Nicomedia. Eventually they were allowed to come back, but Arius was still forbidden to go to Egypt to preach for fear that he would cause more trouble. Eusebius of Nicomedia, on the other hand, was allowed to take back his bishopric. Soon after, Eusebius of Nicomedia began a writing campaign to get more support for the Arian view and to make sure that his Arian friends were put in charge of local churches.

Despite all of the trouble that this issue caused early Christianity, Emperor Constantine eventually allowed Arius back into the church and to go to Egypt. Arius, however, never made it home. A later Christian historian named Socrates Scholasticus (born around 380 and died around 439 CE) wrote a book titled *Ecclesiastical History* and described what happened to Arius in 336 CE (Book 1, Chapter 38):

The emperor being thus convinced, ordered that he should be received into communion by Alexander, bishop of Constantinople. It was then Saturday, and Arius was expecting to assemble with the church on the day following: but divine retribution overtook his daring criminalities. For going out of the imperial palace, attended by a crowd of Eusebian partisans like guards, he paraded proudly through the midst of the city, attracting the notice of all the people. As he approached the place called Constantine's Forum, where the column of porphyry is erected, a terror arising from the remorse of conscience seized Arius, and with the terror a violent relaxation of the bowels: he therefore enquired whether there was a convenient place near, and being directed to the back of Constantine's Forum, he hastened thither. Soon after a faintness came over him, and together with the evacuations his bowels protruded, followed by a copious hemorrhage, and the descent of the smaller intestines: moreover portions of his spleen and liver were brought off in the effusion of blood, so that he almost immediately died. (Schaff, n.d.)

We are also told that people would refuse to use the same toilet for fear of dying in the same way that Arius did. Despite this horrific death (if, of course, it is a true account), the spread of Arius's ideas continued. Eusebius, the bishop of Nicomedia, was made the bishop of Constantinople from 339 until his death in 341 CE. Since Constantinople was the capital city, Eusebius had a lot of power to spread Arian ideas and to place Arians in charge of churches. Arianism was a religious movement throughout the 300s until the time of Emperor Theodosius who ruled from 378 to 395 CE. Theodosius ruled that Arianism was a heretical movement. But this was not the end of Arianism. When Eusebius of Nicomedia and Arius were sent into exile, they went to the northern borders of the Roman Empire and spread their ideas to the people who were not Romans, sometimes called the Barbarians. When these "barbarian" groups invaded the Roman Empire in the late 300s and the 400s, some of them were Arian Christians. Eventually most of them were converted to the Catholic version of Christianity.

Further Reading

Gregg, Robert C. *Arianism: Historical and Theological Reassessments: Papers from the Ninth International Conference on Patristic Studies* (Patristic Monograph). Eugene, OR: Wipf & Stock, 2006.

Hanson, R. P. C. *The Search for the Christian Doctrine of God: The Arian Controversy, 318–381.* Grand Rapids, MI: Baker Academic, 2006.

The Nicene Creed (author's translation).

Rubenstein, Richard E. *When Jesus Became God: The Struggle to Define Christianity during the Last Days of Rome.* New York: Harcourt, 2000.

Schaff, Philip. "Ecclesiastical History." *Socrates and Sozemus: Ecclesiastical Histories.* T&T Clark: Edinburgh, n.d. Available online at http://www.ccel.org/ccel/schaff/npnf202.html.

Williams, Rowan. *Arius: Heresy and Tradition.* Rev. ed. Grand Rapids, MI: William B. Eerdmans, 2002.

ASCETICISM   The word "asceticism" comes from the Greek word meaning "training," as in training for a sport. This is a good description of this early Christian movement since many of the ascetics believed that they were involved in an athletic competition against the Devil. Asceticism was a movement whereby those who practice it usually lived a very hard lifestyle (not eating very much, praying constantly, sleeping very little, and living by themselves) and sometimes tried to isolate themselves in order to worship God. There are many roots to the ascetic movement. The earliest, and probably the most influential, is Jesus. Luke, in 5:16 states that Jesus would "withdraw to deserted places and pray." Matthew, in 4:1-2, tells the story of Jesus going into the desert (or wilderness) for 40 days: "Then Jesus was led up by the Spirit into the wilderness to be tempted by the devil. He fasted forty days and forty nights, and afterwards he was famished." Many people, both men and women, decided to replicate the experience that Jesus had and they did this by seeking out their own wilderness, whether it was in the deserts of Egypt or secluded spots within cities.

Many influential early Christians were ascetics, or tried to live an ascetic lifestyle, including Anthony, Julian Saba, Jerome, and Simeon Stylites. Anthony is probably the most famous ascetic from early Christianity (died around 356 CE). He was a monk who lived in the desert of Egypt from the 270s through the middle part of the 300s CE. The way he lived his life became an example to many early (and modern Christians) who believed that his way of life was better than their own. Anthony was also influential with the local government in his area. Quite a bit is known about Anthony because of a book that survived from antiquity titled *The Life of Anthony*, written by Athanasius, the bishop of Alexandria (328 to 373 CE). The document is very important in shedding light on Anthony and the monks who lived around him. According to *The Life of Anthony*, Anthony's parents were Christian, and after they died, Anthony inherited their wealth. He decided to follow the examples of the apostles when he sold everything and then went to live in the desert. At first he lived in an abandoned tomb (maybe a tomb from the time of Egypt's pharaohs?). The text states that he was tempted and tortured by the devil (here called "the enemy") (section 8):

> Thus tightening his hold upon himself, Antony departed to the tombs, which happened to be at a distance from the village; and having bid one of his acquaintances to bring him bread at intervals of many days, he entered one of the tombs, and the other having shut the door on him, he remained within alone. And when the enemy could not endure it, but was even fearful that in a short time Antony would fill the desert with the discipline, coming one night with a multitude of demons, he so cut him with stripes that he lay on the ground speechless from the excessive pain. For he affirmed that the torture had been so excessive that no blows inflicted by man could ever have caused him such torment. But by the Providence of God—for the Lord never overlooks them that hope in Him—the next day his acquaintance came bringing him the loaves. And having opened the door and seeing him lying on the ground as though dead, he lifted him up and carried him to the church in the village, and laid him upon the ground. And many of his kinsfolk and the villagers sat around Antony as round a corpse. But about midnight he came to himself and arose, and when he saw them all asleep and his comrade alone watching, he motioned with his head for him to approach, and asked him to carry him again to the tombs without waking anybody. (Schaff, "Life of Anthony," n.d.)

We are told that Anthony was attacked many times, but that God rescued him. We are also told that Anthony, despite the fact that he lived in the tomb for decades, did not age. Other men also started to live in the desert around Anthony, seeking his advice and wanting to live like him. They often gathered around him while he taught them about the ascetic life and the Bible. Anthony's way of worshipping was soon followed by many other people.

Another example of an ascetic was a man named Julian Saba (died around 367 CE), who is described by Theodoret, an early Christian historian. Theodoret wrote a book titled *A History of the Monks of Syria*. He states that Julian lived in Mesopotamia in a natural cave. He only ate once a week and this was just barley, bran, salt, and water. Like Anthony, soon many men had heard about Julian and wanted to live like him, and soon he had over 100 disciples. Their usual day consisted of going out into the desert in groups of two, and while one prayed on his knees, the other sang songs from the Old Testament. This continued all day until right before sunset, and at this point they all gathered again in front of Julian and sang songs to him.

Jerome, a Christian writer (died in 420 CE) writes that he retreated into the wilderness for a couple of years. He mentions his experiences in his Letter 22, section 7. Here he talks about wearing sackcloth and eating very little. He states that eating cooked food was frowned upon. As mentioned in the section on Jerome, Jerome was convinced that the ascetic way of living was the correct one for a vast number of Christians, including women. Jerome himself set up a monastery for men and women in the city of Bethlehem. Jerome also wrote a book titled *The Life of Paulus, the First Hermit*. In it Jerome states that many have written about who the first hermit was, and he is convinced that it was a person named Paulus of the Egyptian city of Thebes. We are told that Paulus escaped into the mountains when there were Christians being persecuted. There he found a cave that had a palm tree growing in it because the cave had an opening to the sky. Jerome then writes (in chapter 6):

> Accordingly, regarding his abode as a gift from God, he fell in love with it, and there in prayer and solitude spent all the rest of his life. The palm afforded him food and clothing. And, that no one may deem this impossible, I call to witness Jesus and His holy angels that I have seen and still see in that part of the desert which lies between Syria and the Saracens' country, monks of whom one was shut up for thirty years and lived on barley bread and muddy water, while another in an old cistern (called in the country dialect of Syria Gubba) kept himself alive on five dried figs a day. What I relate then is so strange that it will appear incredible to those who do not believe the words that "all things are possible to him who believes." (Schaff, "Life of Paulus," n.d.)

Jerome also said that Paulus lived to be 113 years old, surviving on the water that sprang up near the palm tree and bread, which was delivered every day by a bird. Before he died, Paulus met probably with Anthony, mentioned above.

The last ascetic we can examine is Simeon Stylites who died around 459 CE. Simeon entered into a monastery at the age of 16. Simeon, however, believed that he should live an extreme ascetic life and was thrown out of the monastery. His fame grew soon after this with hundreds of pilgrims seeking him out for advice and for his blessing. Simeon didn't like this, so he decided to live on top of a pillar, which, when fully built, reached fifty feet high. He lived on an area that has been estimated to be only three feet by three feet. He refused to come down to greet the hundreds of pilgrims, so they ended up building platforms and using ladders to get close to him. He was so influential that emperors either made visits to see him or sent him letters and many people after his death mimicked his living on a pillar.

Asceticism was a very popular movement in early Christianity. Many early church writers either mention the ascetics or were ascetics themselves. Their influence affected all levels of the church, from the lowest monks to the emperors. Despite the difficult lifestyle, many people after the time of Anthony, Julian, and Simeon wanted to live like this. They believed it allowed them to worship God in a better way than if they had continued to live their lives surrounded by luxuries and temptations in the cities.

See also: Jerome.

Further Reading

Brakke, David. *Athanasius and the Politics of Asceticism* (Oxford Early Christian Studies). Oxford: Oxford University Press, 1995.

Brakke, David. *Athanasius and Asceticism*. Baltimore: John Hopkins Press, 1998.

Schaff, Philip. "Life of Anthony." *Athanasius: Select Works and Letters*. Edinburgh: T&T Clark, n.d. Available online at http://www.ccel.org/ccel/schaff/npnf204.html.

Schaff, Philip. "The Life of Paulus the First Hermit." *Jerome: Letters and Select Works*. Edinburgh: T&T Clark, n.d. Available online at http://www.ccel.org/ccel/schaff/npnf206.i.html.

Vaage, Leif E., and Vincent L. Wimbush, eds. *Asceticism and the New Testament*. New York: Routledge, 1999.

Vuolanto, Ville. *Children and Asceticism in Late Antiquity: Continuity, Family Dynamics and the Rise of Christianity*. Dorchester: Dorset Press, 2015.

ATHANASIUS   Athanasius was bishop of Alexandria, Egypt, from 328 to 373 CE. He is probably the most controversial bishop of the fourth century mostly because of his involvement and arguments with the Arians. Although he was bishop of Alexandria for a very long time (45 years), he spent a good part of that time away because of the numerous exiles that he suffered during this period. Athanasius had a long association with the church, even before he became bishop. He was a deacon from 311 CE until the time he became bishop. He was also present at the now-famous Council of Nicea in 325. Athanasius wrote quite a few texts and letters that still survive today, and there are also two documents that chronicle some of his life and letters, written sometime right after his death. Because of these important sources, the later part of his life is well known.

Not much is known about the early life of Athanasius. It is known that he became a deacon of the church in Alexandria, Egypt, in 311 CE under Bishop Alexander. It was just after this period that Bishop Alexander had gotten into a heated discussion with a priest named Arius. Arius openly argued with Alexander over the nature of Christ. Arius believed that God was always in existence, while Christ came into existence at some point after God. Alexander believed that God, Christ, and the Holy Spirit existed all at the same time from the very beginning. The argument soon spread outside of Egypt and was centered primarily in the eastern part of the Roman Empire. The deacon Athanasius sided with Bishop Alexander. In 325 Emperor Constantine I asked that all bishops and their attendants go to Nicea to discuss the problems surrounding the Arian controversy. Alexander, Arius, and Athanasius were all present, although since Athanasius was a deacon, he had no say in the main meeting, which was reserved only for the bishops. Athanasius acted as the secretary of his bishop, so he knew what was happening. Athanasius wrote a little of what happened in the Council of Nicea (especially in his book titled *Defense of the Nicene Definition*). He wrote that the Arians were condemned at this council and specifically mentions the end of the Nicene Creed. Alexander, Athanasius, and those who supported their beliefs walked away from the council victorious in their efforts to get the Arians exiled. However, this celebration did not last long.

Bishop Alexander and Athanasius went back to Alexandria thinking that the Arian controversy was over, but in reality, it was just starting. In either 327 or early 328 Emperor Constantine allowed a number of Arians to rejoin their church, and the emperor demanded that Bishop Alexander take back Arius. Alexander refused to do this. Alexander died in 328 and before his death he picked Athanasius to be the next bishop. This did not occur right after the death of Alexander. It appears that a few months went by, and it isn't absolutely clear what had happened in the meantime. It appears that some did not want Athanasius to become bishop, but by June 328, he was officially anointed. Bishop Athanasius, like Alexander, refused to accept Arius back into the Alexandrian church. This was the beginning of many years of trouble for him. In 335 CE Bishop Athansius was removed from his office for the first time and sent into exile to the western Roman city of Trier. Emperor Constantine died in 339, and his three sons, Constantine II, Constans, and

Constantius II, jointly ruled the Roman Empire. After the death of Emperor Constantine, Athanasius traveled back to Alexandria with the support of Emperor Constantine II, who was ruling over the western part of the empire. However, this return did not last long, and he was once again sent into exile in 339. The emperor of the eastern part of the Roman Empire was Constantius II, who was firmly in the Arian camp and did not like Athanasius. Athanasius, however, was well liked in Rome, but wasn't able to return to Egypt until 346 CE. He was sent into exile again from 356 to 361, in 363 for a short period, and finally in 365 for a year. Each exile was essentially over his sometimes violent opposition to the Arians.

Being away from Alexandria for so long also caused him problems. Some bishops who didn't like him stated that he really should be replaced by someone else, and that he was cowardly for not standing up to the emperors and instead abandoned his flock. Athanasius responded to this with a book titled *Defense of His Flight*. He starts his letter:

> I hear that Leontius, now at Antioch, and Narcissus of the city of Nero, and George, now at Laodicea, and the Arians who are with them, are spreading abroad many slanderous reports concerning me, charging me with cowardice, because indeed, when I myself was sought by them, I did not surrender myself into their hands. Now as to their imputations and calumnies, although there are many things that I could write, which even they are unable to deny, and which all who have heard of their proceedings know to be true, yet I shall not be prevailed upon to make any reply to them, except only to remind them of the words of our Lord, and of the declaration of the Apostle, that "a lie is of the Devil," and that, "revilers shall not inherit the kingdom of God." For it is sufficient thereby to prove, that neither their thoughts nor their words are according to the Gospel, but that after their own pleasure, whatsoever themselves desire, that they think to be good. (Schaff, n.d.)

Athanasius continues to defend himself against the charges all throughout this book. Athanasius also wrote many other books about his trials against his enemies, including one titled *Defense against the Arians*. At the very beginning of the book he explained why he had to write it:

> I supposed that, after so many proofs of my innocence had been given, my enemies would have shrunk from further enquiry, and would now have condemned themselves for their false accusations of others. But as they are not yet abashed, though they have been so clearly convicted, but, as insensible to shame, persist in their slanderous reports against me, professing to think that the whole matter ought to be tried over again (not that they may have judgment passed on them, for that they avoid, but in order to harass me, and to

disturb the minds of the simple); I therefore thought it necessary to make my defense unto you, that you may listen to their murmurings no longer, but may denounce their wickedness and base calumnies. And it is only to you, who are men of sincere minds, that I offer a defense: as for the contentious, I appeal confidently to the decisive proofs which I have against them. For my cause needs no further judgment; for judgment has already been given, and not once or twice only, but many times . . . (Schaff, n.d.)

This book is extremely important because Athanasius preserves a number of letters that were sent (and do not exist anywhere else). Care must be taken, however, with believing everything that Athanasius wrote because, in many cases, we only have his accounts. Regardless, Bishop Athanasius is an extremely important source for our knowledge of what took place in the middle of the 300s CE. Athanasius died in 373 after presiding over the Alexandrian church for 45 years. Although he did not have an easy time, his battles with the Arians helped to cement the theological ideas that were rapidly becoming part of the Catholic Church. His writings were also used by many later Christians and are very important for recreating this interesting time in church history.

See also: Arians; Council of Nicea.

Further Reading

Anatolios, Khaled. *Athanasius* (The Early Church Fathers). New York: Routledge, 2004.

Barnes, Timothy D. *Athanasius and Constantius: Theology and Politics in the Constantinian Empire*. Cambridge, MA: First Harvard University Press, 1993.

Brakke, David. *Athanasius and the Politics of Asceticism* (Oxford Early Christian Studies). Oxford: Oxford University Press, 1995.

Schaff, Philip. "Defense against the Arians." *Athanasius: Select Works and Letters*. Edinburgh: T&T Clark, n.d. Available online at http://www.ccel.org/ccel/schaff/npnf204.

Schaff, Philip. "Defense of His Flight." *Athanasius: Select Works and Letters*. Edinburgh: T&T Clark, n.d. Available online at http://www.ccel.org/ccel/schaff/npnf204.

AUGUSTINE   Augustine, born 354 and died in 430 CE, was another very influential bishop of his time. He was an active writer and his material today can fill up whole bookshelves. We know Augustine very well because of that. Once he became a Catholic, he became one of the leading bishops in North Africa (where he was from) and certainly played a large role in later theology. There are a couple of areas that can be looked at to get a better understanding of Augustine. We can examine his early life, his various religious/philosophical conversions, his writings, and finally, the last section of this life.

Augustine was born in 354 in a North African city called Thagaste. His father was a pagan, or a follower of the Roman religion, while his mother, Monica, was a Catholic. Augustine wrote a very important book titled *The Confessions* and he tells us quite a bit about his early life. He states that he was a very active little kid and teenager who got into various troubles such as stealing pears from his neighbors. He took his studies very seriously, especially Roman philosophy. By all accounts he was a very good student. His book-learning helped him to rise up in terms of social rank. He eventually decided that a type of philosophy called Neoplatonism was the best form of philosophy, and he gathered together a group of his friends to study it. It was really his first conversion.

Soon after this he decided to convert to Manichaeism, a Christian religion that seemed to be popular in North Africa. He believed that this was the best form of Christianity, and he proceeded to convince all of his friends to convert as well. While studying this religion he became a teacher of rhetoric. Rhetoric taught young men how to give persuasive arguments so that they could become lawyers. He seemed to be unhappy with some of his students who were skipping out of paying him, so he decided to move to Italy where there were more opportunities for someone who wanted to climb the social ladder.

He also had a girlfriend, and together they had a son named Adeodatus (which literally means "a gift from God"). Augustine adored his mother, but there is a very famous episode in his *Confessions* in which he tells the story that he had to trick his mother into not coming with him to Italy. He told her when he was going to leave, but then left before that, leaving her behind. When he arrived in Rome he stayed with some of his Manichaean friends. Through some upper-level contacts, Augustine got the job as rhetor in the city of Milan, where his mother soon joined him. This was an extremely important post in that he had to give speeches for people who were high up in the Roman government, including the emperor. During his stay in Milan, at his mother's insistence he left his girlfriend in order to marry a young girl whose family had money (but he never married her in the end). The girlfriend had to return to Africa, but his son Adeodatus stayed with Augustine.

While he was certainly following his dream of having influence and money, he was not happy. Two years after he started, he left his position in Milan, and then his son died at an early age, leaving Augustine with no family except for his mother. He did have many friends, and Augustine spent some time with them to study philosophy. Augustine then decided to get baptized by none other than Ambrose of Milan. Augustine then went to Africa, but unfortunately for him, Monica, his mother, died before they left shore.

A few years after returning to North Africa he went to the city of Hippo and was really forced into becoming a priest by Valerius, the bishop of Hippo. Augustine tells us that he cried because he did not want to be a priest, but it was done. He asked Valerius for some time to study the Bible, and it was during this period that he began to write against his former Manichaean friends and religion. Many books and letters from Augustine have come down to us, and many of them are very argumentative. He wrote against the Manichaeans, against the Donatists, against people who did not follow his form of religion, and against those who followed the Roman religion. It was in 395 CE that Augustine became the bishop of Hippo.

His life was very busy after this point. He would spend his days attending to his congregation and usually spend his nights writing. This was his normal routine for the entire period he was bishop. It did not stop as he got older either. Despite this, he could not control the Roman government or the problems that were plaguing it during the late 300s and into the 400s. These problems centered on the barbarian incursions that were happening more and more frequently, and the Roman emperors could do little to prevent them. One group, named the Vandals, swept through Spain and then went further by sailing to North Africa. During the last year of his life Augustine's city of Hippo was surrounded by the Vandals, but fortunately for Augustine, he did not see his city taken over since they captured it soon after his death in 430. The Vandals, known for their destructive behavior (which is where we get the word "vandal"), conquered North Africa and made it into their own kingdom. But Augustine's influence lasted much longer than the Vandal control of Africa, and even today the Catholic Church recognizes the impact that Augustine had on Catholic theology.

See also: Ambrose; Donatists; Mani, the Founder of Manichaeism; Manichaeans.

Further Reading
Brown, Peter. *Augustine of Hippo: A Biography.* A New Edition with an Epilogue. Berkeley: University of California Press, 2000.

Chadwick, Henry. *Augustine: A Very Short Introduction.* New York: Oxford University Press, 1986.

Levering, Matthew. *The Theology of Augustine: An Introductory Guide to His Most Important Works.* Grand Rapids, MI: Baker Academic, 2013.

O'Donnell, James J. *Augustine: A New Biography.* New York: HarperCollins, 2005.

Vessey, Mark, ed. *A Companion to Augustine* (Blackwell Companions to the Ancient World). Malden, MA: John Wiley and Sons, 2012.

CATACOMBS The catacombs were underground rooms and tunnels where Christians and others would bury their dead in the first centuries of Christianity. There are many catacombs in and around Rome as well as in other major Roman cities. They were an easy place to lay the dead to rest. The tunnels were usually dug for other purposes such as getting access to stone that would then be used in building. The remaining tunnels would then be converted to cemeteries. While Christians were not the first people to bury their dead in catacombs, these catacombs are a very important part of early Christian history, not only for the graves, but also for some of the earliest known Christian artwork that has been found in these tunnels. The art ranges from mosaics to statues to wall paintings, all of which give us a glimpse of what was happening in the lives of early Christians.

Probably the most famous road in early Christianity is the Via Appia, a Latin name sometimes translated as the Appian Way or the Appian Road. This is the road that the apostle Paul traveled on when he was brought to Rome to make his appeal to the emperor. There are now Christian catacombs all along this route and on the roads that criss-cross through this area. There are at least 40 catacombs known, but this number will likely increase when more are discovered. The most famous catacombs are the Catacomb of Saint Sebastian, the Catacomb of Domitilla, and the Catacomb of Saint Callixtus. So where did the idea of burying people in tunnels come from? The answer isn't totally known, but we do know that Jewish people and Romans did the same thing, usually in the same tunnels that the Christians eventually took over. The Christians also just had to look at the New Testament to read that the body of Jesus was put into a rock cave that had a round stone for a door. The rock around Rome also helped with creating tunnels. Many of the stone buildings around Rome were built with a volcanic stone called *tufa*. It is fairly soft, but sturdy enough for building. The stone was carved out, leaving vast tunnels and rooms. In the Christian period the building of the tunnels continued by people who were called *fossores*. This is the Latin word for "bone." There are even some catacomb paintings that show what these *fossores* did when they were digging.

Some of the catacombs are very long and complicated. The catacomb of Callixtus goes for at least 12 miles and is four levels deep. It is named after Callixtus, an early third century administrator of a Christian cemetery, and then later it became an official cemetery of the Catholic Church. The bodies were buried in a few ways. The most common was to dig into the sides of the tunnels to create small niches that were the size of the body being put into it. Once the body was put into the niche, stone or tile was put over the opening. In some cases you could have four of these niches, one on top of the other, and the hallways would be lined in this manner. Sometimes the niche would be deep enough for two bodies, and many times the tile would be decorated and grave objects were put with the bodies. Building a chamber was another way of burying the bodies. A room would be carved out, the body (or bodies in the case of families) would be entombed, and then large tiles would be used to close the body in. Many times these chambers were highly decorated. One example is found in the Catacomb of Saint Callixtus where one chamber is called the Cubicle of the Sacraments. It contains frescoes (or wall paintings) showing the sacraments of baptism and of the Eucharist. The Catacomb of Callixtus also contains the famous tombs of many of the third century popes who reigned from 230 to 283 CE. The earliest pope buried here is Pope Pontian, and the latest is Pope Eutychian. There are also a few bishops who are buried here, and in total it contains 16 graves. The most amazing find from this catacomb is a statue of Christ, showing him as a young shepherd carrying a sheep over his shoulders. This is one of the earliest statues of Christ, and today it can be found in the Vatican Museum in Rome.

Another famous catacomb is the Catacomb of Saint Sebastian. It is thought that Sebastian was killed during the time of Emperor Diocletian and the Great Persecution. A church was built by Emperor Constantine I, and then a more modern church (which still stands today) was built over the old one in the 1500s. The catacomb entrance is right inside the church. This catacomb was originally a Roman cemetery, followed by its use by Christians. This catacomb is famous because it is thought that the bodies of Saint Peter and Saint Paul were held here. If you visit, you will be able to see a small room that is covered with graffiti from centuries of Christians who came to this catacomb and asked Peter and Paul to pray for them.

As mentioned, these catacombs are full of early Christian artwork. Some of the artwork are painted symbols that represent various things that happened in Christianity. For example, a common symbol is of the fish and the loaves, representing the story of when Jesus took a few fish and loaves of bread and miraculously increased them to feed 5,000 people (Matthew 14:16–21). Another symbol is the alpha and the omega, the first and last letters in the Greek alphabet. These represent Christ, who is mentioned in Revelation 1:8 (and elsewhere): "'I am the Alpha and the Omega,' says the Lord God, who is and who was and who is to come, the Almighty."

Early Christians knew about these catacombs and would often venture down into them just to see what they looked like. Jerome, an early church father who lived from the early 340s to 420 CE, gave an eyewitness account of visiting a catacomb after he attended church. He writes (in his *Commentary on Ezekeiel*, 40.5–13):

> When I was a boy at Rome, and was being educated in liberal studies, I was accustomed, with others of like age and mind, to visit on Sundays the sepulchres of the apostles and martyrs. And often did I enter the crypts, deep dug in the earth . . . (Schaff, n.d.)

He also writes that the walls of the tunnels were lined with bodies and, not surprisingly, it was a very dark and scary place. Later in the 600s a "tourist guide" to the catacombs was published, and this led to many more people visiting the graves of the dead. The scientific study of the catacombs did not start until the 1400s and has continued since then. Some of the catacombs can still be visited today.

See also: Diocletian.

Further Reading

Athnos, Gregory S. *The Art of the Roman Catacombs: Themes of Deliverance in the Age of Persecution.* Parker, CO: Outskirts Press, 2011.

Ferrua, A., trans. by I. Inglis. *The Unknown Catacomb: A Unique Discovery of Early Christian Art.* Glasgow: Geddes and Grosset, 1990.

Mancinelli, Fabrizio. *The Catacombs of Rome and the Origins of Christianity.* Firenze: Scala, 1981.

Nicolai, V. F., F. Bisconti, and D. Mazzoleni. *The Christian Catacombs of Rome: History, Decoration, Inscriptions,* rev. ed. Schnell und Steiner, 2009.

Schaff, Philip. "Commentary on Ezekeiel." *Jerome: The Principle Works of Jerome.* Edinburgh: T&T Clark, n.d. Available online at http://www.ccel.org/ccel /schaff/npnf206.

CHRISTOLOGY   Christology is simply the study of Christ. But what is not so simple is who Christ was to ancient Christians. Here are some typical questions we can look at in the study of Christology: Was he the Son of God? Was he God? Was he totally human? If both human and God, how can a human be both God and man at the same time? If both human and God, then what does this tell us about his behavior? Are his thoughts God's thoughts? Or are they different? If Jesus was both God and man, what distinguishes him from God (or for that matter, the Holy Spirit) or is he exactly the same? If he was born a human, then when exactly did he become God? These questions, and many others, plague not only modern scholars but, in particular, plagued ancient Christians. The questions and their answers led to many conflicts in early Christianity, and in some cases these conflicts led to physical violence. Other times they led to multiple church councils that would then try to determine the "correct" answer, and this led to the enforcement of this answer on the lay Christians.

EARLY CHRISTOLOGY

So who exactly was Christ? Was he first a man, and then elevated to God? If he was believed to be a man first, then God later, then this is called "low Christology." In this case some early Christians believed that Jesus was born a regular man, albeit a very special one, and at his baptism, God made him the Son of God. The main scriptural evidence behind this type of Christology was Mark 1:9–11 (and similar verses in Luke 3:21–22):

> In those days Jesus came from Nazareth of Galilee and was baptized by John in the Jordan. And just as he was coming up out of the water, he saw the heavens torn apart and the Spirit descending like a dove on him. And a voice came from heaven, "You are my Son, the Beloved; with you I am well pleased." (NRSV)

Here Jesus is seen as becoming the Son of God at this point. The other side of the coin was the question: was Jesus born of a virgin and the Son of God from the very beginning? Some Christians believed this, and this is called "high Christology." Christ, as God, descended from "high" to be a part of human society as opposed to starting off "low," as a man, who was then elevated to Godship. The main scriptural evidence behind high Christology comes from the Gospel of John, which begins with Jesus being the Word of God (John 1:1–4):

> In the beginning was the Word, and the Word was with God, and the Word was God. He was in the beginning with God. All things came into being through him, and without him not one thing came into being. What has come into being in him was life, and the life was the light of all people. (NRSV)

Related to high Christology, Christians in the second century asked how Christ could be human and divine at the same time. One answer can be found in the writings of Tertullian, a North African church father, who stated that Jesus was a single person, but contained two natures—human and divine. Tertullian's idea made sure that Jesus stayed fully human and at the same time stayed fully God. Tertullian was fighting with a group of people who believed that Jesus was one "mode" of God, meaning that God would become Christ and that God would only be found on the earth (and not in heaven). This form of Christology is called Modalism. This led to lots of problems for some Christians because it meant that God Himself was crucified and suffered when Christ was on the cross. Many refused to believe this, and it led to other Christological controversies.

LATER CHRISTOLOGY

Christians continued to discuss the nature of Christ throughout the 200s and into the 300s. Christology became the biggest reason for Christian infighting during this later period. In the earliest decades of the 300s CE there was no one "correct" form of Christianity—there were many different types. Each group naturally believed that it was the correct one for all of Christianity to follow. In this period there were two main forms: the Nicenes and the Arians. The Nicenes were Christians who would eventually become the Catholics. The Arians would become a major movement in the 300s, would nearly die out by the end of the 300s, only to remerge in the 400s with the "barbarian" invasions. These barbarians were, for the most part, Christian, but of the Arian persuasion.

The main difference between the two was over Christology. The Nicenes believed that God, Jesus, and the Holy Spirit always and forever existed. There was never a time when they were not in existence. The Nicenes ended up using a word *homoousius*, a rarely used word, to explain the relationship between the Three (or the Trinity). *Homoousius* is a mixture of two Greek words: *homo*, meaning "same," and *ousius*, meaning "nature," so, one-nature: God, Jesus, and the Holy Spirit share the exact same nature. They have different functions, but are the same. The Arians, on the other hand, believed that God, Jesus, and the Holy Spirit were not the same nature. Arius, who started this movement, believed that because God is the Father, He must have come first (after all, he would ask, who comes first—a father or a son?). At some point Jesus and the Holy Spirit were brought into existence by the Father. The Nicenes did not like the Arian beliefs for a number of different reasons. The primary one was that if Jesus was not fully God, then he could not forgive sins. The Arians did not like the Nicene Christology because it created two gods (the Father and the Son).

Both sides would turn to the Old and New Testaments to back up their beliefs. This Christological controversy led directly to the Council of Nicea, held in 325. There, a council of bishops created the Nicene Creed, which stated that God, Jesus, and the Holy Spirit were of the same nature, and anyone who did not believe this was deemed to be a heretic. The Council of Nicea did not put an end to the Christological debates. Some Christians focused on the mind of Christ: Did he have a human mind, or did he have the mind of God? If he had the mind of God, how could he be a man at the same time? Did he also have the nature of God? If so, how could he be a man at the same time? This argument was called the Monophysite controversy (from the Greek words *mono*, "one," and *physite*, "nature," or Christ has one nature). However, this Christological controversy falls outside the scope of this book.

See also: Council of Nicea.

Further Reading

Akin, Daniel L. *Christology: The Study of Christ*. The Concise Theology Series. N.p.: Rainer Publishing, 2013.

Brown, Raymond Edward. *An Introduction to New Testament Christology*. Mahwah, NJ: Paulist Press, 1994.

O'Collins, Gerald. *Christology: A Biblical, Historical, and Systematic Study of Jesus*. Oxford: Oxford University Press, 1995.

Rausch, T. P. *Who is Jesus?: An Introduction to Christology*. Collegeville, MN: Liturgical Press, 2003.

Witherington, Ben. *The Christology of Jesus*. Minneapolis: Augsberg Fortress Press, 1990.

CONSTANTINE I   Roman emperor Constantine I was born around 272 CE. His father was Constantius I and his mother was Helena. Constantius I rose up in the army, became the caesar (something like our vice president) under Emperor Maximinius Herculius, and ultimately became emperor of the western Roman Empire in 305 CE. During this early period Constantine was held as a royal hostage by Galerius, the caesar in the east, which was meant to ensure that Constantius I behaved. Constantine was eventually allowed to see his father, who was in Britain at the time. During a battle with the Picts, a group of native Britons, Constantius I was killed. At this point Constantine was elected emperor by the Roman troops. This, however, was against the Tetrarchy that Emperor Diocletian had set up in the late 200s.

Constantine accepted this, but he also had two other contenders for the throne: Severus, who was the rightful caesar and now emperor as well, and Maxentius, the son of Emperor Maximian in the east who felt he should be emperor. Severus was sent to Rome to do battle with Maxentius, but lost and was eventually killed. This left Maxentius and Constantine to battle it out on who would be the sole emperor in the west. This battle took place in 312 in Rome. The battle is famous in Christian history because it was at this point that Constantine had his first glimpse at Christianity. There are two versions of this story that come down to us from contemporaries of Constantine. The first is from Eusebius, the bishop of Caesarea. The second is from Lactantius, a Christian teacher who became friends with Constantine and was the tutor to Constantine's son Crispus. The two accounts are nearly the same, so we can look at what Eusebius of Caesarea had to say about this in his book titled *Life of Constantine*, Book 1, Chapter 28:

> Accordingly he called on him with earnest prayer and supplications that he would reveal to him who he was, and stretch forth his right hand to help him

in his present difficulties. And while he was thus praying with fervent entreaty, a most marvelous sign appeared to him from heaven, the account of which it might have been hard to believe had it been related by any other person. But since the victorious emperor himself long afterwards declared it to the writer of this history, when he was honored with his acquaintance and society, and confirmed his statement by an oath, who could hesitate to accredit the relation, especially since the testimony of after-time has established its truth? He said that about noon, when the day was already beginning to decline, he saw with his own eyes the trophy of a cross of light in the heavens, above the sun, and bearing the inscription, "Conquer by this." At this sight he himself was struck with amazement, and his whole army also, which followed him on this expedition, and witnessed the miracle . . . (Schaff, n.d.)

Constantine followed this advice, put the sign of the cross on his standards, and then went to battle Maxentius at the Milvian Bridge, one of the bridges that crosses the Tiber in Rome. Maxentius was defeated, and after his death Constantine became the sole emperor in the west, while a man named Licinius was the emperor of the east. These two met in 313 CE in Milan, Italy, and it was here where the two men finally stopped the Great Persecution by issuing something that is referred today as the Edict of Milan. This is a very important document in the history of early Christianity because it gave Christians the right to practice their faith openly and without fear of persecution for the very first time. The beginning of the Edict states:

> When I, Constantine Augustus, as well as I, Licinius Augustus, fortunately met near Mediolanum (Milan), and were considering everything that pertained to the public welfare and security, we thought, among other things which we saw would be for the good of many, those regulations pertaining to the reverence of the Divinity ought certainly to be made first, so that we might grant to the Christians and others full authority to observe that religion which each preferred; whence any Divinity whatsoever in the seat of the heavens may be propitious and kindly disposed to us and all who are placed under our rule. . . (Schaff, n.d.)

It is clear from this text that Christianity was not the only religion that was allowed to be practiced in the Roman Empire at the time, but it was very clear that Christians were able to be Christians without being persecuted.

Despite this outward show of unity, the two men did not totally get along, and this uneasiness between the two of then led to two battles, in 314 and then again in 315. There were no victors, and so they remained as co-emperors. But in 321 they went to battle again, and this time Licinius was totally defeated and eventually killed under the orders of Constantine. This left

Constantine as the sole ruler of the entire Roman Empire, and was the last time that the Tetrarchy, developed by Emperor Diocletian only 40 years before, was applied. After his elevation to sole emperor Constantine started to encourage Christians in a number of different ways. He had a number of churches built; he gave tax relief to the clergy and the churches; he made bishops judges over civil cases; he created antipagan laws; and finally, he had a new royal city built: Constantinople.

After securing the safety of Christians who wanted to openly worship, Constantine then built them a number of churches. The most important church was St. Peter's Basilica. This was a five-apse church, meaning that there were five aisles. The front of the church is called the apse, and within the apse is the altar. In the case of this church, Constantine ordered that the apse and altar be built directly over the spot where people believed St. Peter was buried. This church stood from the time of Constantine until the time of Pope Julius II, who in the early 1500s ordered that it be torn down. The Pope then oversaw the building of the new St. Peter's, which still stands today. Constantine also built churches called the Lateran, the Basilica of Saints Marcellinus and Peter, and the Basilica of Saint Paul (among many others). Constantine's mother Helena was also involved in building churches, including the Church of the Nativity and a church on the Mount of Olives, both in Jerusalem.

Almost everyone in the Roman Empire had to pay taxes, but in the early 300s Constantine passed a series of laws that said that the clergy and the Church itself no longer had to pay taxes on its income. People could also, for the first time, leave their estate to the Church when they died. This had a number of effects on the history of Christianity. First, it allowed the church to build up a huge sum of money, which it then spent on building buildings, helping the poor, and supporting widows and orphans. The second effect it had is that even today religious organizations are not taxed, which allows them to do the same things that the ancient Christians did with their extra money.

There is a bit of debate on whether or not Constantine himself ordered antipagan laws. It is known, however, that when his three sons came to power (Constantius II, Constans, and Constantine II), there were antipagan laws. Some scholars argue that it was indeed Constantine who forbade blood sacrifice. They point out that Constantine refused to have sacrifice performed in front of him, and it was probably Constantine who put a law from a collection titled *The Theodosian Codes*, Chapter 16.10.4 on the books. This law also has the name of his son Constans attached to it. It states:

> It is decreed that in all places and all cities the temples should be closed at once, and after a general warning, the opportunity of sinning be taken from the

wicked. We decree also that we shall cease from making sacrifices. And if anyone has committed such a crime, let him be stricken with the avenging sword. And we decree that the property of the one executed shall be claimed by the city, and that rulers of the provinces be punished in the same way, if they neglect to punish such crimes. Constantine and Constans Augusti. (Thatcher 1907)

Finally, Constantine had a new royal city built in the east. Today the city is called Istanbul, and before the time of Constantine it was called Byzantium. Constantine was rarely in Rome and never lived there the entire time that he was emperor (31 years). He seems to have wanted a spot that he could fully rule from that wasn't in the pagan center of the world—Rome. So he created a new city, created a new senate, and this time the city was fully Christian. He named it Constantinople, after himself. The ending *ople* is related to the Greek word *polis*, which means "city," so Constantinople is literally "the city of Constantine." The city was located in a perfect spot. It was on a hill surrounded by cliffs and water on three sides, which made it very hard to capture. Constantine had a wall built on the exposed side, and then later in the fifth century Emperor Theodosius II had another wall built. The walls and secure place for the city allowed it to fend off any attackers until an army sponsored by Venice captured it in 1204, and then finally in 1453 the Muslim Turks captured the city and made it a Muslim capital, eventually renaming it Istanbul.

Emperor Constantine ruled for 31 years, and in all that time he was never baptized. To be baptized on your deathbed was considered normal during this period. The idea was that if you are baptized just before you are about to die, you will enter heaven sinless. So in 331 CE Constantine began to feel ill and wanted to be baptized. He first went to a city named Helenopolis (named after his mother) to pray at a local saint's tomb. He was hoping that this would cure him. However, he did not feel better so he decided to return to Constantinople. On his way he stopped at Nicomedia, a major Roman city in northern Turkey. It was here that he was baptized by the Arian bishop Eusebius of Nicomedia (not to be confused with Eusebius of Caesarea). He died on May 22, 337 CE.

See also: Diocletian.

Further Reading

Kousoulas, D. G. *The Life and Times of Constantine the Great*, 2nd ed. Bethesda, MD: Provost Books, 2003.

Pohlsander, Hans A. *Emperor Constantine* (Lancaster Pamphlets in Ancient History), 2nd ed. New York: Routledge, 2004.

Potter, David. *Constantine the Emperor*. Oxford: Oxford University Press, 2012.

Sayers, Dorothy L. *The Emperor Constantine*. Grand Rapids, MI: W. B. Eerdmans, 1976.

Schaff, Philip. "Edict of Milan." *Eusebius Pamphilius: Church History, Life of Constantine, Oration in Praise of Constantine*. T&T Clark: Edinburgh, n.d. Available online at http://www.ccel.org/ccel/schaff/npnf201.

Schaff, Philip. "Life of Constantine." *Eusebius Pamphilius: Church History, Life of Constantine, Oration in Praise of Constantine*. Edinburgh: T&T Clark, n.d. Available online at http://www.ccel.org/ccel/schaff/npnf201.

Stephenson, Paul. *Constantine: Roman Emperor, Christian Victor*. New York: Peter Mayer Publishers, 2010.

Thatcher, Oliver J., ed. *Codex Theodosianus*. From *The Library of Original Sources*. Milwaukee: University Research Extension Co., 1907, Vol. IV: The Early Medieval World, 69–71. Available online at http://legacy.fordham.edu/halsall/source/codex-theod1.asp.

COUNCIL OF NICEA   The Council of Nicea is one of the most important church councils in the history of Christianity. It was called by Emperor Constantine I in order to deal with the deep divisions that were occurring in Christianity between the Arians and the non-Arians (who would become the Catholics). The emperor was getting tired of all of the arguments and complaints that were coming from both sides. The council is extremely significant in Christian history for a number of different reasons. The first is that it was the very first church council where all bishops were called to attend, both those living in the east and those in the west. The second is that all future church councils followed the plan set down in this first one. The third is that the decisions made by this council affected all of church history. The fourth is that it set the precedent, for a long time to come, of having an emperor preside over and sometimes call for a council to meet.

The Council of Nicea (a city in northwestern Turkey) met in 325 CE in order to find a way to stop the arguing between the Arians and those who would soon be called Catholics. The main reason they were arguing was over theology, and in particular, something called Christology. Christology is the study of Christ. In the early 300s there was a man named Arius who was a priest in northern Egypt. Arius and his supporters believed that God was always in existence and that the Son, Christ, came into existence at some point afterwards. As Arius pointed out, God is called the Father, and he would ask, which comes first, the Father or the Son? On the other side stood his bishop, Alexander. Alexander and his supporters believed that God the Father, Christ the Son, and the Holy Spirit were always in existence and that one did not come before the others. The two sides quickly gathered their supporters, and arguments began.

Sozomen, a church historian who lived between 400 and 450 CE, wrote that when Arius first put forth his ideas, some people in Alexandria liked his ideas, and sometimes those that did not accept Arius fought violently with those who did. Later in the controversy, cities like Constantinople and Alexandria were divided into Arian and non-Arian camps. Socrates Scholasticus, a church historian who died sometime in the 430s CE, wrote that people were killed in rioting. Churches were burned when one form of Christianity took the place of another. Those that weren't burned were invaded by both sides, usually at the same time, and the only way to get them to leave was the use of the troops. Sometimes, usually under political pressure, bishops changed sides. The spread of Arianism and the Nicene/Catholic form of Christianity was rarely a peaceful affair in the fourth century. But that did not stop the two sides from trying to convince the people to accept one or the other. These arguments caught the attention of Emperor Constantine. Constantine had tried to bring the two sides together and sometimes tried to force them to accept the other's beliefs. When this didn't work, the emperor decided to call a church council together to get all of the bishops talking and to get them to all agree on what the true faith actually was.

Emperor Constantine sent letters to all of the bishops, east and west. The Council of Nicea is titled the First Ecumenical Council because of this. In truth, most of the bishops came from the east. A handful came from the west, but not the bishop of Rome, who sent representatives. One of the reasons why there were hardly any western bishops is because of the hardship of travel, despite the fact that the emperor provided free transport to the bishops and their attendants. The exact number of bishops who attended is not known. The traditional number is 318, but it seems to be somewhere between 250 and 300 bishops, plus all of their staff. Arius was also in attendance, as well as Bishop Alexander. When everyone arrived Constantine called the council to order and the discussions began. Constantine really wanted the bishops to find some common ground and to stop fighting over issues that he believed were not important.

After having numerous discussions, the Council created a document and some canons (or church laws) that they hoped would settle the matter forever. In the end, the bishops chose the side of Alexander, or what will be referred to as the Nicene or the Catholic side, and rejected the beliefs of Arius. The document they created is the Nicene Creed, an extremely important document that is still used today. It puts forth what the bishops stated were the correct beliefs for Christians. It stated they believed in God, in Christ who created all things, and in the Holy Spirit. It ended with a curse on the Arians and anybody who believed that the Son came second. As a result of this decision, Arius and a few of his supporters were thrown into exile and had to go up to the far northern border of the Roman Empire. A few months later, Eusebius, the bishop of Nicomedia, was also sent into exile for his support of Arius. The exiles and the Nicene Creed were supposed to stop the arguing between the two groups and to form a united Christian front. However, this was not the case, and the Arians and Nicenes/Catholics continued to fight over this issue for centuries to come. The bishops also created 20 canons or laws that were considered binding on the church. They covered many issues, from the castration of priests to restricting women from living with priests or bishops unless the women were mothers, sisters, or aunts, and to making sure that if a member of the clergy was excommunicated in one area, that excommunication would hold in other areas. These canons dealt mostly with the behaviors of the clergy and were meant to be binding on everyone, both in the east and in the west. Despite their good intentions, many of the canons would be ignored later.

The Council of Nicea set a precedent for all later church councils. Each church council that came after this first one recognized its importance, and usually any official proceedings of later councils mentioned that the Nicene Creed was still followed. All future church councils would also create their own creeds and their own canons, repeating what had happened at Nicea. And because the emperor called the first council, many emperors after would attempt to control the church by calling their own councils. This did not make some bishops happy, especially when the emperors were trying to control the church, but because it was done at Nicea in 325, future emperors decided it was within their right to call councils as well.

See also: Arians; Christology.

Further Reading

Davis, Leo D. *The First Seven Ecumenical Councils (325–787): Their History and Theology* (Theology and Life Series). Wilmington, DE: Michael Glazier, 1983.

Kelly, Joseph F., *The Ecumenical Councils of the Catholic Church: A History.* Collegeville, MN: Liturgical Press, 2009.

Rubenstein, Richard E. *When Jesus Became God: The Struggle to Define Christianity during the Last Days of Rome.* New York: Harcourt, 1999.

DATING   As modern people we rarely question our calendar. However, our lives are ruled by time, and this is particularly the case when we wonder what happened in the ancient world. The keeping of time has a very long history, and many early cultures kept their own calendars, but these did not correspond well with other cultures. The period we can first consider was when early Greeks first started to write what we would call "history."

One of the earliest historians was Herodotus, a Greek who lived in the 400s BCE. He wrote the first large history book, titled *The Histories*. Herodotus wrote primarily about the Greeks, the Persians, and the Egyptians. Herodotus, however, had a hard time dating what had happened in the past, especially when he had to compare what was happening in three different cultures. The reason for this is that there wasn't a standard calendar like there is today. Greeks, Egyptians, and Persians kept calendars, but the numbers didn't correspond to each other. For example, Greeks had city-states and they kept track of time by the number of years of the ruler. So Ruler A could rule for 10 years, and the dating system would state that something had happened in the fifth year of Ruler A. When Ruler A died, the calendar would go back to year one of Ruler B. The same would occur in Persia and in Egypt. This would mean that what happened in the fifth year of Ruler A, for example, would correspond to the 15th year of rule of the King of Persia and the second year of rule for the Egyptian pharaoh. As you can imagine, this was very confusing for Greek and later Roman writers who faced the same problem.

When Christianity appeared, early Christian historians began to date things by the birth of Christ, which for them was Year 0. So if something happened 100 years after Christ, they would refer to it as that—100 years after Christ. It didn't matter which culture they were referring to—Greek, Roman, Egyptian, or Persian. The Christian historians would also refer to things that happened before the time of Christ by subtracting the years. So if something happened 100 years before the time of Christ, eventually this was referred to as Before Christ, or BC as it is called today. Later Christians began to refer to what happened after the birth of Christ as AD. It is sometimes thought that this stands for After Death, but it is two Latin words: *anno domini*, or in the year of (our) Lord.

While this is a good dating system, some people in the modern world do not want to use a religious calendar to date things. Thus to date something 100 years after Christ would be 100 CE or 100 Common Era. To date something 100 years before Christ would be 100 BCE, or Before Common Era. It should be pointed out that 100 CE is still exactly the same as 100 AD, and 100 BCE is exactly the same as 100 BC. Finally, not everyone in the world uses the Christian calendar. The Muslim world dates their calendar from the year that Muhammad moved from Mecca to Medina. This would be year 1 in the Muslim calendar, or 622 CE (or AD) in the Christian calendar. The Jewish calendar is also different from the Christian calendar.

Further Reading
Levy, Thomas, and Thomas Higham, eds. *The Bible and Radiocarbon Dating: Archaeology, Text, and Science*. New York: Routledge, 2005.

THE DECIAN PERSECUTION Emperor Decius ruled from 249 to 251 CE, right in the middle of a period in Roman history called the Third Century Crisis. This was a devastating time for the Romans since they were being attacked on two fronts: by the Persians to the east and by the barbarians to the north. Before becoming emperor, Decius was a senator who was sent by the current emperor, Philip, to Moesia (north of Greece) to lead the army's efforts there. After arriving, the troops decided to raise Decius from senator to emperor. Emperor Philip then took his troops to do battle with Decius, and in the process Philip was killed, leaving Decius as the sole emperor. When Decius arrived back in Rome, he started a new building agenda, but more importantly for our purposes, he decided to persecute the Christians.

It isn't known why he did this. Eusebius of Caesarea, in his book titled *Ecclesiastical History* (Chapter 6.39), stated that Decius hated Philip, implying that Philip was a Christian. Eusebius is probably incorrect here, and he also states that Fabianus (or Fabian), the bishop of Rome, was killed in this persecution. Regardless of his motives, Decius required that all Roman citizens take an oath to the emperor, then make a sacrifice and pour a libation (usually pouring wine in honor of the emperor as the Greeks did when they prayed to their gods). Those that did this received a note, or a *libellus*, proving that they had done as the emperor asked. If Christians refused, then they were usually killed or at least tortured. Some Christians also decided to flee the persecution. The most famous one to flee persecution was Cyprian, the bishop of the North African city of Carthage. Cyprian came under attack later by other Christians because he left his flock during the persecution. Cyprian, however, stated that he needed to flee so that the church would stay whole. If he had been killed during this period, he was worried the whole church in North Africa would collapse. Cyprian remained bishop when he returned and then had to deal with other Christians who also fled, or those Christians who lied when they signed their *libelli*. Cyprian was martyred (killed for his faith) in 258, in a new persecution started by Emperor Valerian.

One of the most famous victims of the Decian Persecution was a Christian scholar named Origen. Origen's father was a Christian and was killed during an outbreak of persecution in 202 CE. We are told that Origen also wanted to die with his father, but his mother hid his clothes so that Origen would not leave the house. It isn't clear how true that story is, but we do know that he was tortured in the Decian persecution. Eusebius of Caesarea writes about his torture in his *Ecclesiastical History* (Chapter 6:39):

> But how many and great things came upon Origen in the persecution, and what was their final result: as the demon of evil marshaled all his forces, and fought against the man with his utmost craft and power, assaulting him beyond

all others against whom he contended at that time. And what many things he endured for the word of Christ: bonds and bodily tortures and torments under the iron collar and in the dungeon; and how for many days with his feet stretched four spaces in the stocks he bore patiently the threats of fire and whatever other things were inflicted by his enemies; and how his sufferings terminated, as his judge strove eagerly with all his might not to end his life; and what words he left after these things, full of comfort to those needing aid, a great many of his epistles show with truth and accuracy. (Schaff, n.d.)

Origen did not die during the persecution itself, but a few years after the persecution stopped. We are told that Origen died because of the wounds he received when he was tortured. Christians went through sporadic persecution in the first three centuries, which created many martyrs. This particular persecution ended with the death of Decius in 251, only to be started again by Emperor Valerian. The last of the Christian persecutions officially ended when the joint emperors Constantine I and Licinius issued the Edict of Milan, which gave Christians the right to practice their religion openly and without fear of death.

See also: Diocletian.

Further Reading

Castelli, Elizabeth. *Martyrdom and Memory: Early Christian Culture Making* (Gender, Theory, and Religion). New York: Columbia University Press, 2004.

Frend, W. H. C. *Martyrdom and Persecution in the Early Church*. Cambridge: James Clarke & Co, 2008.

Moss, Candida. *The Myth of Persecution: How Early Christians Invented a Story of Martyrdom*. New York: HarperCollins, 2013.

Schaff, Philip. "Ecclesiastical History." *Eusebius Pamphilius: Church History, Life of Constantine, Oration in Praise of Constantine*. Edinburgh: T&T Clark, n.d. Available online at http://www.ccel.org/ccel/schaff/npnf201.

Workman, Herbert B. *Persecution in the Early Church*. Bloomington, IN: Clearnote Press, 2014.

DIOCLETIAN   Diocletian is important, not only to Christian history, but also to Roman history in general. Without him and his efforts to rescue the Roman Empire in the late 200s CE, Roman history and thus Christian history would have been very different. There are several episodes we can examine for this period. The first is the Third Century Crisis and what led up to the problems occurring in the Roman Empire. The second is how the Third Century Crisis was solved by Emperor Diocletian. The third is the Great Persecution, a persecution aimed at the Christians in the Roman Empire.

From the time of the first emperor, Augustus, up until the early 200s CE, the Roman Empire was fairly stable. This is not to say that there were not problems, because there were, but in general, the empire had preserved its borders, its type of government, and its economy. However, in the early/middle of the 200s there began a period of severe instability that is usually called the Third Century Crisis. There were a number of factors that led up to this instability. The first and primary one is that the Roman Empire was being attacked both in the east by the Persians and in the north by the so-called barbarians, or the people who were living outside of the empire. The Romans had been at war with the Persians on and off for over 200 years by this point. The flashpoint was usually over Armenia (in northern Mesopotamia) or the area controlled by the Romans called Roman Mesopotamia (which covered modern Syria, Palestine, and Israel). As a result, the Persians and the Romans were usually fighting over these areas. The fighting became particularly bad, especially for the Romans, in the middle of the 200s CE as a result of the great Persian king named Shapur I. Shapur I and his army were responsible for the defeats of two emperors. The first emperor was Gordian III who ruled from 238 to 244 CE. Emperor Gordian was only 13 years old when he was made emperor. Gordian III joined the fighting in Mesopotamia in 243. By 244 the emperor was dead, but it isn't clear how he died. The Roman troops lost to Persia, and it is possible he was injured and died during or after the fighting. The supply lines were cut off to the Roman troops, so it is also possible that his own troops turned on him. Regardless of how he died, the new emperor was Philip. Philip had to negotiate with Shapur to stop the war, and part of the agreement was to pay a massive payment to the Persians, along with a possible annual tribute. This was very humiliating to the Romans, but it was better than having to start fighting again. The other blow that Shapur I dealt to Rome was when the Romans invaded Persia once again under the rule of Emperor Valerian (who ruled from 253–260). In the battle Emperor Valerian was captured by Shapur's troops and was never returned to Rome, nor were there ever any rescue attempts. He died a Persian prisoner.

All of these military problems were compounded because of the sheer number of emperors and economic problems. Within 50 years there were 26 emperors, and many times there were two or more emperors at the same time, so Rome had to deal with not only wars with the barbarians and with the Persians, but also civil wars within their own borders. Of course wars are expensive, and the Romans had to steadily increase the size of the military now that they were fighting on multiple fronts. One way of trying to make the economy better, or at least increase the amount of money available, was through tax increases. But people can only be taxed so far, so the Roman government started to debase its currency, which means that they started to

decrease the amount of precious metals in their coins and replace these with
cheaper metals. For example, you would expect a silver dollar to contain a
dollar's worth of silver. But what the Romans started to do was to replace the
silver in the silver dollar with a cheaper metal, but still say it was worth a dollar. Romans soon found out that their coinage was worth less than what it
should be, and then inflation happened. The price of goods and services sky-
rocketed throughout the empire, leading to an even worse economic crisis.

The person who put an end to the Third Century Crisis was Diocletian,
who ruled from 284–305 CE. He began his life being very poor and decided
to join the military. This was a good move for him since eventually the troops
raised him up to be emperor. Diocletian did a number of things to stop the
Third Century Crisis. This involved making changes to the economy by issuing a Price Edict, doubling the number of provinces, and making fundamental changes to the government.

As mentioned, the Roman economy was in shambles because of the debas-
ing of the currency. Diocletian started to issue laws that increased the amount
of precious metals in coins, and this increased the confidence of the Roman
people in their own money. This was probably started at some point in the
late 280s CE. Along with this, Diocletian issued the Edict of Maximum
Prices. As the name suggests, this document listed the absolute maximum
price or amount for products, services, and wages. For example, a merchant
could charge less, but could not charge more. If they did, the punishment was
death. The Price Edict did quite a bit to stabilize the Roman economy. But
Diocletian also reorganized the Roman government, especially at the top, and
this also had a great effect on the Third Century Crisis.

By the time of Diocletian the Roman Empire stretched from Britain in the
northwest to North Africa in the south and to Egypt and Mesopotamia in the
east. Diocletian decided that it was too much for one emperor to rule, so he
divided the empire into east and west and then decided that there should be
a second emperor. As mentioned, one problem of the Third Century Crisis
was the number of emperors that were ruling for very short periods of time.
It was standard procedure for the army to choose who was going to be the
next emperor. However, Diocletian decided that each emperor needed a caesar and when an emperor died, the caesar would become the next emperor
(much like our own vice president who would become president if anything
happened). This ensured that there would be no more multiple emperors and
therefore no civil wars. This governmental setup is called the Tetrarchy (the
Rule of Four). So with the Maximum Price Edict and the Tetrarchy, Diocletian was able to stop the Third Century Crisis and allowed the Roman Empire to continue on, at least until the early 400s CE when the Western Roman
Empire collapsed under the weight of the barbarian invasion.

The last impact that Diocletian had on the empire was something referred to as the Great Persecution. There is a lot of discussion among early Christian scholars on the extent of persecution of the Christians by the Roman government. Some see a great deal of official persecution, and some see very little. The one persecution that both sides agree on is Diocletian's persecution of the Christians. This persecution started when Diocletian and his caesar Galerius were performing sacrifices in 303 CE. Usually when a sacrifice is done, the animal is opened up and the lines in the liver are read by a priest. The animal that was sacrificed for Diocletian and Galerius had no lines, so they ordered another sacrifice done. When this was started, Galerius noticed that some Christians were making the sign of the cross, and he was furious that they were interfering. He convinced Diocletian to begin persecuting the Christians empire-wide. In reality, most of the persecution focused on the eastern side of the empire.

Lactantius, a Christian who lived from 240 to 320 CE, wrote a book titled *On the Deaths of the Persecutors*. He wrote about this episode in Chapter 10:

> Diocletian, as being of a timorous disposition, was a searcher into futurity, and during his abode in the East he began to slay victims, that from their livers he might obtain a prognostic of events; and while he sacrificed, some attendants of his, who were Christians, stood by, and they put the *immortal sign* on their foreheads. At this the demons were chased away, and the holy rites interrupted. The soothsayers trembled, unable to investigate the wonted marks on the entrails of the victims. They frequently repeated the sacrifices, as if the former had been unpropitious; but the victims, slain from time to time, afforded no tokens for divination. At length Tages, the chief of the soothsayers, either from guess or from his own observation, said, "There are profane persons here, who obstruct the rites." Then Diocletian, in furious passion, ordered not only all who were assisting at the holy ceremonies, but also all who resided within the palace, to sacrifice, and, in case of their refusal, to be scourged. And further, by letters to the commanding officers, he enjoined that all soldiers should be forced to the like impiety, under pain of being dismissed from service. Thus far his rage proceeded; but at that season he did nothing more against the law and religion of God. After an interval of some time he went to winter in Bithynia; and presently Galerius Caesar came thither, inflamed with furious resentment, and purposing to excite the inconsiderate old man to carry on that persecution which he had begun against the Christians. (Schaff, n.d.)

We also have eye-witnesses to this persecution, including Eusebius, the bishop from Caesarea. He wrote a book titled *Ecclesiastical History*, and in Chapter 8.2 he writes:

All these things were fulfilled in us, when we saw with our own eyes the houses of prayer thrown down to the very foundations, and the Divine and Sacred Scriptures committed to the flames in the midst of the market-places, and the shepherds of the churches basely hidden here and there, and some of them captured ignominiously, and mocked by their enemies. When also, according to another prophetic word, "Contempt was poured out upon rulers, and he caused them to wander in an untrodden and pathless way" (Psalms 107.40). (Schaff, n.d.)

The Great Persecution continued throughout the reign of Diocletian, who retired in 305 CE. Galerius became the emperor (according to the Tetrarchy) and continued to persecute Christians until he became very ill. It was at this point that Galerius stopped his persecution of Christians, but it wasn't until 313 CE that emperors Constantine I and Licinius officially stopped the Great Persecution.

Further Reading

Barnes, Timothy D. *The New Empire of Diocletian and Constantine.* Cambridge, MA: Harvard University Press, 1982.

Rees, Roger. *Diocletian and the Tetrarchy* (Debates and Documents in Ancient History). Edinburgh: Edinburgh University Press, 2004.

Schaff, Philip. "Ecclesiastical History." *Eusebius Pamphilius: Church History, Life of Constantine, Oration in Praise of Constantine.* Edinburgh: T&T Clark, n.d. Available online at http://www.ccel.org/ccel/schaff/npnf201.

Schaff, Philip. "On the Deaths of the Persecutors." *Fathers of the Third and Fourth Centuries: Lactantius, Venantius, Asterius, Victorinus, Dionysius, Apostolic Teaching and Constitutions, Homily.* Edinburgh: T&T Clark, n.d. Available online at http://www.ccel.org/ccel/schaff/anf07.

Williams, S. *Diocletian and the Roman Recovery.* New York: Routledge, 2000.

THE DONATISTS   The Great Persecution was started by Emperor Diocletian and Caesar Galerius. This was supposed to be an empire-wide persecution, but centered mostly in the eastern part of the Roman Empire and into North Africa, which was also part of Roman territory. When people were persecuted for their Christian faith, they were usually first given the choice of recanting, or leaving Christianity. There were a few things that they had to do to prove that they really meant it. They usually had to curse Christ in front of a Roman official and turn in any Christian books. They then had to worship the emperor by praying to his statue and/or performing Roman religious rites. After this, people normally had to sign a statement saying they were not Christian. There are many of these forms that still exist today, and they are called *libelli*. Some Christians refused to curse Christ and renounce their faith. If they survived the persecution, they were called Confessors. When the persecution was officially ended, many of the people who had cursed Christ and turned over Christian writings wanted to get back into the church, including priests and bishops. In many places this didn't seem to cause problems for Christian communities, but this was not the case in North Africa. The people who wanted back into the church were sometimes referred to as traitors.

The Donatists are named after Donatus, a priest who then became bishop of Carthage. Donatus firmly believed that those who cursed Christ and left Christianity shouldn't be allowed back in the church without having some form of punishment. He was especially adamant that the priests and bishops who left Christianity during the persecution should not be able to reclaim their ecclesiastical positions. To make matters worse, there were actually two bishops of Carthage—Donatus and a man named Caecilian. The Donatists stated that Caecilian was made bishop by a traitor, and therefore he really wasn't a bishop. For the Donatists, this meant that Donatus was the only true bishop of Carthage.

Emperor Constantine I got involved in this as well. In 313 CE Constantine called together some Donatists and some Nicene/Catholic bishops to discuss their differences, but in the end, it was decided that Donatus was not the bishop. The Donatists appealed this decision, and once again Emperor Constantine was called in. Constantine called for a larger church council to deal with these issues. The bishops met in 314 and decided that Donatus was not the bishop, and that Caecilian was. Again, the Donatists were not happy with the decision, and the matter dragged on. Then in 321 CE Constantine was getting tired of the whole thing, so he issued a letter stating that the Donatists could practice their faith and that the Roman government would not get involved. The Donatists eventually became the majority in North Africa until the Catholics got a firm foothold there in the late 300s and early 400s. At that point the Roman government got involved in these arguments again. In 411 CE the Donatists were forced into becoming Catholics, and their churches were taken away and given to the Catholics. In 412 CE the government issued an edict that forbade them from practicing their faith.

Further Reading

Burns, J. Patout, and Robin M. Jensen. *Christianity in Roman Africa: The Development of Its Practices and Beliefs*. Grand Rapids, MI: William B. Eerdmans, 2014.

Frend, W. H. C. *The Donatist Church: A Movement of Protest in Roman North Africa* (Oxford Scholarly Classics). Oxford: Oxford University Press, 1951.

Tilley, Maureen A. *The Bible in Christian North Africa: The Donatist World*. Minneapolis: Fortress Press, 1997.

EARLIEST FRAGMENT OF THE NEW TESTAMENT   There are no original documents for the New Testament. The New Testament documents that we have today are usually dated from 150 to 300 years after the time of Jesus and the apostles. For example, there are many texts that are dated to the 300s CE, the most famous of which is given the title of the Hebrew letter "Alpha," or the first letter in the Hebrew alphabet. This text, written in Greek, was discovered in a monastery on Mount Sinai and is usually titled the *Codex Sinaiticus*. "Alpha" contains the entire New Testament, written in all capital letters (which was the most common way to write during this period). The manuscript (which is a mix of two Latin words: *manus*, meaning "hand" and *script*, meaning "to write") also contained parts of the Old Testament, but unfortunately this part did not survive. It has been thought that there are over 5,000 Greek manuscripts that contain parts or all of the New Testament. This makes it a challenge for biblical scholars to recreate what might be the original, primarily because there are so many manuscripts and because many of the texts do not agree with each other. These problems do not mean that the text as we have it today is incorrect, but rather that scholars have to examine these early texts (and sometimes fragments of texts) to recreate what would hopefully have been the original. As mentioned, many of the manuscripts are dated to at least 150 years after the time of Christ. However, the earliest fragment of the New Testament (that we know of) has been dated to around the first half of the second century, or between 100 and 150 CE.

This earliest fragment is very small and only contains a few lines from the Gospel of John, written in Greek. It was discovered in a pile of fragments in 1934 by a scholar named C. H. Roberts. It was originally purchased in Egypt, and from this, it has been guessed that the Gospel of John was being read in Egypt at this early stage. This is important because it helps scholars to map out the spread of early Christians. Professor Metzger, in his book titled *The Text of the New Testament: Its Transmission, Corruption, and Restoration*, states (p. 39) that even though it was found in Egypt, it was not written there. The place of origin was in Ephesus, in modern-day Turkey. This is important since it is believed that John, the author of the Gospel, was living in Ephesus and probably wrote his Gospel there. The fragment is titled P52, for Papyrus number 52, and is found at the John Rylands library in Manchester, England.

You can see the fragment and a short description in the University of Manchester Library: http://www.library.manchester.ac.uk/searchresources /guidetospecialcollections/stjohnfragment/.

Further Reading

Comfort, Philip W., Barrett, David P., eds. *The Text of the Earliest New Testament Greek Manuscripts*, corrected and enlarged edition. Carrol Stream, IL: Tyndale House, 2001.

Metzger, Bruce M. *The Text of the New Testament: Its Transmission, Corruption, and Restoration*. Oxford: Oxford University Press, 1992.

Porter, Stanley E. *How We Got the New Testament: Text, Transmission, Translation* (Acadia Studies in Bible and Theology). Grand Rapids, MI: Baker Academic, 2013.

ECCLESIOLOGY   Ecclesiology is the study of the hierarchical structure of the church. The main part of this word, *ecclesia*, comes from the Greek, meaning "an assembly." Those who study ecclesiology examine the various roles that people held in this structure. For example, in the first century there were three main groups of people who were in charge of the Christian faith: the apostles, the teachers, and the prophets. There were also church officials with the titles of deacons, bishops, and presbyters. However, by the fourth century, there were no apostles, teachers, or prophets, but the offices of bishop and deacons continued. The study of this changing structure, and the reasons why it changed, is ecclesiology.

As mentioned, at the beginning of Christianity there was a rudimentary structure: apostles, teachers, prophets, bishops, presbyters, and deacons. The apostles were those people whom Jesus chose to work with him (see Mark 3:14). At first there were 12, but this number grew, as we find many unnamed apostles in the New Testament writings. Paul, too, considered himself to be an apostle even though he never personally met Jesus. These apostles were the ones in charge of the overall structure and spread of Christianity. The prophets of the first century and the early second century were primarily itinerant, meaning that they traveled from town to town. From what little we know of this group, they acted much like prophets of the Old Testament: they gave communities messages that they believed were given to them from God, and the communities were expected to follow their advice. The teachers were also like the prophets—they were itinerant. Like the prophets, we don't know very much about this particular group. By their title, it is assumed that they traveled from town to town teaching the rules and regulations that Christians should be following. Paul certainly ran into other apostles on his tours through the Mediterranean and more than likely met prophets and teachers (he mentions these groups specifically in 1 Corinthians 12:29). However, Paul believed he had the correct view of Christianity and did not like people spreading ideas that were contrary to his own.

Bishops and a group of people given the title of presbyters and deacons were also part of the church hierarchy from very early on in church history. Unfortunately their roles in the early church are not totally understood, primarily because the authors of the New Testament do not discuss their exact roles and because sometimes the bishop and the presbyter seem to be the same role. The deacons were lower on the ecclesiastical scale, and their job was to support the bishop. The bishops came into power through other bishops, meaning that a bishop should be able to trace his ecclesiastical lineage back to the original apostles and ultimately to Jesus. This becomes very important by the second century because there were many people claiming to be legitimate bishops, but they did not fit into the acceptable lineage going back to the original apostles; therefore they were seen as illegitimate. Tracing the lineage back to Jesus is called apostolic succession, and many areas started keeping their own lists to ensure that they had a legitimate bishop.

By the beginning of the second century, it is clear that bishops were becoming the main leaders of the church, and ecclesiology began to evolve. Many early texts from this period refer to bishops and the political power they had over their cities. A good example of this is Polycarp, a second-century bishop of the city of Smyrna (today in the far west-central part of Turkey). He was taken by the Roman authorities to be killed in Rome for being a Christian. As he passed through what is modern-day Turkey, he wrote letters to various Christian groups. It is very clear from his letters that the bishops were now in charge of their churches. He didn't write to the teachers, prophets, or apostles, but to bishops. Hence, by the second century, these three other groups were starting to disappear. It is clear why there were no more apostles: the last apostle was certainly dead by the beginning of the 100s, and there were no more chosen. There is evidence that there were still teachers and prophets, but they were gradually forced out of the hierarchy because they were deemed to be too disruptive to a settled community. As the teachers and prophets were becoming less powerful, the bishops become more powerful.

By the beginning of the second century, there were also bishops that were deemed more important than others, and this is the beginning of the idea of the papacy. These important bishops lived in Rome, Antioch, and Jerusalem. It isn't clear when the office of a singular leader, or pope (from papa/abba meaning father) came into being. Many second-, third-, and even fourth-century Christian leaders rejected the idea that the bishop of Rome was the most important. At the same time the bishops of Rome believed that they were the most important of all the bishops. Rome is where, according to tradition, Peter the disciple was killed. The bishops of Rome believed that because Peter was given the keys to the kingdom by Jesus (Matthew 16:19), they too were in possession of those keys. It was only later in Christian history that the pope, or the main bishop of Rome, was recognized by most Christians as being the head of the Catholic Church. Today, the hierarchy of the Catholic Church consists of the pope at the top, followed by cardinals, archbishops, bishops, and priests.

By the fourth century the church hierarchy was settled (with the exception of having a singular office of the pope). The power of the bishops steadily rose as Christianity became more and more accepted and certainly after it became a legal religion (during the time of Emperor Constantine I in the early 300s). The deacons continued in their work supporting the work of their bishops. By the end of the fourth century we have stories of bishops (such as Ambrose of the Italian city of Milan) openly arguing with the emperors over theology and individual behavior, which shows that the office of the bishop during this period had become very powerful.

Further Reading

Bockmuehl, Markus, and Michael B. Thompson, eds. *A Vision for the Church: Studies in Early Christian Ecclesiology*. Edinburgh: T&T Clark, 1997.

Kaufman, Peter Iver. *Church, Book, and Bishop: Conflict and Authority in Early Latin Christianity*. Boulder, CO: Westview Press, 1996.

Meyendorff, John, ed. *The Primacy of Peter: Essays in Ecclesiology and the Early Church*. Yonkers, NY: St. Vladimir's Seminary Press, 1992.

Prusak, Bernard P. *The Church Unfinished: Ecclesiology through the Centuries*. Mahwah, NJ: Paulist Press, 2004.

EUSEBIUS OF CAESAREA   Eusebius was the bishop of Caesarea, a major city along the eastern coast of the Mediterranean in what is now Israel. He was born around 260 CE and died around 339 CE. He became bishop in 314 CE. Eusebius was a prolific writer, and many of his writings exist today. Probably the most important book that Eusebius wrote was his *Ecclesiastical History*, or the *History of the Church*. It is one of the earliest church histories written, and later historians loved it so much that instead of rewriting early Christian history, they just added on to what Eusebius had written. He also wrote many books about theology and a very important work titled *The Life of Constantine*, and he is also a great primary source for Emperor Diocletian's Great Persecution.

There isn't much known about the early life of Eusebius of Caesarea (not to be confused with Eusebius of Nicomedia who was also living at the same time), despite all that he wrote. He had a famous teacher named Pamphilus. Pamphilus in turn was taught by a very famous Christian named Origen. Origen had written and collected a huge number of texts, and it seems that Eusebius had access to this collection, which must have been one of the best libraries around at the time. This explains how Eusebius was able to write so much. As mentioned, his *Ecclesiastical History* is his most important, and probably the most famous of this writings today. He gives the history of Christianity from the very beginning (as told in Genesis) up through his lifetime. There were really no other writers before him who had taken on the task, and Eusebius recognized that he was the first. Luckily for us Eusebius of Caesarea wrote in his *Ecclesiastical History* exactly why he wrote what he did:

> 1. It is my purpose to write an account of the successions of the holy apostles, as well as of the times which have elapsed from the days of our Savior to our own; and to relate the many important events which are said to have occurred in the history of the Church; and to mention those who have governed and presided over the Church in the most prominent parishes, and those who in each generation have proclaimed the divine word either orally or in writing.
>
> 2. It is my purpose also to give the names and number and times of those who through love of innovation have run into the greatest errors, and, proclaiming themselves discoverers of knowledge falsely so-called have like fierce wolves unmercifully devastated the flock of Christ.
>
> 3. It is my intention, moreover, to recount the misfortunes which immediately came upon the whole Jewish nation in consequence of their plots against our Savior, and to record the ways and the times in which the divine word has been attacked by the Gentiles, and to describe the character of those who at various periods have contended for it in the face of blood and of tortures, as well as the confessions which have been made in our own days, and finally the gracious and kindly succor which our Savior has afforded them all. Since I propose to write of all these things I shall commence my work with the beginning of the dispensation of our Savior and Lord Jesus Christ. (Schaff, n.d.)

This book is still printed by modern publishers since it has been recognized as being very important not only to Christian history but also to historians in general since Eusebius was starting to use a calendar that was based on the birth of Christ. This is something that we do today (for example, 2014 is 2014 years after the birth of Christ).

Caesarea was a very important city in the east, long known as a scholarly city, and being the bishop allowed Eusebius to be very influential, especially in terms of theology. Sometime in the late 310s or early 320s Eusebius of Caesarea received a letter from Eusebius, the bishop of another eastern city named Nicomedia. The letter describes the problems that Arius, an Egyptian priest, was having with his own bishop, Alexander of Alexandria. Eusebius of Caesarea decided to side with Arius in this controversy, which means that Eusebius believed that God was always in existence and the Son came second. Both Eusebius of Nicomedia and Eusebius of Caesarea were very active in supporting the beliefs of Arius, much to the annoyance of people who supported Alexander. Eventually a regional church council was called, and Arius was absolved of any heresy by the two Eusebii. However, this did not make Alexander of Alexandria happy, and in early 325 there was a church council held by supporters of Alexander who decided to punish Eusebius of Caesarea. He was temporarily excommunicated and given time to rethink his Arian position.

A few months later Emperor Constantine I called the Council of Nicea to deal with the issues of Arianism, and Eusebius of Caesarea attended. It appears that Eusebius of Caesarea did change his mind and wrote an early version of the Nicene Creed. While this version was not ultimately accepted, it laid down the groundwork for the actual Nicene Creed. After this Eusebius seems to have been forgiven of his past issues with Arius, and he continued to write. Eusebius of Caesarea was also a friend of Emperor Constantine and seemed to have good relations with his sons after Constantine's death. In fact, soon after the death Eusebius wrote a very important book titled *The Life of Constantine*. Like his *Ecclesiastical History*, he tells his readers why he wrote it:

> Wherefore, if it is the duty of any one, it certainly is mine, to make an ample proclamation of his virtues to all in whom the example of noble actions is capable of inspiring the love of God. For some who have written the lives of worthless characters, and the history of actions but little tending to the improvement of morals, from private motives, either love or enmity, and possibly in some cases with no better object than the display of their own learning, have exaggerated unduly their description of actions intrinsically base, by a refinement and elegance of diction. And thus they have become to those who by the Divine favor had been kept apart from evil, teachers not of good, but of what should be silenced in oblivion and darkness. But my narrative, however unequal to the greatness of the deeds it has to describe, will yet derive luster even from the bare relation of noble actions. And surely the record of conduct that has been pleasing to God will afford a far from unprofitable, indeed a most instructive, study to persons of well-disposed minds. *Life of Constantine* 1.10 (Schaff, n.d.)

This work is very important because it gives us more in-depth glimpses of Constantine. As mentioned, Eusebius was a prolific writer. He wrote many commentaries, or examinations, on some of the books of the Bible. He wrote a book on geography and place-names found in the bible called *Onomasticon*. He also wrote a highly influential book called the *Chronicle* in which Eusebius of Caesarea examined world history by using columns. Many writers afterwards used this method to think about history. Unfortunately, nothing is known about his death, which probably occurred sometime around 340 CE. Despite this, his writings have come down to us and played a large role in how early Christian and world history was written.

See also: Arians; Council of Nicea.

Further Reading

Barnes, Timothy D. *Constantine and Eusebius*, reprint edition. Cambridge, MA: Harvard University Press, 2006.

Grafton, Anthony, and Megan Williams. *Christianity and the Transformation of the Book: Origen, Eusebius, and the Library of Caesarea*. Cambridge, MA: Harvard University Press, 2006.

Johnson, Aaron, and Jeremy Schott, eds. *Eusebius of Caesarea: Tradition and Innovations*. Washington, DC: Center for Hellenic Studies, 2013.

Schaff, Philip. "Ecclesiastical History." *Eusebius Pamphilius: Church History, Life of Constantine, Oration in Praise of Constantine*. Edinburgh: T&T Clark, n.d. Available online at http://www.ccel.org/ccel/schaff/npnf201.

Schaff, Philip. "Life of Constantine." *Eusebius Pamphilius: Church History, Life of Constantine, Oration in Praise of Constantine*. Edinburgh: T&T Clark, n.d. Available online at http://www.ccel.org/ccel/schaff/npnf201.

EUSEBIUS OF NICOMEDIA   Eusebius of Nicomedia (died either in 341 or 342 CE) was one of the more influential bishops during the first 30 years of the fourth century. He moved up from being a bishop in the town of Berytus (modern-day Beirut), then to being bishop of the imperial city of Nicomedia, and ended his career as bishop of Constantinople, the most important city in the eastern Roman Empire. He played a very important role in the spreading and maintaining of Arianism. We know that Eusebius of Nicomedia wrote many letters, but unfortunately only a few survived, so what is known about him comes mostly from his enemies.

Unfortunately, there isn't much known about the early life of Eusebius of Nicomedia (not to be confused with Eusebius of Caesarea, who also lived in this same time period). He became bishop of Berytus sometime during the beginning of the reign of Emperor Licinius (who began to rule in 308 CE). According to Sozomen, an ancient Christian historian, Eusebius of Nicomedia was a favorite in the court of the emperor, and this could explain why he moved from Berytus to Nicomedia, where the emperor lived. He became bishop of Nicomedia in 317 CE, and because this was an imperial city, Eusebius of Nicomedia had a great deal of influence over ecclesiastical affairs in the eastern part of the Roman Empire. There isn't much known about his early theological beliefs, but early on in his bishopric Eusebius of Nicomedia received a letter from a man named Arius, who was a priest in Egypt. This letter changed the course of history for Eusebius.

Arius became entangled in an argument with Alexander, his bishop in the Egyptian city of Alexandria. Arius believed that God was always in existence and that the Son came afterwards. Alexander believed that God, the Son, and the Holy Spirit were always in existence. Sometime between 318 and 321 CE Arius was condemned by a church council held in Egypt and was excommunicated, or kicked out of the church. The views of Arius were very popular in Egypt, and Arius decided to write some letters to bishops that lived outside of Egypt—one of them was Eusebius of Nicomedia. This letter has been preserved, and part of it reads:

> To his very dear lord, the man of God, the faithful and orthodox Eusebius, Arius, unjustly persecuted by Alexander the Pope, on account of that all-conquering truth of which you also are a champion, sends greeting in the Lord . . . that the bishop greatly wastes and persecutes us, and leaves no stone unturned against us. He has driven us out of the city as atheists, because we do not concur in what he publicly preaches, namely, God always, the Son always; as the Father so the Son; the Son co-exists unbegotten with God; He is everlasting; neither by thought nor by any interval does God precede the Son; always God, always Son; he is begotten of the unbegotten; the Son is of God Himself . . . We are persecuted, because we say that the Son has a beginning, but that God is without beginning. This is the cause of our persecution, and likewise, because we say that He is of the non-existent. And this we say, because He is neither part of God, nor of any essential being. For this are we persecuted; the rest you know. I bid thee farewell in the Lord, remembering our afflictions, my fellow-Lucianist, and true Eusebius. (Schaff, n.d.)

Throughout the letter Arius makes it clear that he believes that God came first, then the Son afterwards. Eusebius of Nicomedia must have believed the same thing, because soon after receiving this letter from Arius he begins a letter-writing campaign to support Arius and his ideas. One of the people he wrote to was Alexander, the bishop of Alexandria. Eusebius of Nicomedia asked that Arius be reinstated back into the church and to become a priest again, but Alexander refused. Alexander then wrote more letters to other bishops asking them to reject not only Arius, but Eusebius of Nicomedia.

Ultimately these arguments were heard by Emperor Constantine I, who decided in 325 CE to call the first large church gathering called the Council of Nicea. The Council of Nicea decided to side with Alexander of Alexandria and his belief that God, the Son, and the Holy Spirit were all in existence at once and from the beginning. It also decided to send Arius into exile. Eusebius of Nicomedia was not sent into exile immediately, but a few months after the council finished, he was stripped of his bishopric in Nicomedia and sent into exile in the far north. Arius and Eusebius were reinstated in 327, just two years later, when Constantine changed his mind about their exiles and even allowed Eusebius to take back his office as bishop of Nicomedia.

Arius died in 336, but this did not stop Eusebius of Nicomedia from spreading Arian beliefs. In 337 CE Emperor Constantine began to feel ill and traveled to Nicomedia. It was here that Eusebius of Nicomedia baptized

Emperor Constantine, who then died shortly thereafter. Despite the death of his supporter, Eusebius of Nicomedia was friends with Constantius II, one of the sons of Constantine who became co-emperor with his brothers Constantine II and Constans. Emperor Constantius II called for a church council and decided to make Eusebius of Nicomedia the bishop of Constantinople, the most important city in the east, second only to Rome. This happened in 339 CE, and it gave Eusebius enormous power and influence. He wasted no time installing Arian bishops all over the east. Eusebius only had a few years to really push the beliefs of Arius before he died, probably in 341 CE. It isn't known how he died.

See also: Arians; Council of Nicea.

Further Reading

Gregg, Robert C., and D. E. Groh. *Early Arianism—a View of Salvation*, 1st ed. Minneapolis: Fortress Press, 1981.

Hanson, R. P. C. *The Search for the Christian Doctrine of God: The Arian Controversy, 318–381*. New York: T&T Clark, 2005.

Schaff, Philip. "Letter of Arius." *Theodoret, Jerome, Gennadius, & Rufins: Historical Writings*. Edinburgh: T&T Clark, n.d. Available online at http://www.ccel.org /ccel/schaff/npnf203.

Williams, Daniel H. *Ambrose of Milan and the End of the Arian-Nicene Conflicts* (Oxford Early Christian Studies). Oxford: Clarendon Press, 1995.

Williams, Rowan. *Arius: Heresy and Tradition*, rev. ed. Grand Rapids, MI: William B. Eerdmans, 2002.

THE FORMATION OF THE NEW TESTAMENT   The New Testament as we have it today did not look like this in at least the first three centuries of Christianity. Over time, the collection of Christian canonical (officially recognized) texts sometimes grew larger and sometimes smaller. Today most Bibles consist of at least 27 books written by a variety of people from a number of different places. Before we start discussing specifics, it should also be pointed out that we do not have the originals for any of the New Testament texts. The earliest piece dates to about the middle of the 100s and is part of the Gospel of John. It measures about 2.5 inches by 3.5 inches. We start to find whole manuscripts in Greek that date to about 200 CE. Today there are over 5,000 of these manuscripts, and it is rare that they agree with each other. Some of these manuscripts are divided up by families (or where they were originally written). For example, there is the Alexandrian manuscript family, which were written in Alexandria, Egypt. There are also many other families. What this ultimately means is that the New Testament we have today is just a best guess, put together by New Testament scholars who have examined the thousands of available manuscripts. They then decide what the original probably looked like. It is hoped that it is very accurate, but not everyone agrees, and this explains why there are so many translations of the New Testament today.

The first books in the New Testament are the Gospels of Matthew, Mark, Luke, and John. Even though they are first in this collection, they are not the earliest texts written. The earliest texts come from Paul. More specifically, his letter titled 1 Thessalonians is the earliest document in the New Testament, probably written in either 50 or 51 from the city of Corinth. Paul's letters (and he writes nothing but letters) are to the various Christian groups that he either founded or encouraged to follow his brand of Christianity. Many times he wrote these letters to keep them under his theological control or to encourage them to keep to their faith. He wrote many other letters including I and II Corinthians (54–54 CE), Romans (58 CE), Galatians (54–57 CE), Philippians (60–63 CE), and Philemon (60–63 CE).

There are also a number of letters attributed to Paul in the New Testament that almost certainly were not written by him, but by his own disciples, probably after his death. These are: 2 Thessalonians, Colossians, Ephesians, I and II Timothy, Titus, and Hebrews. There are many reasons why scholars believe these specific texts were not written by Paul. The first is language—there are many words and phrases found in them that are not found in Paul's letters. The second and most compelling reason is that in these letters the church hierarchy appears to be already formed and that it could not have been like this when Paul was alive. Therefore, many believe that indicates the letters were written after the time of Paul by his students or people who were familiar with Paul's genuine writings.

The modern New Testament begins with the Four Gospels: Matthew, Mark, Luke, and John. So why do the Gospels come first? It appears that someone decided that the stories of Jesus's life should be first, rather than Paul's letters. This makes sense if you want to tell the story of Christianity in chronological order. There are some early manuscripts that do not follow this order, but the order of Matthew, Mark, Luke, and John is accepted today. Scholars are also undecided on the dates the Gospels were written. It is thought that they date sometime between the late 60s right up through the early 90s for the Gospel of John. To make matters even more confusing, we don't know who the genuine authors are—the names Matthew, Mark, Luke, and John are added later in the manuscript history.

Despite these problems, by the end of the first century, many Christian groups throughout the Mediterranean were reading different texts, but the core of the Gospels and some of Paul's letters seem to be common among them. Some of the more controversial texts (at least for early Christians) come at the end of the New Testament; in particular, Revelation. The traditionally recognized author is John, the same author as the Gospel of John and I, II, and III John. The topic is what will happen at the end of time. The theme and language of this book is very different from the Gospels and Paul's letters. It wasn't until the early 300s that Revelation was accepted as being part of the original writings that Christians should read.

The New Testament, as we have it today, was a collection of texts that changed over time. By the beginning of the first century, more writings begin to appear and some Christian groups believed that these were just as important as the Gospels and Paul. One text is titled *The Shepherd of Hermas*. Eusebius of Caesarea, writing at the end of the 200s, states that some Christian groups believed the Shepherd text should be canonical (or accepted), but he rejected this. Eusebius of Caesarea also tells us that, as mentioned above, the Apocalypse, or Revelation, was not accepted by many Christian groups. Titus too was also questioned up through the early 300s. There were also people who combined a number of texts together to make one document. Tatian, who died in 180 CE, is a good example of this. He took the four Gospels, combined them into one text, and titled his work *Diatessaron*. His reasoning was that the individual Gospels contain a lot of information that is repeated in the others. He felt that it would be better to unite them into one text and get rid of all of the repeated material. Books were also expensive to produce. Although Tatian's text was popular in Syria, it did not spread, and the four Gospels were kept as individual texts.

Eusebius was not the earliest writer to give a list of texts that Christians should read. Marcion, in the early/middle of the 100s, believed that Christians should not read the Old Testament at all and only included 10 of Paul's letters and Luke as the official Christian texts. However, he did not just accept them as they were written. Marcion went through these 11 texts and cut out anything he deemed to be unacceptable or anything he thought might have been added later. Usually he cut out anything he thought was too "Jewish." There is quite a bit of debate whether Marcion created the first collection of texts that the Christians were supposed to read. His collection then forced other Christians to create their own, leading to the New Testament we have today. Other scholars believe that Christians would have created a list regardless of what Marcion had done with his own.

One the earliest lists we have of Christian texts that resembles the modern New Testament is titled the Muratorian Canon. It was found in the Vatican library by a priest named Muratori and published in 1740 CE. The list itself dates to somewhere around the end of the 100s CE (although this date is controversial). It is essentially a list of texts that Christians should read and a few that they should avoid. In many cases the texts are the same as our New Testament today, but there are some differences. For example, the *Apocalypse of Peter* is included. Today we do not recognize this text as canonical, but in the past many thought it was just as acceptable to read as it was to read Paul's Letter to the Romans. The Muratorian Canon also lists two letters that the author states were attributed to Paul, but Christians were not to use them: *To the Laodiceans* (which might be Paul's Letter to the Ephesians), and another *To the Alexandrians*. The author claims that these letters were created by Marcion. Finally, the author of the Muratorian Canon states that the *Shepherd of Hermas* is acceptable to read, but cannot be read in the church to the people since Hermas was neither a prophet nor an apostle. Scholars are not sure which Christian groups would have followed the advice given in this important list, but it was still at least a century later that the list of Christian readings became official.

What this really means is that by the end of the 100s there was no agreement between Christians about what should and should not be read. The list of "acceptable" readings varied by date and by geography throughout the Mediterranean, and it was a long process to create a canonical list. It wasn't until the early 300s that we finally get a list that resembles the New Testament we have today. This is first found in the writings of an Egyptian bishop named Athanasius. He wrote a series of letters called the *Festal Letters*. Letter 39, written around 367 CE, contains a list of books that Christians should read. It is this list that matches our modern New Testament. A few decades later (397 CE), a Christian named Augustine wrote down the list of canonical books for Christians in his own book titled *On Christian Doctrine*. Despite these early agreements, the official list of texts is still not agreed on. The Catholic Bible is different from the Protestant Bibles, showing that even today Christians still disagree on which texts should be read.

Further Reading

Aland, Kurt, and Barbara Aland. *The Text of the New Testament: An Introduction to the Critical Editions and to the Theory and Practice of Modern Textual Criticism*, 2nd ed. Grand Rapids, MI: William B. Eerdmans, 1989.

Hill, Charles E. and Michael J. Kruger, eds. *The Early Text of the New Testament*. Oxford: Oxford University Press, 2012.

Metzger, Bruce M. *The Text of the New Testament: Its Transmission, Corruption, and Restoration*. Oxford: Oxford University Press, 1992.

THE GREAT FIRE OF ROME   Fires were always a danger for ancient cities, just like they are for modern cities. The difference is that in modern cities, we have a dedicated group of people who fight fires. In the ancient world the development of firefighters was a gradual process, and Rome was no different. Emperor Augustus (who ruled from 31 BCE until his death in 14 CE) had created the city's first firefighters in 6 CE. This certainly helped, but it didn't change the fact that the city of Rome had been prone to fires because of the cramped conditions found within its city walls and that many of the buildings were made out of wood (stone was used primarily for governmental buildings). We know from written and archaeological remains that there were many devastating fires in the city throughout its long history. One of the more dangerous ones happened in July 64 CE during the reign of Emperor Nero, and it is important in Christian history because it is one of the earliest periods when the Roman government singled out the Christians for persecution.

The Great Fire of Rome was a disaster for the city. It burned 10 districts out of 14 and lasted for nearly a week. As far as we know, it started in an area called the Circus Maximus in some shops and quickly spread. The Emperor Nero was not in the city, but at Antium, his hometown. He must have heard about the fire, but at first seemed unconcerned (at least he did not leave Antium right away) but ended up going to Rome when the fire moved towards his palace. By some accounts he took part in the relief effort and even gave some of his own money to help rebuild parts of the city. He also took advantage of the devastation to build his palace even larger, leading some to believe he set the fire to make room for his new palace, the Golden House.

Unfortunately it is not known who started the fire, if anyone. It is possible that it started by accident in one of the Circus Maximus shops, but most of the blame, however, falls on either Emperor Nero or the Christians. There are a few Roman sources that tell us about the Great Fire. One comes from the Roman senator and historian Tacitus. The other two are Suetonius and Dio Cassius. Of these, the more reliable source is Tacitus. Tacitus was a boy when the Great Fire occurred, so it is possible that he actually remembered hearing the news. It wasn't until the year 113 CE that he wrote about the fire in his book titled *The Annals*, Chapter 15, sections 39–44. He tells us that much of Rome was destroyed from this fire and that many lost their lives. While there were now firefighters throughout the city, Tacitus states that they did not fight it because of roving groups of people who were threatening them. Unfortunately Tacitus does not tell us who these people were, but he does state that they possibly had received orders from someone to make sure the fire kept burning. Nero, while helping set up shelters to house those who lost their homes, went to a private stage and sang about the destruction of Troy. Tacitus writes in detail that Nero rebuilt his palace to make it even larger since there was now open land thanks to the destructive force of the fire. The Romans began to state that Nero started it just so he could build a larger palace. According to Tacitus, it is then that Nero blamed the Christians.

While the effects of the fire were devastating to Rome, the city itself would be rebuilt. However, the Christians blamed for the fire were mostly killed by the Roman government. Tacitus describes the horrific torture some Christians suffered when Nero blamed the fire on them. He tells us that they were covered in animal skins and then thrown to the dogs. They were also tied to stakes, flammable liquid was poured on them, and then they were lit on fire. We are told that Nero used these burning people as lights for his garden parties. Nero's treatment of the Christians was not supported by many Romans, and if anything, their treatment led some, like Tacitus, to have sympathy towards them. This sympathy might have helped increase the number of Christians.

Suetonius, a Roman writer and a secretary to Emperor Hadrian, tells us in his book *The Lives of the Twelve Caesars: Nero* (chapter 38) that Nero was to blame. This was written in 121 CE. He set the fire because the city was ugly and the roads were too narrow and crooked. This great fire burned for six days and seven nights. Suetonius also states that Nero dressed up as an actor and sang a song titled "Sack of Ilium" (about the Trojan War), which is where we get the familiar phrase that "Nero fiddled while Rome burned." Dio Cassius, a Roman who wrote a book titled *Roman History* in the late 100s CE, also states that Nero set the fire because he wanted Rome to die when he did (Chapter 62.16–18). Dio Cassius tells us that Nero secretly sent out some agents who burned buildings at various parts of the city. The confusion of the fire led to vandalism and looting, with many people being killed. Like Seutonius, Dio Cassius writes: "and assuming the lyre-player's garb, he sang the 'Capture of Troy,' as he styled the song himself, though to the enemies of the spectators it was the Capture of Rome." The Roman people blamed Nero for the fire.

As can be seen, there are various accounts of the fire and what happened afterwards. Of all the writers who mention the Great Fire, only Tacitus mentions the Christians and the fact that Nero blamed them for the fire. He too only mentions the torture they suffered. It isn't clear why Suetonius and Dio Cassius do not mention the Christians or the idea that Nero blamed them. It is possible that Tacitus had access to other information about this fire and its aftermath than the other two writers. However, if the account of Tacitus is correct, then it is one of the earliest references we have to the Roman government being aware of the Christians as an organized religion.

Further Reading
Champlin, Edward. *Nero*. Cambridge, MA: Harvard University Press, 2003.
Griffin, Miriam. *Nero: The End of a Dynasty*, reprint. New York: Routledge, 2000.
Shotter, David. *Nero Caesar Augustus: Emperor of Rome*. New York: Routledge, 2008.

HEROD THE GREAT   Herod the Great was born around 73 BCE and died around 4 BCE. He ruled over Judea from the year 37 BCE until his death. Herod's father, Antipater II, was awarded Roman citizenship, which passed down to Herod. Just 26 years before this, in 63 BCE, Judea became a Roman province when the Roman general Pompey took it over. There were still Jewish leaders in control, but they were appointed by the Romans, under the thumb of the Romans, and this included the title of "king." Herod became king of Judea primarily because he proved himself capable to Mark Anthony and Octavius, the future Augustus, first emperor of Rome. Josephus, a Jewish historian, in his *Wars of the Jews* (probably finished around 78 CE) wrote about the appointment of Herod as King of Judea (*Wars of the Jews*, 1.14.4):

> So he (Octavius) called the senate together, wherein Messalas, and after him Atratinus, produced Herod before them, and gave a full account of the merits of his father, and his own good-will to the Romans. At the same time they demonstrated that Antigonus was their enemy, not only because he soon quarreled with them, but because he now overlooked the Romans, and took the government by the means of the Parthians. These reasons greatly moved the senate; at which juncture Antony came in, and told them that it was for their advantage in the Parthian war that Herod should be king; so they all gave their votes for it. And when the senate was separated, Antony and Caesar went out, with Herod between them; while the consul and the rest of the magistrates went before them, in order to offer sacrifices, and to lay the decree in the Capitol. Antony also made a feast for Herod on the first day of his reign. (Josephus, n.d.)

Herod was certainly an active king. He spent a great deal of money (after first obtaining the money through taxes) on building up his kingdom, and the list of building projects is impressive. He built a new city, named Caesarea Maritima, where he also built a harbor to guarantee that the new city would become a shipping capital. Much of the harbor walls can still be seen today, mostly under the waves. Herod named the city after Octavius, who was also known as Caesar. He also repaired the Second Temple and greatly expanded its footprint. This included building a massive platform, part of which still exists today and is referred to as the Wailing Wall. He also built a number of fortresses around his kingdom, including Masada.

However, Herod's reputation is mostly remembered for what is told in the New Testament. Herod is mentioned a number of times and plays an important role in the accounts given by those who wrote the New Testament texts. Probably the most famous episode relating to King Herod is the account of the murder of all children two years old and under, which is sometimes referred to as the "Massacre of the Innocents." According to the New Testament, Herod had heard that a king of the Jews had been born. Here is the account from Matthew 2:1–6:

In the time of King Herod, after Jesus was born in Bethlehem of Judea, wise men from the East came to Jerusalem, asking, "Where is the child who has been born king of the Jews? For we observed his star at its rising, and have come to pay him homage." When King Herod heard this, he was frightened, and all Jerusalem with him; and calling together all the chief priests and scribes of the people, he inquired of them where the Messiah was to be born. They told him, "In Bethlehem of Judea; for so it has been written by the prophet: 'And you, Bethlehem, in the land of Judah, are by no means least among the rulers of Judah; for from you shall come a ruler who is to shepherd my people Israel.'" (NRSV)

Herod's next decision made him one of the most infamous characters in the New Testament. The book of Matthew (2:16) tells us that Herod then killed all children two years old and under: "When Herod saw that he had been tricked by the wise men, he was infuriated, and he sent and killed all the children in and around Bethlehem who were two years old or under, according to the time that he had learned from the wise men." Whether this is true or not, Herod had a reputation for being a cruel leader. We know that he executed his wife Mariamne and killed his own children he had with her. Josephus tells us, in his *Jewish Antiquities* 14.9.3, that Herod was "a violent and bold man, and very desirous of acting tyrannically." Modern scholars are starting to see him in a different light, as noted by McCane in his article titled "Simply Irresistible: Augustus, Herod, and the Empire." They are starting to see him as a more reasonable ruler, relying more on archaeological material than was available to previous historians.

Herod died in 4 BCE, and over time the location of his tomb was lost. It was widely reported in 2007 that his tomb location was found. The tomb structures were partially destroyed, but archaeologists found a sarcophagus, grand staircases, and other materials that suggested that this was indeed the tomb of Herod. However, in 2013 another set of archaeologists claimed that what was found in 2007 could not be the tomb of Herod, primarily because the tomb structures were too small and did not fit with the accounts we have of the funeral. Unfortunately it is still a mystery as to where the tomb of Herod stands.

Further Reading

Gelb, Norman. *Herod the Great: Statesman, Visionary, Tyrant*. Lanham, MD: Rowman & Littlefield, 2013.

Grant, Michael. *Herod the Great*, 1st ed. Winter Park, FL: American Heritage Press, 1971.

Josephus. "Wars of the Jews." *Josephus: The Complete Works*. Available online at http://www.ccel.org/ccel/josephus/complete.

Marshak, Adam Kolman. *The Many Faces of Herod the Great*. Grand Rapids, MI: William B. Eerdmans, 2015.

McCane, Byron R. "Simply Irresistible: Augustus, Herod, and the Empire." *Journal of Biblical Literature* 127, no. 4 (Winter 2008): 725–35.

IGNATIUS OF ANTIOCH   Ignatius was the bishop of Antioch. He was born around 50 CE and died sometime between 98 and 117 CE. We know a little bit about Ignatius because he left us a series of letters that discuss his upcoming martyrdom in Rome. His letters also give us a glimpse of some early Christian communities in Asia Minor (modern-day Turkey) and in Rome. For generations of Christians Ignatius was held up as a perfect example of what a Christian should be. Eusebius of Caesarea, the great church historian living in the late 200s and early 300s, wrote:

> At that time Polycarp, a disciple of the apostles, was a man of eminence in Asia, having been entrusted with the episcopate of the church of Smyrna by those who had seen and heard the Lord. And at the same time Papias, bishop of the parish of Hierapolis, became well known, as did also Ignatius, who was chosen bishop of Antioch, second in succession to Peter, and whose fame is still celebrated by a great many. Report says that he was sent from Syria to Rome, and became food for wild beasts on account of his testimony to Christ. (Schaff, *Ecclesiastical History* 3.1–3, n.d.)

The letters written by Ignatius were also treasured by many early Christians. Polycarp, the bishop of Smyrna, stated that he had copies of the letters of Ignatius that he sent along to other Christian communities. They could then use them to learn more about what it meant to be a Christian (see Polycarp, *Letter to the Philippians*, chapter 13). Ignatius was so highly regarded later in Christian history that a number of letters were written in his name, but these are now known to be spurious, or fake.

Ignatius wrote six letters to various communities from Turkey to Rome and wrote at least one personal letter to Bishop Polycarp of Smyrna. These are extremely important letters in the history of early Christianity since they document not only early Christian groups, but also some of the problems these communities were having. It gives a small glimpse into the lives of early Christians. These genuine letters were written by Ignatius when he was being taken to Rome as a prisoner. His journey mimics the journey of Paul when he was taken to Rome in the middle of the first century as a prisoner. The news that Ignatius was being brought through the city must have spread out ahead of his arrival since most of his letters state that local church leaders had met with him. A good example is in the introduction to his *Letter to the Ephesians* (chapter 1) where he states that he knew of the Ephesians and that their bishop, Onesimus, had visited with him: "I received, therefore, your whole multitude in the name of God, through Onesimus, a man of inexpressible love, and your bishop in the flesh, whom I pray you by Jesus Christ to love, and that you would all seek to be like him." Ignatius would usually mention the name of the visiting bishop or the presbyters primarily because he was very interested in pushing the idea that the bishop was the only leader of the congregation. In this early stage of Christian history the roles of the bishop (and other church officials) were still being worked out, but Ignatius firmly believed that the bishop should be in charge of his community. Ignatius could not be clearer on this matter than what he wrote in chapter 5 of his *Letter to the Ephesians*:

> For if in this brief space of time I have enjoyed such fellowship with your bishop—I mean not of a mere human, but of a spiritual nature—how much more do I reckon you happy who are so joined to him as the Church is to Jesus Christ, and as Jesus Christ is to the Father, that so all things may agree in unity! Let no man deceive himself: if anyone be not within the altar, he is deprived of the bread of God. For if the prayer of one or two possesses such power, how much more that of the bishop and the whole Church! He, therefore, that does not assemble with the Church, has even by this manifested his pride, and condemned himself. For it is written, "God resists the proud." Let us be careful, then, not to set ourselves in opposition to the bishop, in order that we may be subject to God. (Schaff, n.d.)

There is a natural order of things for Ignatius in the church. The relationship of the bishop to his flock is like the relationship of Christ to the Father, and as the church to Jesus. If that order is broken, then the order of everything is broken. The hierarchy was extremely important to Ignatius and it is because of his push for an orderly organization that the bishops became the most important figures in early Christianity.

It isn't known what the ultimate fate was of Ignatius. It is assumed that he was taken to Rome and then fed to wild animals as punishment for being a Christian. He certainly writes of his possible fate in his letters and, in particular, he begs his readers not to stand in the way of his upcoming martyrdom. His most famous statement comes in his Letter to the Romans where he writes:

> I write to the Churches, and impress on them all, that I shall willingly die for God, unless you hinder me. I beg of you not to show an unseasonable good-will towards me. Suffer me to become food for the wild beasts, through whose instrumentality it will be granted me to attain to God. I am the wheat of God, and let me be ground by the teeth of the wild beasts, that I may be found the

pure bread of Christ. Rather entice the wild beasts, that they may become my tomb, and may leave nothing of my body; so that when I have fallen asleep [in death], I may be no trouble to anyone. Then shall I truly be a disciple of Christ, when the world shall not see so much as my body. (Schaff, n.d.)

Ignatius died a martyr sometime between 98 and 117 CE. The lessons in his letters and the account of his martyrdom were used as examples for generations of Christians after his death. He played an extremely important role in the development of the church.

Further Reading

Brent, Allen. *Ignatius of Antioch: A Martyr Bishop and the Origin of Episcopacy* (T&T Clark Theology). New York: T&T Clark, 2007.

Robinson, Thomas A. *Ignatius of Antioch and the Parting of the Ways: Early Jewish-Christian Relations*. Peabody, MA: Hendrickson Publishers, 2009.

Schaff, Philip. "Ecclesiastical History." Eusebius Pamphilius: Church History, Life of Constantine, Oration in Praise of Constantine. Edinburgh: T&T Clark, n.d. Available online at http://www.ccel.org/ccel/schaff/npnf201.

Schaff, Philip. "Letters of Ignatius." The Apostolic Fathers with Justin Martyr and Irenaeus. Edinburgh: T&T Clark, n.d. Available online at http://www.ccel.org/ccel/schaff/anf01.

Schoedel, William R. *Ignatius of Antioch: A Commentary on the Letters of Ignatius of Antioch* (Hermeneia: A Critical and Historical Commentary on the Bible). Minneapolis: Fortress Press, 1985.

Vall, Gregory. *Learning Christ: Ignatius of Antioch and the Mystery of Redemption*. Washington, DC: Catholic University of America Press, 2013.

JEROME   Jerome, a Catholic priest who lived from about 345 to about 420 CE, was a prolific writer, so much is known about his life. Many of his books and letters still exist today. He was born in a small Roman town called Stridon, which was northeast of Italy. His parents were Christian and fairly wealthy, which allowed them to send Jerome to Rome for schooling. Jerome was one of the most learned Christians during this period. He started to collect books, and this continued throughout his lifetime. He also wrote his own and sent them out all over the Mediterranean for people to read and comment on. He was an amazing biblical exegete, meaning that he was very good at examining the Bible—either whole books or writing commentaries on individual words. These were written to allow people a greater understanding as to what the Bible meant.

Jerome was also an advocate for asceticism, which is a movement that took place in early Christianity. Ascetics, or people who followed asceticism, were using living their lives studying the Bible. Sometimes ascetics would live totally alone, or they could live in small groups in monasteries. Men and women could be ascetics, and Jerome was a large supporter of this movement. Jerome himself can be considered an ascetic. He had lived for a few years in the wilderness near the Greek town of Chalcis, and when he left Rome he went to Bethlehem and set up his own monastery, one for women and one for men. He did this with the help of his wealthy patrons, especially women. Jerome had made friends with a small group of very wealthy women when he was living in Rome and convinced them to live out their lives as virgins and ascetics. A good example of this is one of his letters to Eustochium, a daughter of a woman named Paula, a friend of Jerome's. He tells Eustochium how she should be living her life while living in the capital city of Rome. One example (of many) is that he tells her that she should not be seeking the company of wealthy women who are only concerned with appearances. Instead, he tells her:

> Let your companions be women pale and thin with fasting, and approved by their years and conduct; such as daily sing in their hearts: "Tell me where you feed your flock, where you make it to rest at noon," (Song of Solomon 1.7) and say, with true earnestness, "I have a desire to depart and to be with Christ" (Philippians 1:23). Be subject to your parents, imitating the example of your spouse (referring to Luke 2:51). Rarely go abroad, and if you wish to seek the aid of the martyrs seek it in your own chamber. For you will never need a pretext for going out if you always go out when there is need. Take food in moderation, and never overload your stomach. For many women, while temperate as regards wine, are intemperate in the use of food. When you rise at night to pray, let your breath be that of an empty and not that of an overfull stomach. Read often, learn all that you can. Let sleep overcome you, the roll still in your hands; when your head falls, let it be on the sacred page. Let your fasts be of daily occurrence and your refreshment such as avoids satiety. It is idle to carry an empty stomach if, in two or three days' time, the fast is to be made up for by repletion. (Letter 22, section 17) (Schaff, n.d.)

His letter is very long, and as can be seen from this small excerpt, Jerome used the Bible to provide examples to Eustochium. He also could use himself as an example of an ascetic when he lived near Chalcis:

> How often, when I was living in the desert, in the vast solitude which gives to hermits a savage dwelling-place, parched by a burning sun, how often did I fancy myself among the pleasures of Rome! I used to sit alone because I was filled with bitterness. Sackcloth disfigured my unshapely limbs and my skin from long neglect had become as black as an Ethiopian's. Tears and groans were every day my portion; and if drowsiness chanced to overcome my struggles against it, my bare bones, which hardly held together, clashed against the

ground. Of my food and drink I say nothing: for, even in sickness, the solitaries have nothing but cold water, and to eat one's food cooked is looked upon as self-indulgence. (Schaff, *Jerome*, Letter 22, section 7, n.d.)

Asceticism was very important to Jerome since he believed it was the way that God wanted some people to live. He also believed that virginity was very important. One very interesting book of Jerome's is titled *The Perpetual Virginity of Blessed Mary*. The question of whether or not Mary was a virgin after giving birth to Christ was a popular one. Jerome argues that Mary was always a virgin, even after the birth of Jesus. A man named Helvidius wrote a book that stated that Mary was not a virgin after the birth of Jesus because the New Testament mentions brothers and sisters of Jesus, which automatically means that she could not have been a virgin for her entire life. Jerome, however, wrote that the "brothers" and "sisters" of Mary were not her own children, but were cousins, or children of Joseph from another marriage. Jerome also argued that virginity for all women was more important than marriage. In the second paragraph of his book he explains why he was writing:

I must call upon the Holy Spirit to express His meaning by my mouth and defend the virginity of the Blessed Mary. I must call upon the Lord Jesus to guard the sacred lodging of the womb in which He abode for ten months from all suspicion of sexual intercourse. And I must also entreat God the Father to show that the mother of His Son, who was a mother before she was a bride, continued a Virgin after her son was born. We have no desire to career over the fields of eloquence, we do not resort to the snares of the logicians or the thickets of Aristotle. We shall adduce the actual words of Scripture. Let him be refuted by the same proofs which he employed against us, so that he may see that it was possible for him to read what is written, and yet to be unable to discern the established conclusion of a sound faith. (Schaff, n.d.)

Jerome argued against Helvidius by writing down what Helvidius had written, and then arguing against it. This was a very popular way of refuting someone's ideas. Jerome also argued with many other people throughout his lifetime, including Augustine, the bishop of Hippo in North Africa. He also argued with others over his translations. The Old Testament that most people read in the West was translated into Greek. Jerome, however, knew the original Hebrew. When he referred to the Old Testament in his writings, he used his translation directly from the Hebrew instead of the Greek, and this caused him some problems because many times the Greek and the Hebrew words differed. Regardless, Jerome was a very important person in the history of early Christianity. He pushed for asceticism for both men and women, and, more importantly, he showed a deep knowledge of the Bible, both New and

Old Testament. When he died in 420, Jerome left a vast number of books, letters, and commentaries that people still read and use today.

Further Reading

Kato, Teppei. "Jerome's Understanding of Old Testament Quotations in the New Testament." *Vigiliae Christianae* 67, no. 3 (2013): 289–315.

Kelly, J. N. D. *Jerome: His Life, Writings, and Controversies*, 1st ed. London: Duckworth and Co., 1975.

Rebenich, Stefan. *Jerome* (The Early Church Fathers). New York: Routledge, 2002.

Schaff, Philip. "Letter 22." *Jerome: The Principle Works of Jerome*. Edinburgh: T&T Clark, n.d. Available online at http://www.ccel.org/ccel/schaff/npnf206.

Schaff, Philip. "The Perpetual Virginity of Blessed Mary." *Jerome: The Principle Works of Jerome*. Edinburgh: T&T Clark, n.d. Available online at http://www.ccel.org /ccel/schaff/npnf206.

JERUSALEM   Jerusalem was probably the most important city in early Christianity, especially since the city was part of the story of Jesus and all of the disciples. It is the spiritual center for Jewish people and Christians, and for Christians it is especially important because the city is where Jesus was put on trial and crucified. The city has a very long history, dating all the way back to the Neolithic period. Closer to our period it became the capital around 1000 BCE for King David's kingdom. The city was built in a spot not necessarily the most typical in the ancient world. But it was probably because of its placement that it was chosen as a capital and then survived until today.

Jerusalem and the surrounding area had multiple overlords throughout its history. In 597 BCE the Babylonians captured Judea and, in the process, destroyed the Temple that had been built by David and expanded by King Solomon. The Babylonians, under King Nebuchadnezzar II, also took many of its leading citizens, including King Zedekiah, back to Babylon (referred to as the Babylonian Captivity). In 539 BCE the Persians arrived and dominated the area. Even though they controlled the political landscape, the Persians were also tolerant of other religions. They allowed the Jewish captives in Babylon to go home and also sponsored the rebuilding of the Temple (referred to as the Second Temple), which had been destroyed by Nebuchadnezzar II. Cyrus the Great was seen as a hero to the Jewish people for doing both of these things, as can be seen in 2 Chronicles 36:22–23:

> In the first year of King Cyrus of Persia, in fulfillment of the word of the LORD spoken by Jeremiah, the LORD stirred up the spirit of King Cyrus of Persia so that he sent a herald throughout all his kingdom and also declared in a written edict: "Thus says King Cyrus of Persia: The LORD, the God of heaven, has given me all the kingdoms of the earth, and he has charged me to

build him a house at Jerusalem, which is in Judah. Whoever is among you of all his people, may the LORD his God be with him! Let him go up. (NRSV)

More details of this account can be found in the beginning of the book of Ezra (1:4–1:11):

[King Cyrus decreed] ". . .and let all survivors, in whatever place they reside, be assisted by the people of their place with silver and gold, with goods and with animals, besides freewill offerings for the house of God in Jerusalem." The heads of the families of Judah and Benjamin, and the priests and the Levites—everyone whose spirit God had stirred—got ready to go up and rebuild the house of the LORD in Jerusalem. All their neighbors aided them with silver vessels, with gold, with goods, with animals, and with valuable gifts, besides all that was freely offered. King Cyrus himself brought out the vessels of the house of the LORD that Nebuchadnezzar had carried away from Jerusalem and placed in the house of his gods. King Cyrus of Persia had them released into the charge of Mithredath the treasurer, who counted them out to Sheshbazzar the prince of Judah. And this was the inventory: gold basins, thirty; silver basins, one thousand; knives, twenty-nine; gold bowls, thirty; other silver bowls, four hundred ten; other vessels, one thousand; the total of the gold and silver vessels was five thousand four hundred. All these Sheshbazzar brought up, when the exiles were brought up from Babylonia to Jerusalem. (NRSV)

The rebuilding of the Temple and the returning of the captives taken by Nebuchadnezzer II affected Jewish history down to the first century CE when the Romans then destroyed the Second Temple.

The Persians were kicked out of Jerusalem when Alexander the Great, the king of Macedon, took control of the area in 332 BCE. Alexander had a very short rule over a very large empire, and when he died his generals took power and crowned themselves kings. The Seleucid family (named after Alexander's general Seleucis) ultimately took control of Jerusalem and the surrounding area. In general the Greek rulers left local religions alone to practice their beliefs, but in 167 BCE King Antiochus IV decided to push Greek religion, and the worship of himself as a god, on the Jewish population of Palestine. The king set up a statue of the Greek god Zeus within the Temple precinct, which desecrated the Temple. This led to a revolt called the Maccabean Revolt, so called because the leaders were from the Maccabean family. Ultimately this revolt was successful. The Jewish people managed to kick out the Greeks and rule themselves for nearly 100 years. The Maccabees cleansed the Second Temple and rededicated it in 164 BCE. This is now celebrated in the holiday of Hanukah.

The Maccabees and their family ruled Palestine with Jerusalem as their capital until their internal problems attracted the attention of the Romans, who were pushing their control into the area. In 63 BCE the Romans made this area into one of their provinces, and then in 40 BCE Mark Anthony and Octavius appointed Herod the king of the area. Herod the Great ruled until his death in 4 BCE, and the Romans allowed his three sons to divide up the territory and to rule as kings.

It was during the time of Herod the Great that Jesus was born and the Christian movement began. The Jewish population had an uneasy relationship with the Romans. On the one hand the Romans were fairly tolerant of the Jewish religion. On the other hand, the Jewish people wanted to rule themselves and, in particular, they intensely disliked paying taxes to Rome. These problems led directly to the Jewish Revolt, which took place between 66 CE and 70 CE. Part of the revolt was instigated by a group of Jewish nationalists called the Zealots. The Zealots had been active since the beginning of the century, and as Rome cracked down on the Jewish population, the Zealots fought back harder and harder. In 66 CE one of the Roman procurators (a governor) named Floris took money from the Second Temple to pay taxes. This money was raised by the Jewish population as tribute to the Temple, and not to pay the Romans. This action led the Jewish population to rise up against their Roman overseers.

The Jewish Revolt technically began when the Romans sent troops to Judea in 66 BCE. In this battle the Jewish fighters routed the Romans. It was hoped that this would be enough to take control of their own area, but the Romans, under Emperor Nero, then decided to send a much larger army under the command of General Vespasian to attack Judea. Vespasian would have to leave the fighting when he was declared emperor in 69 CE. His son Titus continued the fighting, and it was under General Titus that the Romans took control of Jerusalem and then destroyed the Second Temple. Titus was awarded a triumph (a military celebration held in Rome) for his victory and a triumphal arch was built for him in the Roman Forum. This triumphal arch depicts the looting of the Second Temple by the Romans. It was after this period that much of the surviving Jewish population and the growing Christian population fled Judea, going to other cities throughout the Roman Empire as well as fleeing into Persian cities. Despite the loss of Jerusalem to the Romans, the city continued to thrive and to be a center point for Jewish and Christian populations up through 637 CE when the Muslims took control of the area. This control lasted until the First Crusade in 1096 CE when the Christians took back the city. There was then a tug-of-war between the Christians, Jews, and Muslims that continues through today.

See also: Herod the Great; Jesus.

Further Reading

Carroll, James. *Jerusalem, Jerusalem: How the Ancient City Ignited Our Modern World.*
    Boston: Houghton Mifflin Harcourt, 2011.
Galor, Katharina, and Hanswulf Bloedhorn. *The Archaeology of Jerusalem: From the
    Origins to the Ottomans.* New Haven, CT: Yale University Press, 2013.
Horovitz, Ahron. *City of David: The Story of Ancient Jerusalem.* Brooklyn, NY:
    Lambda Publishers, 2009.
Montefiore, Simon Sebag. *Jerusalem: The Biography.* New York: Vintage Books, 2012.

JESUS   Jesus is seen by Christians as being the Son of God and the Savior who died for their sins. There is surprisingly very little we know about the life of Jesus, considering that he is probably the most important figure in Western history. One of the reasons for our lack of knowledge about Jesus is that he is described by people who lived quite a bit of time after his death. The Gospel accounts were written sometime between the middle of the 60s CE and as late as the 90s CE (in the case of the Gospel of John). Another reason is that these writings do not contain what we would call a biography, so what we know comes from the various bits and pieces put together. We don't know the exact year of the death of Jesus, but it probably lies sometime between 30 and 33 CE. This means that at least 30 years had passed since the time of his death and the period when his story was actually written down. This, however, doesn't mean we can't know something about Jesus, since there were almost certainly oral stories about him that were passed down and of course some of the Gospel writers knew Jesus personally.

If Matthew is correct (Matthew 2:1), Jesus was born sometime during the reign of King Herod, who ruled from 37 to 4 BCE. So at the latest Jesus was born in 4 BCE. As mentioned above, we don't know the date of his death, but it has been guessed to be between 30 and 33 CE. Much of our information on the life of Jesus comes from the Gospels, which, according to tradition, were written by people who knew Jesus. Paul, the earliest New Testament writer, had never met the man Jesus so there isn't much in his letters about Jesus as a man.

What we do know is that Jesus was Jewish. Both his human father and mother were Jewish. In fact the first chapter of Matthew quotes a long genealogical list of people from Abraham all the way down to Joseph, the husband of Mary. We know from the sources that he spent time in the Temple when he was growing up, and certainly that he was familiar with the Jewish religion when he was an adult. He celebrated Jewish holidays. Jesus began his ministry when he was an adult, as far as we know (we can't really say what he did when he was a child or even young adult since there is no surviving information). Despite this lack of information, many Christians believed that the coming of

Christ was specifically foretold in the Old Testament. Early Christians certainly knew the Old Testament since many of the early converts were Jewish. These early Christians found statements about Jesus in this collection and believed that the Old Testament prefigured Christ, or told about him before he became a man. For example, see Isaiah 53 and Psalms 82:6. Isaiah 53 is fairly long, but a very important text for seeing Christ in the Old Testament:

> Who has believed what we have heard? And to whom has the arm of the LORD been revealed? For he grew up before him like a young plant, and like a root out of dry ground; he had no form or majesty that we should look at him, nothing in his appearance that we should desire him. He was despised and rejected by others; a man of suffering and acquainted with infirmity; and as one from whom others hide their faces he was despised, and we held him of no account.
>
> Surely he has borne our infirmities and carried our diseases; yet we accounted him stricken, struck down by God, and afflicted. But he was wounded for our transgressions, crushed for our iniquities; upon him was the punishment that made us whole, and by his bruises we are healed. All we like sheep have gone astray; we have all turned to our own way and the LORD has laid on him the iniquity of us all. He was oppressed, and he was afflicted, yet he did not open his mouth; like a lamb that is led to the slaughter, and like a sheep that before its shearers is silent, so he did not open his mouth. By a perversion of justice he was taken away. Who could have imagined his future? For he was cut off from the land of the living, stricken for the transgression of my people. They made his grave with the wicked and his tomb with the rich, although he had done no violence, and there was no deceit in his mouth.
>
> Yet it was the will of the LORD to crush him with pain. When you make his life an offering for sin, he shall see his offspring, and shall prolong his days; through him the will of the LORD shall prosper. Out of his anguish he shall see light; he shall find satisfaction through his knowledge. The righteous one, my servant, shall make many righteous, and he shall bear their iniquities. Therefore I will allot him a portion with the great, and he shall divide the spoil with the strong; because he poured out himself to death, and was numbered with the transgressors; yet he bore the sin of many, and made intercession for the transgressors. (NRSV)

Clearly there are many parallels to the life and death of Christ in this section of Isaiah, and Christians used texts like these to prove that Christ was on earth long before he took a human body. So despite the lack of biographical information in the New Testament, early Christians (and modern ones too) could look to the Old Testament to fill the gaps. In terms of specific information about Christ, we know from the written accounts that he was, among other things, a preacher/teacher, a miracle worker, and a healer.

A PREACHER/TEACHER

While there can be a subtle difference between the role of a preacher and a teacher, the life of Jesus shows that he combined these two. He was definitely teaching the masses while preaching to his various audiences. This is especially the case in his Sermon on the Mount, found in Matthew 5–7. It is here that Jesus addressed a large crowd and taught them the various precepts of what would become the basis of Christianity. This Sermon on the Mount is one of the most moving and informational teachings in the entire New Testament. The New Testament writings also make it clear that Jesus preached nearly everywhere he went. Jesus refers to himself as a teacher a number of times. In John 13:12–17 we are told:

> After he had washed their feet, had put on his robe, and had returned to the table, he said to them, "Do you know what I have done to you? You call me Teacher and Lord—and you are right, for that is what I am. So if I, your Lord and Teacher, have washed your feet, you also ought to wash one another's feet. For I have set you an example, that you also should do as I have done to you. Very truly, I tell you, servants are not greater than their master, nor are messengers greater than the one who sent them. If you know these things, you are blessed if you do them. (NRSV)

His role as teacher comes out very clearly when he speaks in parables. He usually will not give the answer to these riddles, but expects his audience to work out the correct response. For example, in Matthew 9:17 Jesus states: "Neither is new wine put into old wineskins; otherwise, the skins burst, and the wine is spilled, and the skins are destroyed; but new wine is put into fresh wineskins, and so both are preserved." Another one is Matthew 13:1–9:

> That same day Jesus went out of the house and sat beside the sea. Such great crowds gathered around him that he got into a boat and sat there, while the whole crowd stood on the beach. And he told them many things in parables, saying: "Listen! A sower went out to sow. And as he sowed, some seeds fell on the path, and the birds came and ate them up. Other seeds fell on rocky ground, where they did not have much soil, and they sprang up quickly, since they had no depth of soil. But when the sun rose, they were scorched; and since they had no root, they withered away. Other seeds fell among thorns, and the thorns grew up and choked them. Other seeds fell on good soil and brought forth grain, some a hundredfold, some sixty, some thirty. Let anyone with ears hear!" (NRSV)

The purpose of this type of teaching has been extensively written about. Most modern scholars believe that the use of parables in teaching allows Christians to think about their own behavior and how it fits into the message of Jesus. It was and can be now a very effective teaching method.

A MIRACLE WORKER

Before Jesus appeared as a man, Jewish congregations were very familiar with miracles. These miracles were usually performed by God, usually in order to save Israel, or by individuals who were chosen by God (see Kee, *Miracle in the Early Christian World*, p. 147). So when Jesus appeared and did miracles, the early Jewish/Christian communities were not absolutely surprised about this. One telling miracle occurred when Jesus himself was baptized by John the Baptist: the voice of God was heard (Mark 1:9–11, Matthew 3:3–17, and Luke 3:21–23) stating: "You are my Son, the Beloved, with you I am well pleased." Jesus performed his own miracles, the most famous of which is his walking on water (found at Mark 6:45, Matthew 14:22, and John 6:16). Another famous miracle was the changing of a few fish and loaves of bread into food for 4,000 people (Mark 8:1 and Matthew 15:32). These miracles helped to convince people that Jesus was indeed who he said he was—the Son of God. These miracles also were used to increase the number of Christians.

A HEALER

Jesus was probably more famously known as a healer (which can be seen as a subset of doing miracles). He was known for healing a number of people, including a man who was paralyzed (as told in Matthew 9:2) and driving out demons from people who were possessed, as told in Luke 9:37:

> On the next day, when they had come down from the mountain, a great crowd met him. Just then a man from the crowd shouted, "Teacher, I beg you to look at my son; he is my only child. Suddenly a spirit seizes him, and all at once he shrieks. It convulses him until he foams at the mouth; it mauls him and will scarcely leave him. I begged your disciples to cast it out, but they could not." Jesus answered, "You faithless and perverse generation, how much longer must I be with you and bear with you? Bring your son here." While he was coming, the demon dashed him to the ground in convulsions. But Jesus rebuked the unclean spirit, healed the boy, and gave him back to his father. And all were astounded at the greatness of God. (NRSV)

As can be seen from the last sentence, the healings increased the belief that Jesus was indeed the Son of God and thus increased the number of early Christians. Besides being a healer, Jesus was also known as someone who could resurrect the dead. This happens three times in the New

Testament—Matthew 9:25, Luke 7:11–17; probably the most famous is the raising of Lazarus, found in John 11:1–44. The disciples were also given this power when they went out spreading the message of Christ. These miracles (the healing and the resurrection of the dead) really helped to push the message of Jesus that he was the Messiah. And like the other miraculous things Christ did, these also helped to increase the sheer number of people who became Christian.

Jesus could be seen as a bit of a rebel in terms of going against the prominent Jewish groups—the Sadducees and the Pharisees. These Jewish groups fought against Jesus because they did not believe he was the Messiah. We see these two groups fighting with Jesus over and over again in the New Testament, and these fights ultimately lead to the crucifixion of Christ. Finally, the last bit of information we know about Christ is his resurrection and return to heaven. The crucifixion and resurrection account is given in all four Gospels plus many of the other writings found in the New Testament. It is probably the most important account in the entire work since ancient and modern Christians believe that like Christ, they will be resurrected after death as a reward for believing in Christ.

See also: Pharisees; Sadducees.

Further Reading

Crossan, John Dominic. *The Historical Jesus: The Life of a Mediterranean Jewish Peasant*. New York: Harper Collins, 1991.

Ehrman, Bart D. *How Jesus Became God: The Exaltation of a Jewish Preacher from Galilee*. New York: HarperOne, 2014.

Isbouts, Jean-Pierre. *In the Footsteps of Jesus: A Chronicle of His Life and the Origins of Christianity*. Washington, DC: National Geographic, 2012.

Vermes, Geza. *Jesus in His Jewish Context*. Minneapolis: Fortress Press, 2003.

Wright, N. T. *The Challenge of Jesus: Rediscovering Who Jesus Was and Is*. Downers Grove, IL: InterVarsity Press, 1999.

JUDAISM The history of Judaism is extremely important for studying early Christianity since many of the first-century Christians were Jewish (including Jesus). Much of Jewish history, culture, and religious rites were known to early Christians, and many times they borrowed Jewish religious practices when they converted to Christianity. All early Christians were also familiar with the Jewish scripture, the Hebrew Bible, and this collection of documents had a great impact on early Christianity. This history of the Jewish people is a long one. The author of Genesis states that Abraham came from a southern Mesopotamian town named Ur (Gen. 11:31). We don't know the exact date when this might have happened. The rest of Genesis and parts of the beginning of the Old Testament recount the journeys of the Jewish people as they move out of Mesopotamia and into Israel, by way of Egypt, and the creation of the Kingdom of Israel and Judah.

THE BABYLONIAN CAPTIVITY

In 587 BCE the Jewish people suffered a great calamity. They were unfortunate enough to be in the way of King Nebuchadnezzar II, a Neo-Babylonian king. He was trying to expand his territory all the way into Egypt and in the process suffered a series of rebellions, especially by the Jewish population in Judea. The king of Judea at this period was named Jehoiakim, who was captured (which you can read about in 2 Chronicles 36:5–8). A few years later, Nebuchadnezzar II returned, and this time he plundered and then destroyed Jerusalem and its famed Temple (usually referred to as the First Temple). He then took many Jewish people back to Babylonia with him in order to control the population. This episode is referred to as the Captivity period in Jewish history. Writings in the Old Testament tell us that the destruction of Jerusalem and the Captivity was done because God was punishing his people (2 Kings 24:2; Jeremiah 27:6).

The Neo-Babylonians soon lost their kingdom with the rise of the Persians and, in particular, their king Cyrus the Great. After he defeated the Neo-Babylonians, Cyrus allowed the Jewish people to go home (although some ended up staying in the Persian kingdom) and he even gave them back some of the pillaged treasures that Nebuchadnezzar II had taken before he destroyed the First Temple. Cyrus partially gets the title "the Great" because he is fondly remembered by the Jewish people for allowing them not only to go home, but to rebuild their temple, called The Second Temple. Much of the story of Cyrus can be found in the book of Ezra 1:1–1:4:

> In the first year of King Cyrus of Persia, in order that the word of the LORD by the mouth of Jeremiah might be accomplished, the LORD stirred up the spirit of King Cyrus of Persia so that he sent a herald throughout all his kingdom, and also in a written edict declared: "Thus says King Cyrus of Persia: The LORD, the God of heaven, has given me all the kingdoms of the earth, and he has charged me to build him a house at Jerusalem in Judah. Any of those among you who are of his people—may their God be with them!—are now permitted to go up to Jerusalem in Judah, and rebuild the house of the LORD, the God of Israel—he is the God who is in Jerusalem; and let all survivors, in whatever place they reside, be assisted by the people of their place with silver and gold, with goods and with animals, besides freewill offerings or the house of God in Jerusalem. (NRSV)

So the Jewish people rebuilt their Second Temple (which will be destroyed by the Romans in the first century CE) and began to pick up where they had left off after the destruction of Nebuchadnezzar II. The history of Judea, however, was never a peaceful one, and in the late 300s BCE, Persia was conquered by Alexander the Great and his Greek/Macedonian troops, and he claimed this territory as his own.

THE SPREADING OF JUDAISM THROUGHOUT THE MEDITERRANEAN

The period between Cyrus the Great and the building of the Second Temple down until the first century is referred to in Jewish history as a period of Diaspora, which means spreading. During this period the Jewish people moved (and were physically moved from) their homeland in Judea. They spread all throughout the Mediterranean but retained many of the roots of their faith. There were large Jewish populations known to exist in Egypt, Rome, Cyrenaica (North Africa), Persia, Asia Minor (modern-day Turkey), and of course in Judea. The spread of Judaism during this period had profound effects on the growth of Christianity centuries later because many Christians were previously Jewish people who had converted.

HELLENIZATION

With the fall of Persia to Alexander the Great in the 300s BCE, Hellenism was instituted throughout the Mediterranean, including Judea. Many Greeks called themselves Hellenes, and Hellenization is the process of spreading Greek ideas. This included Greek dress, Greek architecture, Greek forms of government, and of course, the Greek language. Judea did not escape this process. With Judea under Greek/Macedonian control in the late 300s BCE, the Greek language and way of life became very common. The Hebrew Scriptures were soon translated into Greek; known as the Septuagint, they became more popular than their Hebrew counterpart. Much of the Jewish population became Hellenized while still respecting their own religious traditions. However, some Jewish groups started to become more and more Hellenized, and some conservative members were not happy about this. This ultimately led to the Maccabean Revolt, which occurred in 168/167 and lasted through 160 BCE.

THE MACCABEAN REVOLT

The Maccabean Revolt began when some Jewish leaders wanted to stop the Hellenization process. This of course meant that part of the Jewish population went to war with their Seleucid/Persian overlords and with members of their own faith. This revolt really started when the king, Antiochus Epiphanes IV, decided to enforce the idea that there should only be one religion—and that was not Judaism. He invaded and desecrated the Temple by setting up a statue and forbade the Jewish population from practicing their faith. The Maccabees were a family that were at the center of resistance by the Jewish population. The Maccabees were successful at fighting off forces of Antiochus Epiphanes IV, and the Temple was rededicated. The celebrations took place over eight days and the historical events are still commemorated by Jewish people all over the world as Hanukkah. Jewish self-rule (to a certain extent) stayed until 63 BCE when the Romans arrived.

THE COMING OF THE ROMANS

Unfortunately the Jewish people did not rule themselves for very long, especially after the coming of the Romans in 63 BCE. The Romans were fairly tolerant of other religions, especially when it could be proven that they were old. Judaism had no problem proving this. The Jewish population was very particular when it came to interacting with their new overlords. They wanted to keep the Temple area clean of outside influences and they managed to do this until the middle/end of the first century. The Romans, who tried to respect Judaism, used Herod as King of Judea to rule the area in their name. Herod, although he gets a bad name in the New Testament, was a fairly good king, especially in terms of the building projects he started that also had the side benefit of making the lives of some Jewish people better. Herod died in 4 BCE, and his sons took over the role of King. In 6 CE Augustus, the first Roman emperor, made Judea a province. The Romans remained fairly neutral in terms of their control of Judea, and the Jewish population, although not content with being ruled by the Romans, were able to continue with their way of life. This remained the case until 39 CE when Emperor Caligula decided to install a statue of himself in the most sacred part of the Second Temple (and in all other temples in the Roman Empire). Luckily Caligula was assassinated before he could cement this policy.

Then in 66 CE, Emperor Nero instituted a number of policies that led directly to an armed Jewish rebellion against their Roman rulers, called the Jewish War. This was started primarily because Nero authorized the governor of Judea to collect money in order to build up the state treasury. The governor apparently was stealing silver from the Second Temple, and this was discovered. At first the Jewish population threw out the Roman infantry that were stationed in Jerusalem, but this did not last very long. The Roman general (and later emperor) Vespasian was sent to quell the violence. He was successful at this and when his son Titus (who also became emperor) arrived to fight, the revolt was put down. Titus expelled the Jewish and Christian population. More than likely Titus did not understand the subtle differences between these two groups—but at that point it didn't really matter because they could no longer live in Jerusalem. Titus also took the step of raiding the Second Temple of its treasure, and then in 70 CE, like Nebuchadnezzar II, the Temple was set on fire. This episode was described by the Jewish historian Josephus in his book titled *Jewish Wars*:

> At which time one of the soldiers, without staying for any orders, and without any concern or dread upon him at so great an undertaking, and being hurried on by a certain divine fury, snatched somewhat out of the materials that were on fire, and being lifted up by another soldier, he set fire to a golden window, through which there was a passage to the rooms that were round about the holy house, on the north side of it. As the flames went upward, the Jews made a great clamor, such as so mighty an affliction required, and ran together to prevent it; and now they spared not their lives any longer, nor suffered anything to restrain their force, since that holy house was perishing, for whose sake it was that they kept such a guard about it. (Josephus, Chapter 6, section 4, subsection 5, n.d.)

The Second Temple was never rebuilt, and all that remains today is a section referred to as the Wailing Wall.

THE ANTI-JEWISH MOVEMENT WITHIN ANCIENT CHRISTIANITY

The Jewish population and the early Christians did not get along all that well even though the roots of early Christianity are thoroughly Jewish. We can see this from Paul's letters (which are the earliest we have that make up the New Testament) where he complains about the lack of Jewish enthusiasm for his message and the fact that many times it was the Jewish population that led to him being tossed out of a number of cities. We can also see some anti-Judaism in other New Testament books, especially from the words of Jesus when he complains about the Pharisees and the Sadducees and their interpretations of the Old Testament. Many early Christians also blamed the Jewish population for killing Jesus. The Gospel of Mark is recognized as the most anti-Jewish of the Gospels.

The anti-Judaism continues in later Christianity—a good example of this is Justin Martyr in his writing titled *Dialogue with Trypho, A Jew*. The exact date he wrote this is unclear, but it was certainly before 165 CE, when Justin died. In the beginning of the *Dialogue* Justin explains to Trypho his conversion experience, from being involved in a number of different philosophies to finally Christianity. Trypho, however, smiles at him and tells him to become Jewish since Christians have invented the figure of Christ. He later tells Justin that being circumcised and following the dietary restrictions and the festivals is the correct form of religion, not following the crucified Jesus. Justin of course disagrees and then uses the Old Testament to try to convince Trypho (and therefore other Jewish people) that the Old Testament itself witnesses to the coming of Christ. In the end Trypho is not convinced, but the message of the *Dialogue* is clear—Christianity is the true outcome of Judaism, and Jewish people should convert.

Further Reading

Collins, John J., and Daniel C. Harlow, eds. *Early Judaism: A Comprehensive Overview*. Grand Rapids, MI: William B. Eerdmans, 2010.

Ferguson, E. *Backgrounds of Early Christianity*, 3rd ed. Grand Rapids: Eerdmans, 2003.

Josephus. "Jewish Wars." *Josephus: The Complete Works*. Available online at http://www.ccel.org/ccel/josephus/complete.

Murphy, Frederick J. *Early Judaism: The Exile to the Time of Jesus*. Grand Rapids, MI: Baker Academic, 2002.

Smith, Mark S. *The Early History of God: Yahweh and the Other Deities in Ancient Israel* (Biblical Resource Series), 2nd ed. Grand Rapids: William B. Eerdmans, 2002.

JULIAN   Julian was emperor from 360 to 363 CE. He clearly did not rule long, but he plays an interesting part in Christian history. As will be discussed, Julian was brought up Christian, but when he became emperor, he tried to bring back the traditional form of Roman religion (sometimes called paganism) and to suppress Christianity. Julian was born in 331 or 332 to Julius Constantius and Basilina. His father was the half-brother of Emperor Constantine I. When Julian was six, Constantine I died, and his three sons, Constantius II, Constans, and Constantine II, were elevated to be co-emperors. When this happened, they decided to kill many of their male family members in order to make sure that no one would try to claim the throne. Unfortunately for Julian, his father Julius was murdered, along with the other half-brothers of Constantine I and their sons. Julian and his brother were not killed, probably because of their young age.

Julian was not allowed to live the life of a family member of Constantine, and as a result he was removed from the limelight and had nothing to do with the governing of the empire, at least in the beginning. He was raised in Nicomedia and was given the best education. We also know that Eusebius of Nicomedia, the Arian bishop, was one of his tutors. As far as we know, Julian had a lonely childhood. He wasn't allowed to have friends other than his tutors. Not surprisingly, he did not like the fact that his family was killed by his own relatives. One of the letters written by Julian that still exist, titled *Letter to the Athenians*, states that his six cousins, his father, his uncles, and finally his brother were all put to death, and he and his brother Gallus were sent into exile. Sozamen, an ancient Christian historian, writes that when Julian was being educated in Nicomedia, he took a vow to renounce his Christian religion and to follow the native Roman religion, but he had to keep this vow secret.

When Julian was just 23, his cousin and emperor Constantius II decided to bring Julian out of his exile, made him a caesar, and then sent him off to Gaul to control some uprisings that were taking place there. Julian, despite not having any military training, was a very successful general, and his troops loved him. This made Constantius II a bit wary since Roman troops were known to raise up a well-loved general to the rank of emperor, and in 360 CE this is exactly what happened to Julian. In 361 Emperor Constantius II rushed from fighting with the Persians to do battle with Julian. Luckily for Julian, Constantius II died, and this left Julian as the sole emperor.

Now Julian could be open with his vow to cause trouble for the Christians. Julian passed a number of laws that promoted the ancient Roman religion while at the same time suppressing Christianity. One law stated that Christians could not be teachers because they would be promoting Christianity instead of teaching the normal subjects. This law was of course unpopular with the Christians, but even pagans thought it was very unfair. He wrote a work called *Against the Galileans*, which was the name he gave to Christians. His letter begins with his argument against Christianity:

> It is, I think, expedient to set forth to all mankind the reasons by which I was convinced that the fabrication of the Galilaeans is a fiction of men composed by wickedness. Though it has in it nothing divine, by making full use of that part of the soul which loves fable and is childish and foolish, it has induced men to believe that the monstrous tale is truth. Now since I intend to treat of all their first dogmas, as they call them, I wish to say in the first place that if my readers desire to try to refute me they must proceed as if they were in a court of law and not drag in irrelevant matter, or, as the saying is, bring counter-charges until they have defended their own views. For thus it will be better and clearer if, when they wish to censure any views of mine, they undertake that as a separate task, but when they are defending themselves against my censure, they bring no counter-charges. (Julian the Apostate, 1923)

He continues throughout this very long work to tear down Christianity. However, even though Julian did not like Christianity, he refused to see them physically persecuted.

Julian did not remain as emperor for very long. Like many Roman emperors before him, Julian decided to go to war against the Persians and to invade Mesopotamia, in 363 CE. He and his army made it part-way into the Persian Empire before the Persian troops and the Persian people began to offer fierce resistance. At Ctesiphon he lost a large part of his army to the Persian troops, but he refused to retreat. Finally, he decided that it was too dangerous to remain in Persia, so he ordered his troops to return home. On their retreat the Persians continued to follow the Romans out of their territory. In one of the battles Julian was hit by a spear and soon died. Julian is sometimes referred to as Julian the Apostate because he grew up as a Christian but then joined another religion. Constantine I, and then his sons Constantius II, Constans, and Constantine II, were all Christian. Julian broke that chain, but he was the last emperor in the history of the Roman Empire to do so—all the rest of the emperors were Christian.

Further Reading

Bowersock, G. W. *Julian the Apostate*. Cambridge, MA: Harvard University Press, 1978.

Browning, Robert. *The Emperor Julian*. Berkeley: University of California Press, 1978.

Julian the Apostate, "Against the Galileans": excerpted from Cyril of Alexandria, *Contra Julianum* (1923), 319–433. Available online at http://www.tertullian.org /fathers/julian_apostate_galileans_1_text.htm.

Murdoch, Adrian. *The Last Pagan: Julian the Apostate and the Death of the Ancient World*. Rochester, VT: Inner Traditions, 2008.

Smith, Rowland B. E. *Julian's Gods: Religion and Philosophy in the Thought and Action of Julian the Apostate*. New York: Routledge, 1995.

MANI, THE FOUNDER OF MANICHAEISM The Manichaeans were a Christian/Jewish offshoot that began in the area of Babylon in the middle of the third century CE. It was a world religion that lasted for 1,400 years across the world from France to China. The founder was named Mani, who was born in 216 CE in Babylon near the twin cities of Seleucia/Ctestiphon, the capital of the Persian Empire. Much is known about Mani, especially from a tiny manuscript called the *Cologne Mani Codex*, called this because it is kept in Cologne, Germany. It was discovered in 1969. This codex is a biography of Mani. The amazing thing about this work is its size: the pages only measure 1.8 inches by 1.4 inches. There is an average of 23 lines of Greek on each page. It was written by at least 4 scribes.

From this text we know that when Mani was little he was taken from his mother and went to live with his father in a Christian/Jewish group called the Elchasaites. There isn't much known about this group, except that they were baptizers. The text states that at the age of 12 Mani was visited by his "heavenly twin" who told him some secrets of the universe. These secrets included the origin of mankind and what will happen to it at the end of time. He was also told how the universe was put together and that he should begin to spread this new religion throughout the entire world. Mani did not act on these secrets, and at the age of 24 he was visited again. After this he left the Elchasaites because he was convinced that he had the correct interpretation of Christianity. Mani was possibly forced out as well, since the *Cologne Mani Codex* talks about him almost being beaten to death by one of the leaders of the Elchasaites.

Mani left with his father and began to travel. He talks about going to India first, and then he headed back into Persia where he met the brother of the Persian king, Shapur I, the King of Kings, who ruled from 240–272 CE. We have a story in a language called Middle Persian that states that Mani met the brother and discussed the Manichaean religion with him. The brother was unimpressed with Mani's ideas until Mani gave him a vision of paradise. The brother was converted to Manichaeism and told the king, Shapur I. It appears from a number of different Manichaean texts that King Shapur and Mani got along with each other very well, so much so that Shapur allowed Mani total access to the kingdom in order to preach.

At this time Persia followed a religion called Zoroastrianism, but there must have been something in the message of Mani that convinced King Shapur that Mani's religion was acceptable. A good reason for this is a text titled the *Shaburagan*, written in a language called Middle Persian. The *Shaburagan* was written by Mani just for Shapur. Some of the text states that the religious message that Mani was spreading was also brought by Buddha, Zoroaster, and Jesus. Mani just happened to be the last messenger. Unfortunately the entire text does not exist, but it is known that there are Manichaean deities that were given Zoroastrian names, which made it look like a Persian religion. This was not done in an underhanded manner, however, since Mani believed that he had founded a universal religion and that Zoroaster, the founder of Zoroastrianism, was nothing but an earlier apostle of the Manichaean faith. This is also the case with Buddha and Jesus. Hence Buddha, Zoroaster, and Jesus were apostles, while Mani was the final apostle to be sent to mankind (as seen from the passage of the *Shaburagan*).

The list of previous Manichaean apostles can be found in other Manichaean documents, such as the *Kephalaia*, a Manichaean book found in Egypt, written in Coptic (an Egyptian language). Here the list of Manichaean apostles goes all the way back to Adam up through Jesus. Mani believed his religion was different because unlike Buddha, Zoroaster, and Jesus, Mani took the time to write his teachings down, and therefore the teaching would remain pure until the end of time. This is probably why the religion of Manichaeism had so much success in the Persian Empire.

It is known that Mani even traveled with King Shapur I on some of his military campaigns, and it is possible that he might have even been present when the Roman emperor Valerian was captured in 260 by Shapur. The connection between Mani and the Persians caused the Manichaeans many problems when they begin to make their way into the Roman territory, especially since they were seen as Persian infiltrators. Shapur I died in 272 and his son Ormizd took over. Mani seemed to get along well with him, but Ormizd died in 273 and Shapur I's other son Vahram I took over. Vahram I was an ardent follower of Zoroastrianism and didn't like the fact that Mani had access to the people of the kingdom to spread his own religion. We are told that one day King Vahram I summoned Mani to his court. At this meeting Vahram I told Mani that he was no longer welcome in the Persian kingdom. Mani was then seized and thrown into prison. Mani was never allowed to leave, and 26 days later he was put to death, in 276 CE. While this made Mani a martyr (someone who dies for their faith), the Manichaeans never forgave the Zoroastrian king and priesthood for murdering their last prophet to mankind.

See also: Mani, the Founder of Manichaeism; Manichaeans.

Further Reading

Coyle, K. *Manichaeism and Its Legacy* (Nag Hammadi and Manichaean Studies). Leiden: Brill, 2009.

Gardner, Iain, and S. N. C. Lieu, eds. *Manichaean Texts from the Roman Empire*. Cambridge: Cambridge University Press, 2004.

Tardieu, Michel. *Manichaeism*, translated edition. Paris: Presses Universitaires de France; English translation by Board of Trustees of the University of Illinois, 2008.

MANICHAEANS   There were many different types of Christianity in the ancient world, just as there are many different types of Christianity in the modern world. For example, in the modern world there are Protestants, Catholics, and Orthodox Christians, not to mention all of the subgroups found within each of these. In ancient Christianity one such Christian group was the Manichaeans. They started in Persia in the 200s CE and soon spread throughout a large part of Europe and Asia. They were still an active religion in China until the 1600s.

This new Christian movement started with Mani, the founder of Manichaeism. He was born in 216 and died either in 276 or 277. According to the *Cologne Mani Codex* (named because it is now in Cologne, Germany), Mani was visited by his "spiritual twin" when he was little. At that point he and his father were part of a Jewish-Christian group called the Elchasaites, who were known for their ritual baptisms. His spiritual twin wanted him to start his own religious movement, which he eventually did. Mani, his father, and some followers broke away from the Elchasaites and started to spread his version of Christianity.

From early Manichaean texts we know that Mani became friends with the Persian king Shapur I. Shapur I allowed Mani to travel around Persia spreading his new form of Christianity, which incorporated parts of the native Persian religion of Zoroastrianism. We are told by the Manichaean texts that Shapur I and Mani were friends. After Shapur I died, however, the following kings did not like Mani, began to persecute him, and forced his followers out of Persia. It was under King Vahram I that Mani was imprisoned and killed, making Mani a martyr. His murder did not stop his religion from spreading, and, if anything, the persecution caused it to spread, both westward into the Roman Empire and north and eastward into Central Asia and eventually China.

The Manichaeans were essentially dualists, meaning they believed that there was a totally good God and its opposite, a totally evil God, referred to as the Two Principles. They divided time up into three segments (called the Three Times in Manichaean texts)—the Beginning, the Middle, and the End. In the beginning before the world was created the Good and the Evil were absolutely separated. In the Middle Time, the Good and Evil became mixed together, which caused humanity many problems. The Manichaeans believed that the Evil God causes humans to commit evil acts. The End time consisted of a total separation of the Good from the Evil, and then the imprisonment of the Evil so that it would never be able to do any harm again. Mani believed he was the last prophet to mankind. Because they were Christians, they believed that Jesus would play a part in the salvation and rescue of humanity.

The Manichaean ecclesiology (or church structure) consisted of two parts: the Elect (who acted as bishops) and the Hearers, who were the laity. This structure is very similar to what would become the Catholic ecclesiology. The Elect had certain rules that they had to follow. For example, they had to be vegetarian. They could not grow their own food for fear of injuring the plants. Their main duty was to teach the Hearers about the teachings of Mani. The Hearers' duty was to take care of the Elect—to feed them, house them, and of course, listen to their instructions.

We don't know exactly when Manichaeism found its way to the Roman Empire. It is thought that sometime in the 260s or 270s representatives were already there, before the death of Mani. Certainly the persecution of the

Manichaeans and the killing of Mani by Vahram II helped to spread the teachings outside of the Persian borders. We know that the Manichaeans were in Egypt in the 290s because the governor of Egypt sent Emperor Diocletian a letter stating that the Manichaeans were causing trouble. Emperor Diocletian had traveled to Egypt, and while he was there he issued an edict ordering their persecution. They weren't necessarily persecuted because of their religious beliefs but because of their ties to Persia (an enemy of Rome). The edict ordered that their books and leaders be burned and ordered the followers to leave or receive the same punishment as their leaders. This persecution continued throughout the entire time they were in the Roman Empire. As mentioned above, they also moved into Asia.

See also: Mani, the Founder of Manichaeism; Manichaeans.

Further Reading

BeDuhn, Jason David. *Augustine's Manichaean Dilemma*, Volume 1: *Conversion and Apostasy, 373–388 C.E.* (Divinations: Rereading Late Ancient Religion). Philadelphia: University of Pennsylvania Press, 2010.

BeDuhn, Jason David. *The Manichaean Body: In Discipline and Ritual.* Baltimore: John Hopkins University Press, 2002.

Lieu, S. N. C. *Manichaeism in the Later Roman Empire and Medieval China: A Historical Survey*, rev. 2nd ed. Manchester: Manchester University Press, 1992.

Rudolph, Kurt. *Gnosis: The Nature and History of Gnosticism*, English version. New York: HarperCollins, 1987.

MARCION   Marcion was born sometime in the early second century CE in the Roman province of Pontus, which is now northern Turkey. He more than likely grew up as a Christian as his father might have been a Christian bishop. We don't know very much about his early life, as with most people from this time, but we do know much more about Marcion the adult, primarily because of Tertullian, a second-century Christian who wrote against the ideas of Marcion. We have to be careful with the information we have because our primary source for the life and ideas of Marcion is written by his opponent, but there are still some facts that can be gleaned about his life and work. He was a Christian but had some different ideas about what Christianity meant. He believed that Christians should not use the Old Testament, which was tied to his belief that there were two gods, the totally good one from the New Testament and the evil one from the Old. He also believed that there were a small number of texts that Christians should read (his list is much smaller than our current New Testament). These ideas had a significant impact on later Christian belief and practice.

Christians from the first century were very familiar with what we now call the Old Testament. It was their scripture, and early Christian writers refer to it all the time. It was and is the basis of Christian morality and how Christians view God. As Christianity became more organized, there was a need to regulate what Christians read and believed. There are a few reasons for this. The first is that more and more writings were appearing that carried the names of the apostles, but were clearly not written by them. The second is that there were legitimate Christians writing material about Christianity, but some believed they should not be in the same category as the writings by the apostles. The third is that there were more and more Christian groups forming in the late first century and early second century, and these groups, sometimes referred to as Gnostics (from the Greek word meaning "knowledge"), wrote their own material.

Marcion was one such writer in the second century. He had many problems with what some Christians were believing, so he decided to write his own books and to also spread his ideas by travelling from his hometown to Rome, the center of Christianity in the second century. Tertullian was a Christian who wrote a book titled *Against Marcion*, and in it he states that Marcion went to Rome to convince people that his ideas were correct. Hippolytus, also a second-century Christian, stated that Marcion's father was a bishop and that it was his own father who excommunicated him. Marcion must have been fairly wealthy: he apparently used his own ship to sail to Rome, and when he arrived he donated a great deal of money to the church, which brought him influence. However, when he started to openly talk about his ideas, the church kicked him out and returned his donation. This didn't stop Marcion, however. He went on to found his own churches, which lasted into the fifth century. Tertullian certainly did not like him. He wrote that Marcion was "more uncouth than a Scythian, more unsettled than a wagon-dweller, more uncivilized than a Massagete, with more effrontery than an Amazon, darker than fog, colder than winter, more brittle than ice, more treacherous than the Danube, more precipitous than Caucasus" (*Against Marcion* 1.1). All of these were clearly insults.

Marcion had some interesting ideas. The first is that he believed there were two gods. The best one was the good and loving God described in the New Testament. Marcion believed that this God was revealed by Jesus. There was also an evil god described in the Old Testament. This god did terrible things (at least according to Marcion) and could not be the true God described by Jesus. To prove his point, he wrote a book called *Antitheses*. As the title suggests, Marcion listed various passages from the Old Testament and then found the opposite message in the New. In doing this he hoped to convince people that the Old Testament was not something that Christians should be reading. One example from his *Antitheses* was his use of Genesis 3:8–10, which states:

> They heard the sound of the LORD God walking in the garden at the time of the evening breeze, and the man and his wife hid themselves from the presence of the LORD God among the trees of the garden. But the LORD God called to the man, and said to him, "Where are you?" He said, "I heard the sound of you in the garden, and I was afraid, because I was naked; and I hid myself." (NRSV)

Marcion then compared this passage to Luke 9:46–48:

> An argument arose among them as to which one of them was the greatest. But Jesus, aware of their inner thoughts, took a little child and put it by his side, and said to them, "Whoever welcomes this child in my name welcomes me, and whoever welcomes me welcomes the one who sent me; for the least among all of you is the greatest." (NRSV)

Marcion was trying to show that God, in the Genesis passages, did not know where Adam and Eve were, which is why God had to ask. But Jesus (seen as God), in Luke 9:47 clearly knows what the apostles were thinking, and therefore the God of the Old Testament was not the true God because he was ignorant while Jesus (God) in the New Testament was clearly the true God because He knew everything.

Another example Marcion used was to compare Exodus 21:23–25 with Matthew 5:38–45. Exodus 21:23–25 states, "If any harm follows, then you shall give life for life, eye for eye, tooth for tooth, hand for hand, foot for foot, burn for burn, wound for wound, stripe for stripe." Matthew 5:38–45 states:

> "You have heard that it was said, 'An eye for an eye and a tooth for a tooth.' But I say to you, Do not resist an evildoer. But if anyone strikes you on the right cheek, turn the other also; and if anyone wants to sue you and take your coat, give your cloak as well; and if anyone forces you to go one mile, go also the second mile. Give to everyone who begs from you, and do not refuse anyone who wants to borrow from you. You have heard that it was said, 'You shall love your neighbor and hate your enemy.' But I say to you, Love your enemies and pray for those who persecute you, so that you may be children of your Father in heaven; for he makes his sun rise on the evil and on the good, and sends rain on the righteous and on the unrighteous." (NRSV)

Again, Marcion compared these two passages to show that the God of the Old Testament was evil in that He wanted to punish people with violence, while the passage in the New Testament contradicts the passage in the Old—do not strike back at someone who hits you, but in fact, show your other cheek and let them slap that one as well. For Marcion, it was clear that there were two very different messages between the Old and New Testaments, and thus he believed that Christians should not be using the Old Testament.

Marcion also did not believe that all of the works written by Christians should be the official ones read by them. He believed that some of the apostles' writings had been corrupted by Jewish people and that they should not be included in official list of what should be read. So what Marcion ended up doing was to edit some of the texts from the New Testament, and he also refused to have Christians read others. He created his own list and reasons for making this list in his *Apostolicon*. Marcion did a few things with this book. First of all he decided that not all texts written by the apostles were valid or accurate enough to be read by Christians, so they were not included in his list. He did include Luke (as the only Gospel), plus 10 letters of Paul, which were Galatians, 1 and 2 Corinthians, Romans, 1 Thessalonians, 2 Thessalonians, Laodiceans (which may have been Ephesians), Colossians, Philippians, and Philemon. He didn't like 1 and 2 Timothy or Titus because he didn't consider them to be written by Paul. And once he created his official list, he then went through and edited these to take out anything he thought was included later. This included the Gospel of Luke. Tertullian tells us that Marcion removed from Luke "the narratives of the annunciation and the nativity, as well as Christ's baptism and temptation, his genealogy, and all mention of Bethlehem and Nazareth." The reason for this is that Marcion did not want Jesus associated with being born as a flesh-and-blood man.

Marcion had a large impact on the early church. Other Christians made the argument that the Old Testament must be part of the Christian readings, and their insistence could be tied to Marcion's argument that it shouldn't. We also know that other Christians started to compile their own lists of texts for Christians to read. These lists were different from Marcion's, and some scholars believe the new lists were created to counter the one made by him. As mentioned, Marcion founded his own churches, which must have happened soon after he left Rome because in the 150s a Christian named Justin Martyr wrote:

> And there is Marcion, a man of Pontus, who is even at this day alive, and teaching his disciples to believe in some other god greater than the Creator. And he, by the aid of the devils, has caused many of every nation to speak blasphemies, and to deny that God is the maker of this universe, and to assert that some other being, greater than He, has done greater works. (*1 Apology*, chapter 26)

Further Reading

BeDuhn, Jason D. *The First New Testament: Marcion's Scriptural Canon*. Salem, OR: Polebridge Press, 2013.

Harnack, Adolf. *Marcion: The Gospel of the Alien God*, reprint ed. Eugene, OR: Wipf & Stock Publishers, 2007.

Lieu, Judith M. *Marcion and the Making of a Heretic: God and Scripture in the Second Century*. New York: Cambridge University Press, 2015.

Meeks, Wayne. *The First Urban Christians*. Yale: Yale University Press, 2003.

Schaff, Philip. "Against Marcion." *Latin Christianity: Its Founder, Tertullian*. Edinburgh: T&T Clark, n.d. Available online at http://www.ccel.org/ccel/schaff /anf03.

Schaff, Philip. "Antitheses." *Latin Christianity: Its Founder, Tertullian*. Edinburgh: T&T Clark, n.d. Available online at http://www.ccel.org/ccel/schaff/anf03.

Schaff, Philip. "1 Apology." *Latin Christianity: Its Founder, Tertullian*. Edinburgh: T&T Clark, n.d. Available online at http://www.ccel.org/ccel/schaff/anf01.

Tyson, Joseph B. *Marcion and Luke-Acts: A Defining Struggle*. Columbia: University of South Carolina Press, 2006.

NAG HAMMADI COLLECTION   One of the most famous textual finds of the 20th century happened soon after the end of World War II. In December 1945 some Egyptian farmers discovered a large clay jar that was buried near the town of Nag Hammadi. The people who found it broke into the jar and discovered, probably to their disappointment, that it was filled with manuscripts (and not treasure!). Not knowing what the texts said (they were written in an Egyptian language called Coptic), some of them were used for fueling a fire. They did save some of them, and ultimately the collection was purchased by a number of different people. Translation of the texts began in the 1950s.

The Nag Hammadi collection found in this jar consists of 13 books, each of which contains a number of smaller books. The total number is 52 writings, some of which are copies. The language of these important texts is Coptic, an Egyptian language that evolved from hieroglyphs as a mixture of Egyptian in a mostly Greek alphabet. The Christians who wrote these down put them down on papyrus, the ancient Egyptian form of paper. These Christians are usually given the title Gnostic Christians. *Gnostic* comes from the Greek word for knowledge. A common pattern found in gnostic writings is that secret knowledge is usually required to get to heaven, and these texts reveal the knowledge that one would need to be saved.

What scholars found, after the texts were translated, was amazing. They discovered manuscripts that were almost certainly used by early Christians living in Egypt. What is surprising about them is that they are not biblical texts as we would name them today. They are primarily Christian texts, with a few titles that would fall into the category of philosophy, such as a part of

Plato's *Republic*. It isn't known who these Christians were, but now we certainly know what they read, and from that we know a bit about what they believed. The Nag Hammadi collection has opened up many new avenues of research into early Christianity and shows that early Christians were reading more than just what we call the Bible today.

Many of these letters look like they were written by the original apostles, such as the Letter of Peter to Philip and the Gospel of Thomas. Other examples are the "Prayer of the Apostle Paul," the "Gospel of Philip," and the "Acts of Peter and the Twelve Apostles." You can find many of these texts online, especially at the Early Christian Writings Web site (http://www.earlychristianwritings.com/gnostics.html) or in a book titled *The Nag Hammadi Library*, by James M. Robinson. There are also many other texts that mention the original disciples, but their names are not found in the titles of the books.

Here is one example of a text found in the Nag Hammadi collection. It is purportedly a letter written from the disciple Peter to the disciple Philip. I have only translated part of it (to see the rest, please see *The Nag Hammadi Library* by Robinson).

> The Letter of Peter which he sent to Philip.
>
> Peter, the apostle of Jesus Christ, to Philip, our brother in Love and our brother-apostle, and to the brothers who are with you.
>
> Now I wish you to understand, our brother, that we received the commandments from him, our Lord and Savior of all the world, that we will come together so that we will teach and proclaim this salvation which he promised to us by our lord Jesus Christ. You were separate from us and did not desire that we come together and to learn that we organize ourselves in order for us to tell the Good News. Therefore if it is agreeable to you, our brother, come according to the commandments of our God Jesus.
>
> And when Philip, in glory and rejoicing, received and read these things, he went to Peter. Then Peter gathered the others. They went upon the mountain which was called Olives, the place which they used to gather along with the blessed Christ when he was in the body. Then the apostles came and they went down on their knees and prayed, saying "Father, Father, Father of Light who possessed the incorruptions, hear us in the manner which you have (heard) your holy child, Jesus Christ." (author's translation)

The letter continues with a conversation between Christ and the disciples. Another more famous text is the Gospel of Thomas, which is a series of statements given by Jesus. The collection is very important because it may give us a glimpse as to other things that Jesus might have said. A good example is the very first saying (out of 114): "Whoever finds the interpretation of these sayings will not experience death." Another (number 25): "Love your brother like your soul, guard him like the pupil of your eye." Many of the sayings given by Jesus are in response to questions by the disciples. For example, in Number 20, the disciples ask what the kingdom of heaven will be like, and Jesus states that it will be like a mustard seed, which starts off small but ends up being a very large plant. This saying is very similar to what is found in the New Testament. There are also other texts in the Nag Hammadi collection that are supposedly written by other people found in the Bible who were not disciples.

Probably the most famous example is the Gospel of Mary (Mary Magdalene), which was not found in the Nag Hammadi texts but has been considered to be so similar that it is usually included in the published lists of Gnostic texts. The Gospel of Mary was written in the form of a dialogue with Mary, the disciple Peter, and the Savior (the text calls him Savior and not Jesus). Unfortunately the first six pages of the manuscript are missing, so it isn't clear what it might have contained. The surviving text starts with some-one asking about whether all physical objects will be destroyed, and the Savior answers. The text continues in this manner until the Savior leaves. The disciples who were there start to weep because he left them, but Mary stands up and gives them a "pep talk." She tells them that the grace of the Savior was on them and protected them, so there was no reason to weep. Peter then tells her, in probably the most famous line of this text, that Mary Magdalene was the woman whom the Savior loved more than any other woman. Mary then tells them a secret that the Savior had only told to her. However, Andrew the disciple states openly that he believes the Savior did not say what Mary re-peated. Peter too questions whether the Savior would tell a secret to a woman and not the men. Mary then starts to cry and can't believe that Peter would think she was lying. At the end of the text we are again told that Mary was loved more than the male disciples and that all of them, Mary included, should go out to proclaim the gospel.

This text caused quite the stir when it was discovered, for two reasons. The first and most obvious is that it elevated a woman, Mary Magdalene, above all the other apostles. The second is that Mary Magdalene was believed to be a prostitute, which would make the claim that she was loved more than the male disciples even more surprising. However, most scholars reject the idea the Mary Magdalene was a prostitute. These Nag Hammadi texts show that early Christians read a number of different texts than what we commonly read today, and that they certainly had different beliefs.

Further Reading

Early Christian Writings. (http://www.earlychristianwritings.com/gnostics.html.

Ehrman, Bart D. *Lost Scriptures: Books That Did Not Make It into the New Testament.* Oxford: Oxford University Press, 2005.

Hedrick, Charles W., and Robert Hodgson Jr., eds. *Nag Hammadi, Gnosticism, and Early Christianity*. Eugene, OR: Wipf & Stock, 2005.

Pagels, Elaine. *The Gnostic Gospels*. New York: Vintage Books, 1989.

Robinson, James M. ed. *The Nag Hammadi Library*. Leiden: Brill, 1978.

THE OLD TESTAMENT   For many early first-century Christians, there was only one collection of sacred texts. They called it Scripture, and we refer to it as the Old Testament or the Hebrew Bible. Christians refer to it as the Old Testament because they believed it contained the message of God before the coming of Christ. They believed not only this message but also that Old Testament texts were written specifically for them. Early Christians, especially in the first century, were very familiar with the Old Testament primarily because many of the earliest generations of Christians were originally Jewish, including all of the disciples and Jesus.

The Old Testament is broken up into three major sections: the Torah or the Law, the Prophets, and the Writings. The Torah consists of the first five books: Genesis, Exodus, Numbers, Leviticus, and Deuteronomy. It is believed by some that these were written by Moses. The Prophets contain Joshua, Judges, 1 and 2 Samuel, 1 and 2 Kings, Isaiah, Jeremiah, Ezekiel, and others (from Hosea to Malachi). The writings contain all the other texts not mentioned above.

During the first century CE there were two versions of the Old Testament—the Greek and the Hebrew. For many Jewish people and many Christians the Greek version, called the Septuagint, was the most popular. The Mediterranean was thoroughly Hellenized, and Greek was the common language for many people, so it isn't surprising that the text would be translated into Greek. We don't know the exact details, but sometime in the third century BCE (at least according to tradition) a group of Jewish people got together and translated the original Hebrew texts into Greek. The most common story about this translation can be found in a letter titled *Letter of Aristeas*. Aristeas describes how a request was made to translate the Hebrew Bible into Greek so that it could be kept with all of the other books at a massive library in Alexandria, Egypt. Seventy-two Hebrew scholars were brought together to translate the Hebrew into Greek. According to the letter, the process took them 72 days to finish translating the entire Hebrew Bible, and when they were finished it was read out to a crowd, deemed to be perfect and that no one in the future would be able to change a single word. They also decided that if anyone changed the text at all, they would be cursed. Later tradition states that it was only 70 scholars, and this is where the title of this Greek Jewish bible comes from: *Septuagint* means "the Seventy." This Greek transla-
⸗n allowed more people to read it rather than having to first learn Hebrew.

The Old Testament was extremely important to early Christians for a number of reasons. Most importantly, it showed the foreshadowing of Christ, meaning that Christians believed that the Old Testament predicted the coming of Christ and even referred to him. Here is an example from Isaiah 61:1:

> The spirit of the Lord GOD is upon me, because the LORD has anointed me; he has sent me to bring good news to the oppressed, to bind up the broken-hearted, to proclaim liberty to the captives, and release to the prisoners. . . (NRSV)

Christians believed that the "me" in this text is Christ, especially when they compared the ministry of Christ to this statement. Isaiah 35:4–7 was another commonly mentioned passage proving (at least for Christians) that the Old Testament talked about Christ:

> Say to those who are of a fearful heart, "Be strong, do not fear! Here is your God. He will come with vengeance, with terrible recompense. He will come and save you." Then the eyes of the blind shall be opened, and the ears of the deaf unstopped; then the lame shall leap like a deer, and the tongue of the speechless sing for joy. For waters shall break forth in the wilderness, and streams in the desert; the burning sand shall become a pool, and the thirsty ground springs of water; the haunt of jackals shall become a swamp, the grass shall become reeds and rushes. (NRSV)

Again, the Christians saw in this passage a perfect description of Christ and what he did: he healed the blind, the deaf, and those who were lame. This proved to them that the coming of Jesus was predicted in the Old Testament writings. You can also find many places in the New Testament where the authors use the Old Testament to describe what happened in the New. Matthew 1:18–23 is a good example:

> Now the birth of Jesus the Messiah took place in this way. When his mother Mary had been engaged to Joseph, but before they lived together, she was found to be with child from the Holy Spirit. Her husband Joseph, being a righteous man and unwilling to expose her to public disgrace, planned to dismiss her quietly. But just when he had resolved to do this, an angel of the Lord appeared to him in a dream and said, "Joseph, son of David, do not be afraid to take Mary as your wife, for the child conceived in her is from the Holy Spirit. She will bear a son, and you are to name him Jesus, for he will save his people from their sins." All this took place to fulfill what had been spoken by the Lord through the prophet: "Look, the virgin shall conceive and bear a son, and they shall name him Emmanuel," which means, "God is with us." (NRSV)

The prophet mentioned is Isaiah and the original passage can be found at Isaiah 7:14: "Therefore the Lord himself will give you a sign. Look, the young woman is with child and shall bear a son, and shall name him Immanuel." There are many other places in the New Testament where the writers used the familiar Old Testament to prove their point or to explain what was currently happening. One example is found in John 2:15–17 where Jesus is driving out the bankers who had set up in the Temple:

> Making a whip of cords, he drove all of them out of the temple, both the sheep and the cattle. He also poured out the coins of the money changers and over-turned their tables. He told those who were selling the doves, "Take these things out of here! Stop making my Father's house a marketplace!" His disciples remembered that it was written, "Zeal for your house will consume me." (NRSV)

The disciples are referring to Psalms 69:9, "It is zeal for your house that has consumed me; the insults of those who insult you have fallen on me," to explain the behavior of Jesus.

There were also other reasons why the Christians used the Old Testament. It told them of their early history before the coming of Christ, and related to that, the stories of the Old Testament made it clear to them that what had happened to them in the first century CE was already predicted in the Old Testament (not just about Jesus, but about Christians as a whole), showing that they really were the chosen ones.

Not everything was accepted as described in the Old Testament, especially in terms of rituals. Jewish men needed to be circumcised, and when people like Paul were trying to get non-Jewish people to convert to Christianity, many men did not want to go through this surgical procedure. Paul convinced the other church leaders that circumcision was not a required part of being a Christian. Rituals relating to food and what should and should not be eaten were also changed. The book of Leviticus contains many rules and regulations about what should not be eaten (for example, shellfish and pork). Again, many people who were not Jewish did not want to change their diets just to join a new religion. This time it was the Apostle Peter who allowed people to eat nearly anything they wanted, with the exception of blood and animals that have been strangled. This can be seen in Acts 15:28–29:

> For it has seemed good to the Holy Spirit and to us to impose on you no fur-ther burden than these essentials: that you abstain from what has been sacri-ficed to idols and from blood and from what is strangled and from fornication. If you keep yourselves from these, you will do well. Farewell. (NRSV)

Not all Christians were enthusiastic about using the Old Testament. In the second century CE, Marcion, a Christian, wanted Christians to reject the entirety of the Old Testament and to only read certain parts of what we now call the New Testament. He believed that the coming of Jesus broke with the old (he also believed that the God of the Old Testament was different from the God of the New). Many scholars believe that Marcion's rejection of the Old Testament forced many Christians to do just the opposite: to actively read and accept the Old Testament as part of Christianity. This is still the case today, and most Christians fully accept the Old Testament as being part of the Christian Bible.

See also: Marcion.

Further Reading

Arnold, Bill T., and Bryan E. Beyer. *Encountering the Old Testament: A Christian Survey* (Encountering Biblical Studies). Grand Rapids, MI: Baker Academic, 1999.

Boadt, Lawrence. *Reading the Old Testament: An Introduction*, 2nd ed, revised and updated by Richard Clifford and Daniel Harrington. Mahwah, NJ: Paulist Press, 2012.

Coogan, Michael D. *The Old Testament: A Historical and Literary Introduction to the Hebrew Scriptures*, 3rd ed. Oxford: Oxford University Press, 2013.

"Letter of Aristeas." Available online at http://www.ccel.org/c/charles/otpseudepig /aristeas.htm.

Matthews, Victor H. and James C. Moyer. *The Old Testament: Text and Context*, 3rd ed. Grand Rapids, MI: Baker Academic, 2012.

Wright, Christopher J. H. *Knowing Jesus Through the Old Testament* (Knowing God Through the Old Testament Set). Downers Grover, IL: IVP Academic, 1995.

PAUL   The apostle Paul is one of the more famous people from early Christianity. He is a complicated figure to describe because most of our information about him comes from his own writings. This does not mean they are totally unreliable, but care must be taken when examining his books and what he has to say about himself. Paul is mentioned occasionally outside of his own writings: he is mentioned in Acts (written by Luke) and very briefly in 2 Peter, but we are mostly reliant on Paul for a description of himself. He is also a complicated figure in terms of his actions and his behavior. As we will examine, he called himself an apostle of Jesus Christ even though he had never met the earthly Jesus. He made it his mission to spread this newfound faith outside of Jewish circles and into the rest of the population (referred to as the Gentiles). He is largely responsible for setting up and maintaining new Christian communities throughout Asia Minor (modern-day Turkey) and for allowing new converts to not follow some of the ritual practices of Judaism.

He was heavily persecuted for trying to spread this message, and even though we do not know exactly what happened to him, Paul was probably killed during the Christian persecution of Emperor Nero in the 60s CE.

We don't know as much as we would like about the early life of Paul. He grew up in Tarsus, a city in the southwestern part of Asia Minor. We know that he was a Roman citizen, and it has been thought that he received his citizenship through his parents. He definitely spoke Hebrew and, not surprisingly given the Hellenistic atmosphere of the Mediterranean, also spoke Greek. Paul tells us that he was in the type of Judaism called Pharisee, and Luke, in Acts, states that Paul had a famous Jewish teacher named Gamaliel (Acts 22:3). He himself mentions this in Philemon 3:4–8. We know that he persecuted Christians. He states in 1 Corinthians 15:9: "For I am the least of the apostles, unfit to be called an apostle, because I persecuted the church of God." In Galatians 1:13–14 he writes: "You have heard, no doubt, of my earlier life in Judaism. I was violently persecuting the church of God and was trying to destroy it. I advanced in Judaism beyond many among my people of the same age, for I was far more zealous for the traditions of my ancestors."

At some point he had his famous conversion to Christianity on the road to Damascus, Syria. Paul barely mentions this, and mostly what we know about this famous episode comes from Luke, in Acts 22:6–16:

> "While I was on my way and approaching Damascus, about noon a great light from heaven suddenly shone about me. I fell to the ground and heard a voice saying to me, 'Saul, Saul, why are you persecuting me?' I answered, 'Who are you, Lord?' Then he said to me, 'I am Jesus of Nazareth whom you are persecuting.' Now those who were with me saw the light but did not hear the voice of the one who was speaking to me. I asked, 'What am I to do, Lord?' The Lord said to me, 'Get up and go to Damascus; there you will be told everything that has been assigned to you to do.' Since I could not see because of the brightness of that light, those who were with me took my hand and led me to Damascus. A certain Ananias, who was a devout man according to the law and well spoken of by all the Jews living there, came to me; and standing beside me, he said, 'Brother Saul, regain your sight!' In that very hour I regained my sight and saw him. Then he said, 'The God of our ancestors has chosen you to know his will, to see the Righteous One and to hear his own voice; for you will be his witness to all the world of what you have seen and heard. And now why do you delay? Get up, be baptized, and have your sins washed away, calling on his name.'" (NRSV)

As mentioned, Paul himself barely talks about this. His conversion, however, did not convince many Christians that he was now actually one of them. As we know from his letter to the Galatians, Paul was well known in Christian communities for persecuting them, and this was one of the reasons why he had a hard time convincing Christians that they should follow his form of Christianity. Despite his difficulties, Paul referred to himself as an apostle of Jesus Christ (see, among others, Romans 1:1, 1 Corinthians 1.1) even though he was not directly appointed as a disciple by Christ (like all of the other apostles). For Paul, hearing Christ's voice on the road to Damascus was enough to convince him that Christ had indeed called him to be a disciple/apostle.

After his conversion, Paul began his mission to convert people, mostly from the Jewish population. At some point he realized that for Christianity to grow, the target for conversion had to be people who were not Jews, but Gentiles (non-Jewish people). He writes in Galatians (1:15–17):

> But when God, who had set me apart before I was born and called me through his grace, was pleased to reveal his Son to me, so that I might proclaim him among the Gentiles, I did not confer with any human being, nor did I go up to Jerusalem to those who were already apostles before me, but I went away at once into Arabia, and afterwards I returned to Damascus. (NRSV)

Part of his reason too for converting Gentiles was that he was rejected by many Jewish communities when he tried to convert them. He mentions getting whipped five times (2 Corinthians 11:24) by the Jewish authorities. His rejection led him to want to convert the Gentiles, and he is primarily responsible for the large increase in Christians during this period. Despite this, many of the original apostles, who had set up their own church in Jerusalem with James, the brother of Jesus, in charge, were not convinced that Gentiles should be allowed to be Christian. Part of what was holding them back was that Jesus was Jewish, and all of the people who were called by Jesus were also Jewish. Being Jewish meant that people had to follow specific behaviors such as eating certain foods and worshipping in specific ways. When they converted to Christianity, many wanted to keep these same behaviors. Paul, however, wanted to go outside of this population, and he began this without getting permission from those in Jerusalem. News of what he was doing reached Jerusalem, and Paul and his companions were summoned to the holy city to explain what they were doing. This meeting, probably taking place in 48 CE, is considered to be the first church council that met in order to deal with problems in the growing religion. It was here that James and Peter allowed Gentiles in.

Paul further had to argue that the Gentiles who wanted to convert would not have to live by some of the Jewish rites such as circumcision. This was a painful procedure for adult males, and many clearly did not want to go through this just to join a religion. It was decided that Gentile males would not have to be circumcised when they converted but that they had to abstain from eating blood. Paul was now free to go back to Tarsus and Asia Minor in general to begin his missions, which numbered three. He was also sent to Rome for trial by the authorities, and on the way there and certainly when he arrived he continued with his mission even though he was held under house arrest.

Paul, by all accounts, was successful at what he did. It was not an easy journey, however, as shown above by the number of whippings he received. Paul would usually go to the village or city synagogue when he entered a new area. Here he would try to convert the Jewish population to his new faith. When that didn't work, he would move on to the Gentiles. Paul too met fellow Christians who were also doing what he was doing, converting people. He appears to have not gotten along with these Christians, especially if they were teaching a different message from his own. Because of that, once he converted people (both Jewish and Gentile) he would then have to make sure that these new converts stayed on the right path. He did this by writing letters, the very letters that make up nearly half of the New Testament. Paul was obsessed about making sure his converts stayed true to his message, and if they did not, he would threaten them with coming back and correcting them. He also sent others on his behalf if there were any problems. This is clear from his earliest letter, 1 Thessalonians. In chapter 3:5 he tells the Thessalonians that he sent Timothy to check up on them. He wrote his first letter to the Corinthians because he had heard about arguments that were occurring over who was more important in the newly formed Christian community (1 Corinthians 1:11). He was particularly upset with the Galatians. He barely gives them a greeting before writing (Galatians 1:6–1:8):

> I am astonished that you are so quickly deserting the one who called you in the grace of Christ and are turning to a different gospel—not that there is another gospel, but there are some who are confusing you and want to pervert the gospel of Christ. But even if we or an angel from heaven should proclaim to you a gospel contrary to what we proclaimed to you, let that one be accursed! (NRSV)

As mentioned, Paul made three journeys throughout the Mediterranean. His last one was important because it took him to Rome. This was not done to convert people (although no doubt he was doing this on the way). Paul got into trouble with the Roman authorities. He was imprisoned in Caesarea for two years (Acts 24:27), and was brought to trial and accused of many crimes against the Jewish population. Paul denied all of them, but the Jewish authorities pressed to have him executed. Paul, as a Roman citizen, then applied to have his case heard before the emperor. This was agreed to, and he was put on a ship that then sailed to Italy. Luke doesn't tell us what happened to him when he arrived in Italy.

Unfortunately there are no contemporary accounts on what happened to him either. We just don't know the fate of Paul. Paul mentions that he planned on going to Spain when he was finished converting those in Asia Minor (Romans 15:24), so some have thought that it is possible that his appeal to the emperor was successful and that he continued to Spain. It is only later in the second century that Ignatius, the bishop of Antioch, stated Paul was a martyr, meaning he was killed for his faith (Letter to the Ephesians, chapter 12). And later someone wrote the Acts of Paul. This work is supposedly written by Paul, but all scholars recognize that this was written much later. It discusses Paul's various journeys and gives an account of his death (just remember that this is fictional and not based on history, as far as we know). It states that Paul was beheaded and that his body then bled milk and not blood. Again, this is not real history, and was written sometime in the second century CE. The truth is that Nero was the emperor at the time when Paul might have been taken to Rome. We know from the Roman senator Tacitus that Nero did not like Christians at all (in fact, he blamed them for a devastating fire in Rome that took place in 64 CE). Because of this it is unlikely that Nero would have let him go. If he was killed during a Neronian persecution, it had to be before the middle of 68 CE since this is the time that Nero committed suicide.

Further Reading

Pollock, John. *The Apostle: A Life of Paul*, 3rd ed. Colorado Springs: David C. Cook, 2012.

Meeks, Wayne A. *The First Urban Christians: The Social World of the Apostle Paul*, 2nd ed. New Haven, CT: Yale University, 2003.

Schnelle, Udo, trans. M. Eugene Boring. *Apostle Paul: His Life and Theology*, English version. Grand Rapids, MI: Baker Academic, 2005.

Tabor, James D. *Paul and Jesus: How the Apostle Transformed Christianity*. New York: Simon & Schuster, 2012.

Wilson, A. N. *Paul: The Mind of the Apostle*. New York: W. W. Norton, 1998.

PERSECUTION IN THE FIRST CENTURY   Many of the early persecutions that Christians faced in the first century came from their conflicts with the Jewish population. Many Jewish people had difficulties understanding how fellow Jews could start believing that Jesus was the Messiah. The problems among the Jews and Christians leaked over into the Roman sphere when the Jewish leadership could not put someone like Jesus to death without the approval of Rome. By the middle of the first century Christians had become sufficiently different in the beliefs from their Jewish counterparts that they now became a target of the Romans (although this was not always the case). The question of how severe the persecution actually was is a current topic among some scholars. Some believe that the Christians were definitely persecuted by the Roman government, while others believe that there was no organized persecution. The jury is still out as to what actually happened, but it is true that there were some early Christians who died for their belief in Jesus.

Of course the earliest and most famous story of persecution (at least murder) of the early Christians is the crucifixion of Christ. We don't know the exact year when this happened, but it is thought that it occurred sometime between 30 and 33 CE. The next persecution was described in Acts 6–8, in which the apostle Stephen was stoned to death for telling the Jewish people that they did not keep to the laws of God that Moses had brought down from Mount Sinai. Acts 7:54–8:1 states (the Saul figure mentioned will later be the apostle Paul):

> When they heard these things, they became enraged and ground their teeth at Stephen. But filled with the Holy Spirit, he gazed into heaven and saw the glory of God and Jesus standing at the right hand of God. "Look," he said, "I see the heavens opened and the Son of Man standing at the right hand of God!" But they covered their ears, and with a loud shout all rushed together against him. Then they dragged him out of the city and began to stone him; and the witnesses laid their coats at the feet of a young man named Saul. While they were stoning Stephen, he prayed, "Lord Jesus, receive my spirit." Then he knelt down and cried out in a loud voice, "Lord, do not hold this sin against them." When he had said this, he died. And Saul approved of their killing him. That day a severe persecution began against the church in Jerusalem, and all except the apostles were scattered throughout the countryside of Judea and Samaria. (NRSV)

As can be seen from Acts 8:1, the stoning of Stephen led to Christians being forced to leave Jerusalem in order to escape the persecution. More than likely this led to Christians going beyond "Judea and Samaria" as the text of Acts states. According to Acts 12:1, the next persecution of the Christians happened under the rule of Herod Agrippa, who was the grandson of King Herod the Great. Herod Agrippa ruled Judea from 41 to 44 CE. Acts 12:1–5 states:

> About that time King Herod laid violent hands upon some who belonged to the church. He had James, the brother of John, killed with the sword. After he saw that it pleased the Jews, he proceeded to arrest Peter also (this was during the festival of Unleavened Bread). When he had seized him, he put him in prison and handed him over to four squads of soldiers to guard him, intending to bring him out to the people after the Passover. While Peter was kept in prison, the church prayed fervently to God for him. (NRSV)

The next period of persecution happened to Christians not living in Judea, but in Rome. In July 64 CE a fire broke out in the city and destroyed a large portion of Rome. The emperor at the time was Nero, and he blamed the Christians for starting the fire. Tacitus, a Roman senator and historian, wrote about this in his book titled *Annals*. He states in chapter 15:44 that Nero rounded up a number of Christians, put animal skins on some of them, and fed them to wild animals as entertainment. Others he doused with flammable liquid, tied to stakes, and lit on fire. He used the light of the flames to host his garden parties. Below is part of the account given by Tacitus:

Such indeed were the precautions of human wisdom. The next thing was to seek means of propitiating the gods, and recourse was had to the Sibylline books, by the direction of which prayers were offered to Vulcan, Ceres, and Proserpina. Juno, too, was entreated by the matrons, first, in the Capitol, then on the nearest part of the coast, whence water was procured to sprinkle the fane and image of the goddess. And there were sacred banquets and nightly vigils celebrated by married women. But all human efforts, all the lavish gifts of the emperor, and the propitiations of the gods, did not banish the sinister belief that the conflagration was the result of an order. Consequently, to get rid of the report, Nero fastened the guilt and inflicted the most exquisite tortures on a class hated for their abominations, called Christians by the populace. Christus, from whom the name had its origin, suffered the extreme penalty during the reign of Tiberius at the hands of one of our procurators, Pontius Pilatus, and a most mischievous superstition, thus checked for the moment, again broke out not only in Judaea, the first source of the evil, but even in Rome, where all things hideous and shameful from every part of the world find their center and become popular. Accordingly, an arrest was first made of all who pleaded guilty; then, upon their information, an immense multitude was convicted, not so much of the crime of firing the city, as of hatred against mankind. Mockery of every sort was added to their deaths. Covered with the skins of beasts, they were torn by dogs and perished, or were nailed to crosses, or were doomed to the flames and burnt, to serve as a nightly illumination, when daylight had expired. Nero offered his gardens for the spectacle, and was exhibiting a show in the circus, while he mingled with the people in the dress of a charioteer or stood aloft on a car. Hence, even for criminals who deserved extreme and exemplary punishment, there arose a feeling of compassion; for it was not, as it seemed, for the public good, but to glut one man's cruelty, that they were being destroyed. (*Annals of Tacitus* 1906: 304–5)

According to Tacitus, this particular persecution did not lead to more hate against the Christians, but just the opposite: he wrote that it led to compassion for the Christians because they were being tortured and killed just to please the cruelty of the emperor. For the most part, the first century was peaceful for the Christians, but the periods of persecution highly affected the spread of Christianity. As seen, harassment against the early Christians did not slow down the spread of Christianity—in fact, it was the opposite. Every time the Christians were persecuted, they left where they had been living, moved to new areas, and continued to practice their religion.

See also: The Great Fire of Rome.

Further Reading

Annals of Tacitus, translated by Alfred John Church and William Jackson Brodribb. London: Macmillan, 1906.

Castelli, Elizabeth. *Martyrdom and Memory: Early Christian Culture Making* (Gender, Theory, and Religion). New York: Columbia University Press, 2004.

Moss, Candida R. *Ancient Christian Martyrdom: Diverse Practices, Theologies, and Traditions* (Anchor Yale Bible Reference Library). New Haven, CT: Yale University Press, 2012.

Workman, Herbert B. *Persecution in the Early Church*. Bloomington, IN: Clearnote Press, 2014.

PHARISEES   There were three main groups found in Judaism during the earliest part of Christianity—the Sadducees, the Pharisees, and the Essenes. Here we will examine the Pharisees. After the first century CE this group became the dominant form of Judaism and still exists today in what is referred to as Rabbinic Judaism. They became the dominant form for a number of reasons, but the main one is that in 70 CE the Second Temple, built in 516 BCE, was looted and destroyed by the Romans. The Sadducees disappeared from history after the center of their religious world disappeared. The Pharisees were not focused on the Temple itself, and when it was destroyed, their religious practices and beliefs survived. The Pharisees often argued with the Sadducees and, in particular, did not like the control that they had over Judaism. The Sadducees controlled the Temple, and with that they controlled many aspects of Jewish life, especially in Jerusalem where the Temple stood.

The most famous ex-Pharisee was the apostle Paul. He made it very clear in his writings that he was a Pharisee. He wrote in his Letter to the Philippians (3:4–6): "If anyone else has reason to be confident in the flesh, I have more: circumcised on the eighth day, a member of the people of Israel, of the tribe of Benjamin, a Hebrew born of Hebrews; as to the law, a Pharisee; as to zeal, a persecutor of the church; as to righteousness under the law, blameless." Like Paul, many early Christians in the first century were originally Jewish, and many of these converts were from the Pharisees. The main reason for this is that many of the beliefs of the Pharisees were similar to those of the early Christians. The Pharisees believed in the resurrection of the body, which is something that the Sadducees rejected. Bodily resurrection was a cornerstone to early Christian beliefs. Another cornerstone for early Christians was the idea that there was an afterlife, which is something that the Pharisees also believed in. The Sadducees rejected the belief that the soul was immortal and that there was some type of afterlife. The last major belief of the Pharisees that allowed them easy entry into Christianity was that they believed that a messiah would be coming at some point in the future. These beliefs certainly parallel the major beliefs held by the early Christians, and it can be seen that these were borrowed from their Jewish past and put to use in Christianity.

The Pharisees are mentioned nearly 100 times in the New Testament, primarily in the four Gospels and Acts, and in nearly all of these places the Pharisees and the Sadducees are not seen in the best light. Many times we hear, in the New Testament, of the Pharisees (and the Sadducees) challenging Jesus on some point, especially when this point conflicted with their interpretation of the law. One example of this is found in Matthew 12:2, where Jesus was confronted by the Pharisees when he and the disciples went through a field to gather grain to eat. They happen to be doing this on the Sabbath, and for the Pharisees, it was against the law to be doing work on the Sabbath. Jesus responds: "Have you not read what David did when he and his companions were hungry? He entered the house of God and ate the bread of the Presence, which it was not lawful for him or his companions to eat, but only for the priests. Or have you not read in the law that on the Sabbath the priests in the temple break the Sabbath and yet are guiltless?" We are also told that the Pharisees "conspired against him" when Jesus healed a maimed hand on the Sabbath (Matthew 12:10–14), which again was considered against the law because no work was to be done on this particular day.

As shown in the New Testament, the Pharisees were also concerned with ritual purity, meaning that they cleaned themselves before doing something spiritual. This often led to them being very legalistic. In Luke 11:38 Jesus was invited to eat with a Pharisee. The Pharisee did not like that Jesus did not first wash before he ate. Jesus responds by stating: "Now you Pharisees clean the outside of the cup and of the dish, but inside you are full of greed and wickedness. You fools! Did not the one who made the outside make the inside also?" Jesus is stating that it is much more important to be clean on the inside of a person than it is on the outside. The Pharisees were not happy with this line of reasoning, and we are told later in Luke that the Pharisees started to watch Jesus more closely for the times when he went against their interpretation of the law.

The New Testament is not the only ancient source we have about the behaviors of the Pharisees. Josephus was a Jewish writer who, towards the end of the first century CE, wrote a book titled *Antiquities of the Jews*. In one part of it he describes the actions of the Pharisees (18.1.3):

Now, for the Pharisees, they live sparsely, and despise delicacies in diet; and they follow the conduct of reason; and what that prescribes to them as good for them they do; and they think they ought earnestly to strive to observe reason's dictates for practice. They also pay a respect to those who are older; nor are they so bold as to contradict them in anything which they have introduced . . . They also believe that souls have an immortal rigor in them, and that under the earth there will be rewards or punishments, according as they have lived virtuously or viciously in this life; and the latter are to be detained in an everlasting prison, but that the former shall have power to revive and live again. On account of these doctrines they are able greatly to persuade the body of the people, and whenever they do divine worship, prayers, and sacrifices, they perform them according to their direction, so much so that the cities give great attestations to them on account of their entire virtuous conduct, both in the actions of their lives and their discourses also. (Josephus, n.d.)

Even though the Pharisees were seen in a bad light all throughout the New Testament, there can be no denying that their beliefs, from the immortality of the soul to the resurrection of the body, and especially their ideas on the coming of the Messiah, impacted many aspects of early Christianity. Their excessive legalism was used as a backdrop by the New Testament writers to showcase the words and actions of Jesus. Despite their bad light in the New Testament, the Pharisees and their brand of belief survives through today. The Sadducees were reliant on the Temple in Jerusalem, and when this was destroyed by the Romans, the Pharisees were really the only major Jewish movement left.

See also: Qumran; Sadducees.

Further Reading

Bowker, John. *Jesus and the Pharisees*. Cambridge: Cambridge University Press, 1973.

Falk, Harvey. *Jesus the Pharisee: A New Look at the Jewishness of Jesus*. Eugene, OR: Wipf & Stock, 2003.

Josephus. "Antiquities of the Jews." *Josephus: The Complete Works*. Available online at http://www.ccel.org/ccel/josephus/complete.

Neusner, Jacob, and Bruce D. Chilton. *In Quest of the Historical Pharisees*. Waco, TX: Baylor University Press, 2007.

Saldarini, Anthony J. J. *Pharisees, Scribes, and Sadducees in Palestinian Society: A Sociological Approach*. Grand Rapids, MI: William B. Eerdman, 2001.

THE PILATE INSCRIPTION   There is probably no non-Christian person more famous from the New Testament than Pontius Pilate, the governor of Judea from 26 to 36 CE. Pilate's role in the crucifixion was an important part in the story of Christ, and he is mentioned in all four Gospels, plus Acts and 1 Timothy. Here is an example from Mark 15:1–5:

> As soon as it was morning, the chief priests held a consultation with the elders and scribes and the whole council. They bound Jesus, led him away, and handed him over to Pilate. Pilate asked him, "Are you the King of the Jews?" He answered him, "You say so." Then the chief priests accused him of many things. Pilate asked him again, "Have you no answer? See how many charges they bring against you." But Jesus made no further reply, so that Pilate was amazed. (NRSV)

And a bit later in Mark 15:9–15:

> Then he answered them, "Do you want me to release for you the King of the Jews?" For he realized that it was out of jealousy that the chief priests had handed him over. But the chief priests stirred up the crowd to have him release Barabbas for them instead. Pilate spoke to them again, "Then what do you wish me to do with the man you call the King of the Jews?" They shouted back, "Crucify him!" Pilate asked them, "Why, what evil has he done?" But they shouted all the more, "Crucify him!" So Pilate, wishing to satisfy the crowd, released Barabbas for them; and after flogging Jesus, he handed him over to be crucified. (NRSV)

Early Christian scholars sometimes have to guess whether some of the people mentioned in the New Testament were actually real, especially when no outside evidence exists other than what the New Testament has to say. However, this is not the case for Pontius Pilate. We know a bit about him from later writers like Tacitus (56–120 CE), Philo (20 BCE to 50 CE), and Josephus (37–100 CE). Tacitus writes (in his book titled *The Annals* 15.44): "Christus, from whom the name had its origin, suffered the extreme penalty during the reign of Tiberius at the hands of one of our procurators, Pontius Pilatus." Josephus writes (in his book titled *The Jewish War*, 2.169–174):

> Pilate, being sent by Tiberius as prefect to Judaea, introduced into Jerusalem by night and under cover the effigies of Caesar which are called standards. This proceeding, when day broke, aroused immense excitement among the Jews; those on the spot were in consternation, considering their laws to have been trampled under foot, as those laws permit no image to be erected in the city; while the indignation of the townspeople stirred the countryfolk, who flocked together in crowds.

Philo writes: "Pilate was an official who had been appointed prefect of Judaea. With the intention of annoying the Jews rather than of honoring Tiberius, he set up gilded shields in Herod's palace in the Holy City."

So we do know a little more about him. More importantly, more external evidence (outside of the New Testament) exists in the form of an inscription carved on limestone that was discovered in the town of Caesarea Maritima in 1961. This inscription is referred to as the Pilate Inscription or the Pilate Stone. Only part of the inscription survives. The Latin text reads: "Tiberium. . .(Pon)tius Pilatus (Prae)fectus Iuda (aea)." The English translation is ". . .Tiberium. . . Pontius Pilate, Prefect of Judaea." The Tiberium would be a temple dedicated to the Emperor Tiberius. There were also words on the left side of the inscription, but they have been lost.

Further Reading

Bond, Helen K. *Pontius Pilate in History and Interpretation*. Cambridge: Cambridge University Press, 1998.

Carter, Warren. *Pontius Pilate: Portraits of a Roman Governor*. Collegeville, MN: Liturgical Press, 2003.

Strauss, Mark L. *Four Portraits, One Jesus: A Survey of Jesus and the Gospels*. Grand Rapids, MI: Zondervan, 2007.

POLYCARP OF SMYRNA   Polycarp was the bishop of Smyrna, located in western Turkey. As with most early Christians, we don't know his exact birthdate or when he died, but it is thought that he was born somewhere around 80 CE and died sometime between 155 and 177 CE. Polycarp is important to early Christianity because of the account of his martyrdom. He also wrote letters to various people, but unfortunately almost all of those are lost. A few writers such as Irenaeus (died in the early 200s) and Tertullian (died around 220) mention Polycarp, and both of them believed that he knew the apostle John and was in fact instructed by him.

Despite the loss of most of his writings, we do have one of the letters that he wrote to the Philippians, which is the same group of people that the apostle Paul wrote to. It appears that Polycarp was asked to write this particular letter, and in it he exhorts them to read Paul's letter to them. Polycarp's letter is a very important document for studying early Christianity because he makes a series of statements about the behavior of people, which then can be used to study the Christian community at Philippi. For example, he writes about the behavior of wives, children, and widows:

Next, [teach] your wives [to walk] in the faith given to them, and in love and purity tenderly loving their own husbands in all truth, and loving all [others] equally in all chastity; and to train up their children in the knowledge and fear of God. Teach the widows to be discreet as respects the faith of the Lord, praying continually for all, being far from all slandering, evil-speaking, false-witnessing, love of money, and every kind of evil; knowing that they are the altar of God, that He clearly perceives all things, and that nothing is hid from Him, neither reasoning, nor reflections, nor any one of the secret things of the heart. (Schaff, n.d.)

Polycarp was also concerned with what people believed about Jesus. There were some people who believed that Jesus was not a true human, but really a phantom or a ghost when he was on earth. This belief is called Docetism, which comes from the Greek word *dokein*, meaning "to seem," so Christ seems to be a man. This belief implies that Jesus was not really crucified and therefore people were not saved by his death, because he was not real in the first place. Polycarp warns his readers that these people are the "first-born of Satan." Docetism was a popular movement in early Christianity, and Polycarp felt it was his duty to warn his readers against falling in with these people. The rest of his letter is spent telling the Philippians to do good things and to follow the words of the Bible.

Polycarp was also famous in early Christianity because of the way he was killed. Polycarp was a martyr (a person killed for his/her beliefs), and someone wrote a letter titled *On the Martyrdom of Polycarp*. Martyrdom stories were used by Christian communities as sources of strength when persecutions began. The martyrs were held up as near-perfect Christians who, despite being tortured, maimed, and usually killed, never denied Christ or left Christianity. Denying Christ or leaving Christianity would have meant that the torture would have stopped and they could have continued living. In fact, according to the *Martyrdom of Polycarp*:

All the martyrdoms, then, were blessed and noble which took place according to the will of God. For it becomes us who profess greater piety than others, to ascribe the authority over all things to God. And truly, who can fail to admire their nobleness of mind, and their patience, with that love towards their Lord which they displayed?—who, when they were so torn with scourges, that the frame of their bodies, even to the very inward veins and arteries, was laid open, still patiently endured, while even those that stood by pitied and bewailed them. But they reached such a pitch of magnanimity, that not one of them let a sigh or a groan escape them; thus proving to us all that those holy martyrs of Christ, at the very time when they suffered such torments, were absent from the body, or rather, that the Lord then stood by them, and communed with them. And, looking to the grace of Christ, they despised all the torments of this world, redeeming themselves from eternal punishment by [the suffering of] a single hour. For this reason the fire of their savage executioners appeared cool to them. For they kept before their view escape from that fire which is eternal and never shall be quenched, and looked forward with the eyes of their heart to those good things which are laid up for such as endure; things "which ear hath not heard, nor eye seen, neither have entered into the heart of man," but were revealed by the Lord to them, inasmuch as they were no longer men, but had already become angels. And, in like manner, those who were condemned to the wild beasts endured dreadful tortures, being stretched out upon beds full of spikes, and subjected to various other kinds of torments, in order that, if it were possible, the tyrant might, by their lingering tortures, lead them to a denial [of Christ]. (Schaff, n.d.)

This document is a testimony to the power the martyrs had in early Christian communities. Christians held up these martyrs as examples of perfect Christians who resisted the Roman government. This particular martyrdom also gives examples of what would happen to Christians who were pulled out of their positions in society to be persecuted in front of the crowds. We are told that Polycarp had the option of cursing Christ and swearing "to the fortune of Caesar," but he refused to do so. The proconsul (governor) asked Polycarp to do this multiple times, but each time Polycarp stated he was a Christian and believed in Christ. Polycarp's punishment for being Christian was that he was tied to a stake that was placed on a pile of wood, which was then lit. We are told that the fire did not burn Polycarp. Then a soldier decided to stab him, and when he did this, a dove flew out of the wound and blood gushed out and put the fire out. After this Polycarp died, and soldiers then burned his body. The text states that believers gathered the bones of Polycarp because they were holy, and Christians would then celebrate the anniversary of his martyrdom.

Further Reading

Aquilina. Mike. *The Fathers of the Church: An Introduction to the First Christian Teachers*, 3rd ed. Huntington, IN: Our Sunday Visitor, 2013.

D'Ambrosio. Marcellino. *When the Church Was Young: Voices of the Early Fathers.* Cincinnati: Servant Books, 2014.

Hartog, Paul, ed. *Polycarp's Epistle to the Philippians and the Martyrdom of Polycarp: Introduction, Text, and Commentary* (Oxford Apostolic Fathers). Oxford: Oxford University Press, 2013.

Howell, Kenneth J. *Ignatius of Antioch and Polycarp of Smyrna* (Early Christian Fathers). Zanesville, OH: CHR Resources, 2009.

Jurgens, William A., trans. *Faith of the Early Fathers*. Liturgical Press, 1979.

Schaff, Philip. "Epistle to the Corinthians." Polycarp, found in *The Apostolic Fathers with Justyn Martyr and Irenaeus*. Edinburgh: T&T Clark, n.d. Available online at http://www.ccel.org/ccel/schaff/anf01.

Schaff, Philip. "Martyrdom of Polycarp." *The Apostolic Fathers with Justyn Martyr and Irenaeus*. Edinburgh: T&T Clark, n.d. Available online at http://www.ccel.org /ccel/schaff/anf01.

PUBLIC DEBATES Public debates on issues related to the church were very important in early Christianity. Usually people who had differing opinions on which form of Christianity was the best would gather together in a public place like the town square or a church. Judges would be appointed, and they would decide who the victor was in the debate. The winner's version of Christianity would be declared as the true version, while the loser would be run out of town and the alternate version would be considered heretical. As can be seen, the ability to speak persuasively was a skill that was needed for these debates, and luckily for many Christians, the ability to speak persuasively was something that was taught in school (called rhetoric). There were many debates that helped shape the form of Christianity today. The first two debates we can examine took place between Augustine, the bishop of the North African city of Hippo, and his Manichaean and Donatist opponents. The third we can look at took place sometime around 402 CE between a Manichaean woman named Julia and a bishop in the city of Gaza.

Augustine, a Catholic church father (born in 354 and died in 430 CE), made use of public debates many times with people who disagreed with his theology. Probably his most famous debates are the ones he held with two Manichaeans, Fortunatus and Felix, along with a public debate with the Donatists. The main result of his debates with Fortunatus and Felix was that Augustine ended up driving most of the Manichaeans from North Africa. The result of his debates on Donatism was that the Roman Empire created a series of edicts that outlawed this particular brand of Christianity. For Augustine, the debate was a useful tool to use against groups of people he considered to be heretics.

We can first look at his debate with Fortunatus, a priest in the Manichaean Christian religion. This debate took place on September 5, 392, in the town of Hippo where Augustine was a priest, in the public baths. It took place over two days, and it was during this period when both men could state their beliefs publically and also defend them. It was assumed that the loser of the debate would have to leave. We know that Fortunatus lived in Hippo for a period of time and had Manichaean followers. The debate began with Augustine telling Fortunatus that he used to be a Manichaean, but was no more. He also listed the beliefs that the Manichaeans held. Fortunatus replied:

> Because I know that you have been in our midst, that is, have lived as an adherent among the Manichaeans, these are the principles of our faith. The matter now to be considered is our mode of living, the falsely alleged crimes for which we are maltreated. Therefore let the good men present hear from you whether these things with which we are charged and which we have thrown in our teeth are true or false. For from your instruction, and from your exposition and

explanation, they will have been able to gain more correct information about our mode of life, if it shall have been set forth by you. (Schaff, n.d.)

Unfortunately for Fortunatus, Augustine did not really want to talk about morals, but about faith. The two men sparred back and forth through most of the first day. At the end, Fortunatus stated that Christ could not have flesh, and he quoted 1 Corinthians 15:50: "What I am saying, brothers and sisters, is this: flesh and blood cannot inherit the kingdom of God, nor does the perishable inherit the imperishable." For Fortunatus, Christ could not have flesh and still inherit the kingdom. However reasonable this might have sounded to him, we are told that it caused an uproar in the crowd which was listening:

> Here a clamor was made by the audience who wished the argument to be conducted on rational grounds, because they saw that Fortunatus was not willing to receive all things that are written in the Codex of the apostle. Then little discussions began to be held here and there by all, until Fortunatus said that the Word of God has been fettered in the race of darkness. At which, when those present had expressed their horror, the meeting was closed. (Schaff, n.d.)

The crowd was being too unruly in their discussions, and more than likely a riot was feared, so the organizers shut the debate down for the day. Augustine and Fortunatus met on the following day, presumably in the same place with the same judges. Both men used the New Testament to support their arguments, but unlike the first day when Fortunatus held his ground, it is clear in the second day that he was having difficulties with his arguments against Augustine. At the end of the day, after a lengthy debate, Fortunatus stopped and wanted to talk to his superiors because he could not adequately answer Augustine's questions. He said:

> Without prejudice to my profession I might say: when I shall have reconsidered with my superiors the things that have been opposed by you, if they fail to respond to this question of mine, which is now in like manner proposed to me by you, it will be in my contemplation (since I desire my soul to be liberated by an assured faith) to come to the investigation of this thing that you have proposed to me and that you promise you will show.
> Augustine said: Thanks be to God. (Schaff, n.d.)

We do not know if Fortunatus ever got back to Augustine with the answer from his superiors, but it is clear from Augustine's response (just above this section) that he then lectured the audience about his brand of Christianity after Fortunatus left. This is a typical debate on theological issues. The same style of debate was held with another Manichaean named Felix, probably in 404 CE. The difference between this debate and his previous debate with Fortunatus is that this time Augustine was the bishop of Hippo, and because of this, Felix was summoned by Augustine to the palace of the bishop to do the debate. The rules, however, were the same. Judges were chosen, the two had to debate in front of the public, and the loser of the debate had to leave or convert. It is not surprising to hear that Augustine won this debate as well, and at the very end, we see that Felix cursed Mani and his beliefs. We can assume that Felix then went on to become a Catholic (although that is just a guess). We also know that Augustine held a public debate with one of the Donatist leaders and the outcome was the same: Augustine won. The Donatists were then forced to convert to Catholicism and to give up their churches to the Catholics.

The final debate we can look at took place around 402 CE, a few years before Augustine's debate with Felix. It was a very interesting debate between a Manichaean woman named Julia and Porphyry, the bishop of Gaza. Julia had arrived in Gaza leading a band of Manichaean Christians. They were spending their time trying to convert people to the Manichaean form of Christianity. Porphyry had heard about her and, like Augustine, summoned her to his palace to debate in public. Julia was asked to leave the Manichaeans, but she refused and told the bishop to "speak and listen, persuade or be persuaded," which is of course exactly what a public debate was. The bishop told her to show up at dawn on the next day. Julia held her ground during the debate. She refused to budge from her position, and when it was clear that Porphyry could not win the debate by his voice, he called God down to punish her. We are told that she became very still and stopped speaking, and still speechless, died an hour later. This was an absolute win for Porphyry, and we are told that her companions and other Manichaeans in the audience fell at the feet of the bishop, were baptized, and were later brought into the Catholic Church.

These debates were powerful and effective tools to combat what some would call heresy. They were done in public so that everyone who was interested could hear both sides. Of course, the main reason to have these debates was really to crush the enemy and drive them from the city, along with any of their followers who refused to switch to the winning side. This is seen over and over again.

See also: Donatists; Mani, the Founder of Manichaeism; Manichaeans.

Further Reading

Brown, Peter. *Augustine of Hippo: A Biography.* A New Edition with Epilogue. Berkeley: University of California Press, 2013.

Drake, H. A. *Constantine and the Bishops: The Politics of Intolerance* (Ancient Society
    and History). Baltimore: Johns Hopkins University Press, 2002.
Schaff, Philip. "Against Fortunatus." *Augustine: The Writings against the Manichaeans
    and against the Donatists*. Edinburgh: T&T Clark, n.d. Available online at http://
    www.ccel.org/ccel/schaff/npnf104.
Simmons, Michael Bland. *Universal Salvation in Late Antiquity: Porphyry of Tyre and
    the Pagan-Christian Debate* (Oxford Studies in Late Antiquity). Oxford: Oxford
    University Press, 2015.

QUMRAN   After his death his generals split up and fought over control
of this territory. Ultimately General Seleucis and his successors controlled
Judea through the 160s BCE, when King Antiochus IV decided to push
Greek religion on the Jewish population. This led to the Maccabean Revolt,
which kicked the Greeks out of the Holy Land. Many Jewish people, however,
were unsatisfied with the Maccabees of Judea who took control after the
revolt had finished. It appears that some of them left the cities and moved
east to the desert and specifically, among the plains near the Dead Sea. One
community in particular, the Essenes at Qumran, spent their time trying to
make the perfect Jewish society. They lived in Qumran from the late 100s
BCE through 68 CE when the Romans destroyed the village during the first
Jewish War. While they lived on the plain, close to them were steep cliffs, and
it was here that they decided to hide their religious texts from the Romans,
probably just as the Romans were attacking. They are important for the
study of early Christianity because some scholars believe that the early
Christians might have integrated some of the rules of the Qumran community
into their own.

   Before the archaeological digs in Qumran, scholars had known about the
Essenes primarily from the writings of Josephus, a Jewish historian who lived
in the first century CE. The following passage is long but very important,
since he describes many of the practices that were later described in their own
texts (*Jewish Antiquities*, 18.1.5):

> The doctrine of the Essenes is this: That all things are best ascribed to God.
> They teach the immortality of souls, and esteem that the rewards of righteous-
> ness are to be earnestly striven for; and when they send what they have dedi-
> cated to God into the temple, they do not offer sacrifices because they have
> more pure lustrations of their own; on which account they are excluded from
> the common court of the temple, but offer their sacrifices themselves; yet is
> their course of life better than that of other men; and they entirely addict
> themselves to husbandry. It also deserves our admiration, how much they ex-
> ceed all other men that addict themselves to virtue, and this in righteousness;
> and indeed to such a degree, that as it has never appeared among any other

men, neither Greeks nor barbarians, no, not for a little time, so it has endured a long while among them. This is demonstrated by that institution of theirs, which will not suffer anything to hinder them from having all things in common; so that a rich man enjoys no more of his own wealth than he who hath nothing at all. There are about four thousand men that live in this way, and neither marry wives, nor are desirous to keep servants; as thinking the latter tempts men to be unjust, and the former gives the handle to domestic quarrels; but as they live by themselves, they minister one to another. They also appoint certain stewards to receive the incomes of their revenues, and of the fruits of the ground; such as are good men and priests, who are to get their cereals and their food ready for them. None of them differ from the Essenes in their way of living, but do the most resemble those Dacae who are called Polistae (dwellers in cities). (Josephus, n.d.)

The Essenes and their community at Qumran came to the attention of the public in 1947 when some Bedouins discovered some broken jars in a cave just above the abandoned village of Qumran. By the jars were leather scrolls. Since then there have been a number of caves and texts discovered in and around Qumran. At first scholars didn't think that the Essenes were the ones who had created the scrolls, but subsequent archaeology in Qumran shows that the Essenes were definitely copying religious texts. Within their community archaeologists have discovered a "scriptorium," or a place where things were written. They found many inkpots, writing utensils, and other material, which shows for certain that those who lived in Qumran created and copied their religious texts and rules for their community. Archaeologists also found a series of cisterns (water tanks carved from the rock) that allowed the community to live in the desert, a large meeting hall that could sit up to 200 people, as well as extensive burial sites for the people who lived at Qumran.

These texts can tell us quite a bit about Qumran. The texts contain parts of many of the Old Testament books including Genesis, Exodus, and Judges, along with commentaries (statements written about some of the Old Testament books). There are also quite a few texts that are not biblical but discuss the inner workings of the Qumran community. Probably the most well known of these Qumran texts is the so-called *Manual of Discipline*, also called *The Community Rule*. The text was found in Cave 1 and is dated to sometime between 100 to 75 BCE. This very important document contains statements on how the Qumran community was to live and work together as a functioning society. Some of the rules discuss how one could become a member. For example, all who wanted to join would have to promise to follow the commandments of God. The new member would have a year to prove that he was pure in his heart and deeds, and if the community believed him, he would then hand over all of his wealth (including property) to an overseer. He was then given another year to prove himself worthy, and at the end of the second year, if he had done what the community asked, then he would be allowed in. If he had not, then the text states that the person would not be allowed to join the community. Once someone was allowed to enter, there were also rules that then governed their lives. They would have to submit to the priests and to the men who made up the community. The new members would have to take a binding oath to follow all of the rules, and then they would be baptized. After this the text states that they would all eat, pray, and study together, even though the members would be ranked, with the priests at the top and the new members at the bottom. If they did not follow the rules, the entire community was to shun that person. Not surprisingly, the text also lists the rules and the punishments if the rules were broken. For example, if someone insulted another member, that person would be given a fine and then excluded from the community for one year.

Further Reading

Collins, John J. *Beyond the Qumran Community: The Sectarian Movement of the Dead Sea Scrolls*. Grand Rapids, MI: William B. Eerdmans, 2010.

Davis, Michael Thomas, and Brent A. Strawn, eds. *Qumran Studies: New Approaches, New Questions*. Grand Rapids, MI: William B. Eerdmans, 2007.

Josephus. "Jewish Antiquities." *Josephus: The Complete Works*. n.d. Available online at http://www.ccel.org/ccel/josephus/complete.

Magness, Jodi. *The Archaeology of Qumran and the Dead Sea Scrolls* (Studies in the Dead Sea Scrolls and Related Literature). Grand Rapids, MI: William B. Eerdmans, 2002.

Schiffman. Lawrence H. *Reclaiming the Dead Sea Scrolls: The History of Judaism, the Background of Christianity, the Lost Library of Qumran*. New York: Doubleday, 1995.

SADDUCEES   Judaism during the period of the first century CE was made up of a number of different groups. There were, however, three main ones: the Sadducees, Pharisees, and Essenes. The Pharisees are examined in another section of the book. The atmosphere of Palestine was very multicultural, with many different languages and ideas all mixed within this one area. The Jewish population was also affected by this multiculturalism. In order to examine the Sadducees (and the Pharisees), it is important to look at some historical events that took place in the second century BCE. When Alexander the Great took over this area in the late 300s BCE, he and his advisors left their Greek mark on the area. This is referred to as Hellenism (the Greeks called themselves Hellenes), and it is a period when Greek ideas, cultures, and architecture all spread through the areas that Alexander the Great conquered. The Jewish people had no choice but to live under Greek rule, and many of them adapted to this new condition. For the most part, the Greek rulers accommodated the various religions that they now oversaw, and this certainly included Judaism. However, in 167 BCE, the current ruler, Antiochus IV, decided to impose strict Hellenistic laws on all of the inhabitants of Judea (see 1 Maccabees). He forced the Jewish people to abandon their religion and even went so far as to put a statue of Zeus in the Temple (the main cultic building for all of Judaism). This led to a rebellion (167 BCE), and under the leadership of Judas Maccabee, the Greek rulers were kicked out of Palestine and the Jewish people cleansed their Temple and rededicated it. Here is an account from 2 Maccabees 5:11–16:

> When news of what had happened reached the king [Antiochus IV], he took it to mean that Judea was in revolt. So, raging inwardly, he left Egypt and took the city by storm. He commanded his soldiers to cut down relentlessly everyone they met and to kill those who went into their houses. Then there was massacre of young and old, destruction of boys, women, and children, and slaughter of young girls and infants. Within the total of three days eighty thousand were destroyed, forty thousand in hand-to-hand fighting, and as many were sold into slavery as were killed. Not content with this, Antiochus dared to enter the most holy temple in all the world, guided by Menelaus, who had become a traitor both to the laws and to his country. He took the holy vessels with his polluted hands, and swept away with profane hands the votive offerings that other kings had made to enhance the glory and honor of the place. (NRSV)

After this period you have the priests who tried to control all aspects of the Jewish faith. These are the Sadducees. It should be pointed out that we only know of the Sadducees from their detractors, so caution should be applied when trying to examine what they believed and practiced. As far as we can tell, they were the conservatives of their time—they wanted Judaism to remain in the control of the priestly caste, which meant that they alone could interpret the Torah. Their opponents were the Pharisees, who wanted to move Judaism away from the Temple cult and away from the control of the Sadducees; they too were priests. Because the Sadducees considered themselves to be the true priests, it is natural that they believed they controlled the Temple and all that happened there. This group was usually wealthy and were also influential in other aspects of Jewish culture. They too were influenced by Hellenism, and it is this influence that kept getting them into trouble with the Pharisees.

The Sadducees are mentioned in the New Testament in a few places, and in many cases they are tied in with the Pharisees. One place is Matthew 16.1, which describes the Sadducees and the Pharisees gathering together to test Jesus and to ask for a sign from heaven. In Matthew 16:11 Jesus himself warns his disciples against listening to what the Sadducees and the Pharisees have to say. This group is sometimes mentioned on its own as well. An important verse is Matthew 22:23. Here the Sadducees ask Jesus a question about the Resurrection, and Jesus tells them that they do not understand the Bible (here he is referring to the Old Testament). They tell Jesus that there is no resurrection. The same version of this appears in Mark 12:18 and Luke 20:27. The fact that they didn't believe in resurrection also appears in Acts 4:2, so it is a good guess that they actually did not believe that the dead would be raised up. The Resurrection was a very important part of early Christian belief, and there must have been many arguments between the Jewish population and the early Christians over this idea. We can possibly get more information about the Sadducees from other parts of the New Testament. Acts 23:8 tells us that they did not believe in the Resurrection and that they did not believe in angels or spirits. Some scholars have questioned the accuracy of this statement because there were many texts in Judaism that contain stories about angels. Unfortunately the authors of the New Testament do not mention the Sadducees further.

One other source for our information on the Sadducees comes from another first-century writer named Josephus. Josephus, who was Jewish, wrote a number of important books on the history of Judaism, including one titled *Antiquities*. In Book 18, Chapter 1.4 he describes the beliefs of the Sadducees: the soul dies with the body, they refuse to adhere to anything but the Torah, and they are argumentative with philosophers who differ in beliefs. He also states that sometimes the Sadducees would start believing what the Pharisees believe so that they could remain in their jobs as judges. Unfortunately Josephus, in this book, doesn't tell us much more about this group.

The Sadducees as a group disappeared soon after 70 CE when the Romans ended a revolt by the Jewish population in Judea. This revolt, sometimes referred to as the Jewish War, started in 66 CE when many Jewish people rose up against Roman rule. At first they were successful and drove the Romans out, but the rebellion was put down after a Roman general named Vespasian was sent in and then Vespasian's son Titus arrived in 70. After the Romans put down the revolt, they sacked and destroyed the Second Temple that was built in 516 BCE. With the Second Temple destroyed, the center of their religious practice was gone. The Romans then forbade the Jewish and Christian population to remain in Judea. Many fled in what is now called the Diaspora. Because the Sadducees were heavily involved in the rites centered on the Temple, when it was taken down, the focal point of the group was gone. More than likely they melted in with the rest of the Jewish population who had to flee Judea when the Romans kicked them (and the Christians) out of this area. With their disappearance we have the rise of the Pharisees, or Rabbinical Judaism.

Further Reading

Fishman, Sylvia Barack. *The Way Into the Varieties of Jewishness*. Woodstock, VT: Jewish Lights Publishing, 2007.

Saldarini, Anthony J. J. *Pharisees, Scribes, and Sadducees in Palestinian Society* (Biblical Resource). Grand Rapids, MI: William B. Eerdmans, 2001.

Scott, J. Julius, Jr. *Jewish Backgrounds of the New Testament*. Grand Rapids, MI: Baker Press, 2000.

Skarsaune, Oskar. *In the Shadow of the Temple: Jewish Influences on Early Christianity*. Downers Grove, IL: InterVarsity Press, 2002.

TERTULLIAN Tertullian was born in the North African city of Carthage, and as with many early Christians, we aren't sure exactly when he was born and when he died. The dates are probably about 160 to the early 200s. Tertullian was a prolific writer, so we know a little bit about his life. He was educated, which implies that his family had some wealth. Jerome, writing in his *Lives of Illustrious Men* (chapter 53), states that Tertullian's father was a centurion (an officer in the Roman military) and that he lived to a very long age. He was able to write in Greek and in Latin, and in fact is one of the earlier Latin Christian writers. He wrote a letter titled "To His Wife," so it can be assumed that he was married. The last concrete thing we know about Tertullian is that towards the end of his life he embraced a form of Christianity called Montanism. The Montanists believed that they directly received revelations from God and, more importantly for Tertullian, were an ascetic movement, which affected how he wrote about certain topics, especially in regards to women. A few examples we can examine are his *Letter to His Wife*, *On the Apparel of Women*, and *On the Veiling of Virgins*. Tertullian also wrote against those whom he considered to be heretics.

Tertullian had some very strong views in terms of the behavior of women. He believed that they can get married, but if their husband died, they must not get married again. Around 207 CE Tertullian wrote a letter to his wife, which still survives. In it he tells her that she needs to remain unmarried if he dies. He points out that Jesus himself stated that although people get married in this life, they will not be married in heaven, nor will there be marriage (Luke 20:34–36): "Jesus said to them, 'Those who belong to this age marry and are given in marriage; but those who are considered worthy of a place in that age and in the resurrection from the dead neither marry nor are given in marriage. Indeed they cannot die anymore, because they are like angels and are children of God, being children of the resurrection.'" With this evidence from the Bible, Tertullian writes to her:

> The precept, therefore, which I give you is, that, with all the constancy you may, you do, after our departure, renounce nuptials; not that you will on that score

confer any benefit on me, except in that you will profit yourself. But to Christians, after their departure from the world no restoration of marriage is promised in the day of the resurrection, translated as they will be into the condition and sanctity of angels. Therefore no solicitude arising from carnal jealousy will, in the day of the resurrection, even in the case of her whom they chose to represent as having been married to seven brothers successively, wound any one of her so many husbands; nor is any (husband) awaiting her to put her to confusion. The question raised by the Sadducees has yielded to the Lord's sentence. Do not think that it is for the sake of preserving to the end for myself the entire devotion of your flesh, that I, suspicious of the pain of (anticipated) slight, am even at this early period instilling into you the counsel of (perpetual) widowhood. There will at that day be no resumption of voluptuous disgrace between us. No such frivolities, no such impurities, does God promise to His (servants). But whether to you, or to any other woman whatever who pertains to God, the advice which we are giving shall be profitable, we take leave to treat of at large. (Schaff, n.d.)

Unfortunately we don't know the response of his wife to receiving this letter (he actually wrote two to her about this topic). It is known that she died before him, so she never had to take his advice. But it is clear from his writings that Christian women should not get married again after the death of their husbands.

Tertullian also had views on how women should dress. He believed that women should dress modestly. In his book titled *On the Apparel of Women* he wrote that women should not be wearing jewelry of any kind and that women should certainly not dye their hair, as he writes about in chapter 6:

I see some (women) turn (the color of) their hair with saffron. They are ashamed even of their own nation, (ashamed) that their procreation did not assign them to Germany and to Gaul: thus, as it is, they transfer their hair (thither)! It is bad, very bad, and it does not bode well for themselves with their flame-colored head, and think that they are being graceful when (in fact) they are polluting! And moreover, the force of the cosmetics burns the hair; and the constant application of even any undrugged moisture, lays up a store of harm for the head; while the sun's warmth, too, so desirable for imparting to the hair at once growth and dryness, is hurtful. What "grace" is compatible with "injury?" What "beauty" with "impurities?" Shall a Christian woman heap saffron on her head, as upon an altar? . . . But, however, God says, "Which of you can make a white hair black, or out of a black a white?" (Matthew 5:36). And so they refute the Lord! "Behold!" say they, "instead of white or black, we make it yellow,—more winning in grace." (Schaff, n.d.)

Not only that, Tertullian believed that women should veil their entire heads. He wrote a book titled *On the Veiling of Virgins* and gave, in detail, his arguments that women must be veiled. Even though he addressed this to virgins (unmarried women), he also wanted married women to continue wearing the veil. To the virgins he wrote (chapter 26):

> It remains likewise that we turn to (the virgins) themselves, to induce them to accept these (suggestions) the more willingly. I pray you, whether you are a mother, or sister, or virgin-daughter—let me address you according to the names proper to your years—veil your head: if you are a mother, wear a veil for your sons' sakes; if a sister, for your brethren's sakes; if a daughter for your fathers' sakes. All ages are periled in your person. Put on the exhibition of modesty; surround yourself with the stockade of bashfulness; rear a rampart for your sex, which must neither allow your own eyes egress nor ingress to other people's. Wear the full garb of woman, to preserve the standing of virgin. Deny somewhat of your inward consciousness, in order to exhibit the truth to God alone. And yet you do not deny yourself in appearing as a bride. For you are wedded to Christ: to Him you have surrendered your flesh; to Him you have espoused your maturity. Walk in accordance with the will of your Espoused. Christ is He who bids the espoused and wives of others veil themselves; (and) of course, much more His own. (Schaff, n.d.)

As can be seen in all of these examples, Tertullian used the Bible to justify his demands. This was extremely common in early Christianity, as it is still common today. Tertullian didn't just write about women. He was also a prolific writer against those who believed differently. Probably one of his most famous books is titled *Against Marcion*. Marcion lived in the middle of the second century and believed something quite different from Tertullian. For example, Marcion believed that Christians should not use the Old Testament and that Christians should only read certain writings by the apostles. Tertullian was adamantly against this. *Against Marcion* is a massive book, and it made a large impact on later writers. Marcion wrote his own books, which unfortunately do not survive today. But Tertullian, in *Against Marcion*, copied down some of Marcion's writings. Tertullian then argued against what Marcion wrote. Many Christians after the time of Tertullian argued against people using the same tactics. Tertullian's writings were very influential after his death, especially his writings that defended Christianity. He was one of the earliest Christians to write in Latin, and this brought many Greek ideas into the Christian, Latin-speaking world.

See also: Asceticism; Marcion.

Further Reading
Dunn, Geoffrey D. *Tertullian* (The Early Church Fathers). New York: Routledge, 2004.

Osborn, Eric. *Tertullian, First Theologian of the West*. Cambridge: Cambridge University Press, 1997.

Rankin, David. *Tertullian and the Church*. Cambridge: Cambridge University Press, 1995.

Schaff, Philip. "On the Apparel of Women." *Fathers of the Third Century: Tertullian, Fourth Part; Minucius Felix; Commodian; Origen, Parts First and Second*. Edinburgh: T&T Clark, n.d. Available online at http://www.ccel.org/ccel/schaff/anf04.

Schaff, Philip. "On the Veiling of Women." *Fathers of the Third Century: Tertullian, Fourth Part; Minucius Felix; Commodian; Origen, Parts First and Second*. Edinburgh: T&T Clark, n.d. Available online at http://www.ccel.org/ccel/schaff/anf04.

Schaff, Philip. "To His Wife." *Fathers of the Third Century: Tertullian, Fourth Part; Minucius Felix; Commodian; Origen, Parts First and Second*. Edinburgh: T&T Clark, n.d. Available online at http://www.ccel.org/ccel/schaff/anf04.

Still, Todd D., and David Wilhite, eds. *Tertullian and Paul* (Pauline and Patristic Scholars in Debate). New York: Bloomsbury T&T Clark, 2013.

WOMEN IN EARLY CHRISTIANITY   There is no doubt that many women were involved in the early Christian communities. Nearly all the books of the New Testament mention women, especially in their support roles for the apostles. They were wives to some of the original apostles. Wealthy women spent their own money funding the apostles, in particular Paul, who could have never done what he did without this financial support. Women too had roles in the early church hierarchy, at least in the first century. They were teachers, prophets (especially in the second century), and in some cases, deaconesses. Women also were killed during the sporadic persecutions that took place in the early centuries. The Christianity of today would look very different if women had not been involved in the support and spread of Christianity in the first couple of centuries.

THE APOSTLE'S WIVES

The first role we can examine for women in the early church was the role of wife. Several of the apostles were married, at least according to Paul. He wrote in 1 Corinthians 9:3–5: "This is my defense to those who would examine me. Do we not have the right to our food and drink? Do we not have the right to be accompanied by a believing wife, as do the other apostles and the brothers of the Lord and Cephas?" Paul's words state clearly that many apostles were married, along with the brothers of Jesus and, more importantly, that the wives traveled with their husbands. Unfortunately Paul does not name names, but we do know that the apostle Peter was definitely married. Luke 4:38 mentions that Jesus left the synagogue and went to Peter's house. It was here that he met Peter's mother-in-law and healed her from her fever. It is clear from this text that Peter was married, although we don't hear anything specific about his wife. Paul, however, was definitely not married since he states in 1 Corinthians 7:8 that it is better for a Christian man to remain unmarried like himself ("To the unmarried and the widows I say that it is well for them to remain unmarried as I am"). It is unfortunate that Paul does not tell us what these wives were doing when they were traveling with their husbands, but we do get some clues from his descriptions of other women.

THE FEMALE DEACON

Paul, in his letter to the Romans, mentions many women who were helping him and other Christians. One in particular, Phoebe, is given the title of deacon. Phoebe was given an introduction by Paul so that she could do her work and so that other people could help her in whatever she needed. There is quite a bit of scholarly discussion on whether Phoebe was an actual deacon of the church, but there is no reason to believe that she was not. Paul insists that she was of great help to him and clearly she had a mission to fulfil, and Paul wanted to make sure that she did her work unobstructed. Here is part of Paul's letter (Romans 16:1–7):

> I commend to you our sister Phoebe, a deacon of the church at Cenchreae, so that you may welcome her in the Lord as is fitting for the saints, and help her in whatever she may require from you, for she has been a benefactor of many and of myself as well. Greet Prisca and Aquila, who work with me in Christ Jesus, and who risked their necks for my life, to whom not only I give thanks, but also all the churches of the Gentiles. Greet also the church in their house. Greet my beloved Epaenetus, who was the first convert in Asia for Christ. Greet Mary, who has worked very hard among you. Greet Andronicus and Junia, my relatives who were in prison with me; they are prominent among the apostles, and they were in Christ before I was. (NSRV)

Prisca, or Pricilla as she is named in other New Testament translations, was also a prominent woman in Paul's writing (as seen from above). She is mentioned many times in the New Testament (Acts 18, Romans 16:3, 1 Corinthians 16:19, and 2 Timothy 4:19) and it is clear that she played an important part in the spreading and supporting of Christianity. In fact, in Acts 18:26 it was Prisca and her husband Aquila who pulled aside a Jewish man named Apollos to teach him about Christianity. Acts tells us that Apollos was teaching in the synagogue, where Prisca and Aquila heard him and decided to instruct him on the "correct" belief. Junia (sometimes referred to as Julia) too was specifically pointed out by Paul in his letter to the Romans (16:7). She and her husband Andronicus were said to be "prominent among the apostles," which could either mean that they were both considered to be apostles or that the apostles knew of the two of them since they were actively working to spread the faith. We still do not have an accurate picture of what these early Christian women were doing.

WIDOWS

Widows (women who were married but whose husbands have died) played a prominent role in early Christian communities. Theirs was usually a passive one, in that their care was the responsibility of the whole Christian community. People living in the premodern era did not have the luxury of having a social security system, and if a woman did not have any children or family to take care of her when she was old, she was in serious trouble. This is where the church stepped in to help (along with helping orphans). However, it appears that as the church stepped in to help these widows, some women began taking advantage of the system. The author of 1 Timothy was very concerned about these women, and new rules were set down in order to prevent the abuse. According to this author (1 Timothy 5:3–16):

> Honor widows who are really widows. If a widow has children or grandchildren, they should first learn their religious duty to their own family and make some repayment to their parents; for this is pleasing in God's sight. The real widow, left alone, has set her hope on God and continues in supplications and prayers night and day; but the widow who lives for pleasure is dead even while she lives. Give these commands as well, so that they may be above reproach. And whoever does not provide for relatives, and especially for family members, has denied the faith and is worse than an unbeliever. Let a widow be put on the list if she is not less than sixty years old and has been married only once; she must be well attested for her good works, as one who has brought up children, shown hospitality, washed the saints' feet, helped the afflicted, and devoted herself to doing good in every way. But refuse to put younger widows on the list; for when their sensual desires alienate them from Christ, they want to marry, and so they incur condemnation for having violated their first pledge. Besides that, they learn to be idle, gadding about from house to house; and they are not merely idle, but also gossips and busybodies, saying what they should not say. So I would have younger widows marry, bear children, and manage their households, so as to give the adversary no occasion to revile us. For some have already turned away to follow Satan. If any believing woman has relatives who are really widows, let her assist them; let the church not be burdened, so that it can assist those who are real widows. (NRSV)

It was, first of all, the responsibility of the family to take care of its elderly members, but if the woman did not have anyone to take care of her, the Christian community would do so. But she had to be over a specific age (60 years old). Widows were also held up by Jesus as being exemplary members of the community when they donated some of what they had even when they did not have a lot to give. Jesus gave an example of this in Mark 12:41–44:

> He sat down opposite the treasury, and watched the crowd putting money into the treasury. Many rich people put in large sums. A poor widow came and put in two small copper coins, which are worth a penny. Then he called his disciples and said to them, "Truly I tell you, this poor widow has put in more than all those who are contributing to the treasury. For all of them have contributed out of their abundance; but she out of her poverty has put in everything she had, all she had to live on." (NRSV)

WOMEN MARTYRS

Although the majority of martyrs that we know of are men, we do know that there were also many women who were killed for their faith. Probably the most famous female martyrs were Perpetua and her friend Felicity. These women were killed sometime in the late 190s or early 200s in the North African city of Carthage. The text is thought to be Perpetua's own words about what happened to her. Here is a section, written towards the beginning of her account:

> After a few days we were taken into the dungeon, and I was very much afraid, because I had never felt such darkness. O terrible day! O the fierce heat of the shock of the soldiery, because of the crowds! I was very unusually distressed by my anxiety for my infant. There were present there Tertius and Pomponius, the blessed deacons who ministered to us, and had arranged by means of a gratuity that we might be refreshed by being sent out for a few hours into a pleasanter part of the prison. Then going out of the dungeon, all attended to their own wants. I suckled my child, which was now enfeebled with hunger. In my anxiety for it, I addressed my mother and comforted my brother, and commended to their care my son. I was languishing because I had seen them languishing on my account. Such solicitude I suffered for many days, and I obtained for my infant to remain in the dungeon with me; and forthwith I grew strong and was relieved from distress and anxiety about my infant; and the dungeon became to me as it were a palace, so that I preferred being there to being elsewhere. (Schaff, n.d.)

Perpetua is sent to the dungeon along with her pregnant friend Felicity. She was eight months pregnant, and the Roman authorities would not put her to death because of her pregnancy, so she prayed and she gave birth so that she too could be a martyr. Towards the end of her account we are told that both women were killed in the arena when they refused to recant Christianity. There are also many other accounts of women martyrs located throughout the Roman Empire. These women were held up in early communities as examples of behavior that people should exhibit when confronted with persecution.

It is clear the women played an extremely important role in early Christianity. They were wives who helped their husbands when they were doing their missionary duties. They held positions of office in the early church, and, even though their roles are not totally clear, they were held in high esteem by not only the other apostles but also by the Christian communities. They were widows who were taken care of by the church and who in turn had their own caregiver roles in the community. And finally, among other roles, they were very public martyrs who willingly died for their beliefs. They suffered just as horribly as early Christian men and were held up as virtuous examples to other Christians during times of persecution.

Further Reading

Brown, Peter. *The Body and Society: Men, Women, and Sexual Renunciation in Early Christianity*. New York: Columbia University Press, 1988.

Miller, Patricia Cox. *Women in Early Christianity: Translations from Greek Texts*. Washington, DC: Catholic University of America Press, 2005.

Schaff, Philip. "Martyrdom of Perpetua." *Latin Christianity: Its Founder, Tertullian*. Edinburgh: T&T Clark, n.d. Available online at http://www.ccel.org/ccel /schaff/anf03.

Swan, Laura. *The Forgotten Desert Mothers: Sayings, Lives, and Stories of Early Christian Women*. Mahwah, NJ: Paulist Press, 2001.

Torjesen, Karen J. *When Women Were Priests: Women's Leadership in the Early Church and the Scandal of Their Subordination in the Rise of Christianity*. New York: HarperSanFrancisco, 1995.

Primary Source Documents

1 THESSALONIANS

1 Thessalonians is the earliest writing we have of what is now called the New Testament, despite the fact that it is the 13th text. It was written by the apostle Paul in the early 50s CE, nearly 20 years after the death of Christ. Paul was writing from Corinth. He had started to travel around what is now Turkey in order to convert people to the new religion of Christianity. His letter to the Thessalonians (Thessalonia, Turkey) is followed by 2 Thessalonians in the New Testament, but scholars are unsure if Paul is the actual author of that particular text. In this passage Paul lists a number of behaviors the Thessalonians should follow.

1 Thessalonians 3:1–5:28

3:1 Therefore when we could bear it no longer, we decided to be left alone in Athens; 3:2 and we sent Timothy, our brother and co-worker for God in proclaiming the gospel of Christ, to strengthen and encourage you for the sake of your faith, 3:3 so that no one would be shaken by these persecutions. Indeed, you yourselves know that this is what we are destined for. 3:4 In fact, when we were with you, we told you beforehand that we were to suffer persecution; so it turned out, as you know. 3:5 For this reason, when I could bear it no longer, I sent to find out about your faith; I was afraid that somehow the tempter had tempted you and that our labor had been in vain. 3:6 But Timothy has just now come to us from you, and has brought us the good news of your faith and love. He has told us also that you always remember us kindly and long to see us—just as we long to see you. 3:7 For this reason, brothers and sisters, during all our distress and persecution we have been encouraged about you through your faith. 3:8 For we now live, if you continue to stand firm in the Lord. 3:9 How can we thank God enough for you in return for all the joy that we feel before our God because of you? 3:10 Night and day we pray most earnestly that we may see you face to face and restore whatever is lacking in your faith. 3:11 Now may our God and Father himself and our Lord Jesus direct our way to you. 3:12 And may the Lord make you increase and abound in love for one another and for all, just as we abound in love for you. 3:13 And may he so strengthen your hearts in holiness that you may be blameless before our God and Father at the coming of our Lord Jesus with all his saints.

4:2 For you know what instructions we gave you through the Lord Jesus. 4:3 For this is the will of God, your sanctification: that you abstain from fornication; 4:4 that each one of you know how to control your own body in holiness and honor, 4:5 not with lustful passion, like the Gentiles who do not know God; 4:6 that no one wrong or exploit a brother or sister in this matter, because the Lord is an avenger in all these things, just as we have already told you beforehand and solemnly warned you. 4:7 For God did not call us to impurity but in holiness. 4:8 Therefore whoever rejects this rejects not human authority but God, who also gives his Holy Spirit to you. 4:9 Now concerning love of the brothers and sisters, you do not need to have anyone write to you, for you yourselves have been taught by God to love one another; 4:10 and indeed you do love all the brothers and sisters throughout Macedonia. But we urge you, beloved, to do so more and more, 4:11 to aspire to live quietly, to mind your own affairs, and to work with your hands, as we directed you, 4:12 so that you may behave properly toward outsiders and be dependent on no one. 4:13 But we do not want you to be uninformed, brothers and sisters, about those who have died, so that you may not grieve as others do who have no hope. 4:14 For since we believe that Jesus died and rose again, even so, through Jesus, God will bring with him those who have died. 4:15 For this we declare to you by the word of the Lord, that we who are alive, who are left until the coming of the Lord, will by no means precede those who have died. 4:16 For the Lord himself, with a cry of command, with the archangel's call and with the sound of God's trumpet, will descend from heaven, and the dead in Christ will rise first. 4:17 Then we who are alive, who are left, will be caught up in the clouds together with them to meet the Lord in the air; and so we will be with the Lord forever. 4:18 Therefore encourage one another with these words. 5:1 Now concerning the times and the seasons, brothers and sisters, you do not need to have anything written to you. 5:2 For you yourselves know very well that the day of the Lord will come like a thief in the night. 5:3 When they say, "There is peace and security," then sudden destruction will come upon them, as labor pains come upon a pregnant woman, and there will be no escape! 5:4 But you, beloved, are not in darkness, for that day to surprise you like a thief; 5:5 for you are all children of light and children of the day; we are not of the night or of darkness. 5:6 So then let us not fall asleep as others do, but let us keep awake and be sober; 5:7 for those who sleep, sleep at night, and those who are drunk get drunk at night. 5:8 But since we belong to the day, let us be sober, and put on the breastplate of faith and love, and for a helmet the hope of salvation. 5:9 For God has destined us not for wrath but for obtaining salvation through our Lord Jesus Christ, 5:10 who died for us, so that whether we are awake or asleep we may live with him. 5:11 Therefore encourage one another and build up each other, as indeed you are doing. 5:12 But we appeal to you, brothers and sisters, to respect those who labor among you, and have charge of you in the Lord and admonish you; 5:13 esteem them very highly in love because of their work. Be at peace among yourselves. 5:14 And we urge you, beloved, to admonish the idlers, encourage the faint hearted, help the weak, be patient with all of them. 5:15 See that none of you repays evil for evil, but always seek to do good to one another and to all. 5:16 Rejoice always, 5:17 pray without ceasing, 5:18 give thanks in all circumstances; for this is the will of God in Christ Jesus for you. 5:19 Do not quench the Spirit. 5:20 Do not despise the words of prophets, 5:21 but test everything; hold fast to what is good; 5:22 abstain from every form of evil. 5:23 May the God of peace himself sanctify you entirely; and may your spirit and soul and body be kept sound and blameless at the coming of our Lord Jesus Christ. 5:24 The one who calls you is faithful, and he will do this. 5:25 Beloved, pray for us. 5:26 Greet all the brothers and sisters with a holy kiss. 5:27 I solemnly command you by the Lord that this letter be read to all of them. 5:28 The grace of our Lord Jesus Christ be with you.

Source: New Revised Standard Version Bible, copyright © 1989 National Council of the Churches of Christ in the United States of America. Used by permission. All rights reserved.

CLEMENT OF ROME, *FIRST LETTER TO THE CORINTHIANS* 45–49

Clement was the bishop of Rome in the late first century and wrote this text sometime towards the very end of his life. News had reached Clement of some problems that were taking place in the church at Corinth. Even though at this early stage many churches in the Roman Empire did not acknowledge the importance of the bishop of Rome, Clement took it upon himself to write to the congregation to get them to settle their differences. The section of his letter given below is probably the angriest part of the entire letter. The section ends with his plea for unity.

Chapter 45

You are fond of contention, brethren, and full of zeal about things which do not pertain to salvation. Look carefully into the Scriptures, which are the true utterances of the Holy Spirit. Observe that nothing of an unjust or counterfeit character is written in them. There you will not find that the righteous were cast off by men who themselves were holy. The righteous were indeed persecuted, but only by the wicked. They were cast into prison, but only by the unholy; they were stoned, but only by transgressors; they were slain, but only by the accursed, and such as had conceived an unrighteous envy against them. Exposed to such sufferings, they endured them gloriously. For what shall we say, brethren? Was Daniel cast into the den of lions by such as feared God? Were Ananias, and Azarias, and Mishaël shut up in a furnace of fire by those who observed the great and glorious worship of the Most High? Far from us be such a thought! Who, then, were they that did such things? The hateful, and those full of all wickedness, were roused to such a pitch of fury, that they inflicted torture on those who served God with a holy and blameless purpose [of heart], not knowing that the Most High is the Defender and Protector of all such as with a pure conscience venerate His all-excellent name; to whom be glory for ever and ever. Amen. But they who with confidence endured [these things] are now heirs of glory and honor, and have been exalted and made illustrious by God in their memorial for ever and ever. Amen.

Chapter 46

Let us cleave to the righteous: your strife is pernicious. Such examples, therefore, brethren, it is right that we should follow; since it is written, "Cleave to the holy, for those that cleave to them shall [themselves] be made holy." And again, in another place, [the Scripture] says, "With a harmless man you shall prove yourself harmless, and with an elect man you shall be elect, and with a perverse man you shall show yourself perverse" (Psalms 18:25–26). Let us cleave, therefore, to the innocent and righteous, since these are the elect of God. Why is there strife and tumults, and divisions, and schisms, and wars among you? Have we not [all] one God and one Christ? Is there not one Spirit of grace poured out upon us? And have we not one calling in Christ? Why do we divide and tear to pieces the members of Christ, and raise up strife against our own body, and have reached such a height of madness as to forget that "we are members one of another" (Romans 12:5)? Remember the words of our Lord Jesus Christ, how He said, "Woe to that man [by whom offences come]! It were better for him that he had never been born, than that he should cast a stumbling-block before one of my elect. Yea, it were better for him that a millstone should be hung about [his neck], and he should be sunk in the depths of the sea, than that he should cast a stumbling-block before one of my little ones." Your schism has subverted [the faith of] many, has discouraged many, has given rise to doubt in many, and has caused grief to us all. And still your sedition continues.

Chapter 47

Take up the epistle of the blessed Apostle Paul. What did he write to you at the time when the Gospel first began to be preached? Truly, under the inspiration of the Spirit, he wrote to you concerning himself, and Cephas, and Apollos, because even then parties had been formed among you. But that inclination for one above another entailed less guilt upon you, inasmuch as your partialities were then shown towards apostles, already of high reputation, and towards a man whom they had approved. But now reflect who those are that have perverted you, and lessened the renown of your far-famed brotherly love. It is disgraceful, beloved, yes, highly disgraceful, and unworthy of your Christian profession, that such a thing should be heard of as that the most steadfast and ancient Church of the Corinthians should, on account of one or two persons, engage in sedition against its presbyters. And this rumor has reached not only us, but those also who are unconnected with us; so that, through your infatuation, the name of the Lord is blasphemed, while danger is also brought upon yourselves.

Chapter 48

Let us return to the practice of brotherly love. Let us therefore, with all haste, put an end to this [state of things]; and let us fall down before the Lord, and beseech Him with tears, that He would mercifully be reconciled to us, and restore us to our former seemly and holy practice of brotherly love. For [such conduct] is the gate of righteousness, which is set open for the attainment of life, as it is written, "Open to me the gates of righteousness; I will go in by them, and will praise the Lord: this is the gate of the Lord: the righteous shall enter in by it" (Psalms 118:19–20). Although, therefore, many gates have been set open, yet this gate of righteousness is that gate in Christ by which blessed are all they that have entered in and have directed their way in holiness and righteousness, doing all things without disorder. Let a man be faithful: let him be powerful in the utterance of knowledge; let him be wise in judging of words; let him be pure in all his deeds; yet the more he seems to be superior to others [in these respects], the more humble-minded ought he to be, and to seek the common good of all, and not merely his own advantage.

Chapter 49

Let him who has love in Christ keep the commandments of Christ. Who can describe the [blessed] bond of the love of God? What man is able to tell the excellence of its beauty, as it ought to be told? The height to which love exalts is unspeakable. Love unites us to God. Love covers a multitude of sins. Love bears all things, is long-suffering in all things. There is nothing base, nothing arrogant in love. Love admits of no schisms; love gives rise to no seditions; love does all things in harmony. By love all the elect of God have been made perfect; without love nothing is well-pleasing to God. In love has the Lord taken us to Himself. On account of the Love he bore us, Jesus Christ our Lord gave His blood for us by the will of God; His flesh for our flesh, and His soul for our souls.

Source: Schaff, Philip. "First Epistle of Clement to the Corinthians." *The Apostolic Fathers with Justin Martyr and Irenaeus*. Edinburgh: T&T Clark, n.d. Available online at http://www.ccel .org/ccel/schaff/anf01.

MATTHEW 1:15–4:25

Matthew 1:15–4:25 is one of the most important sections in this Gospel and was written sometime in the 60s CE. It begins with a long genealogical list of the ancestors of Joseph, the husband of Mary. It is thought that this list was given in order to make it clear that the baby Jesus had a father and that his human father had ancestors who stretched all the way back to Abraham, the father of the Jewish people. The text then introduces the birth story of Jesus, who is now called the Messiah or savior, followed by his importance in that his birth was represented by a star. John the Baptist is introduced, Jesus is then baptized in the Jordan River, and then we hear of the temptation of Christ by the devil. In chapter 4 we see that Jesus is now an adult and is choosing his disciples. We are given an introduction to the life and ministry of Jesus throughout these four chapters.

1:15 . . . and Eliud the father of Eleazar, and Eleazar the father of Matthan, and Matthan the father of Jacob, 1:16 and Jacob the father of Joseph the husband of Mary, of whom Jesus was born, who is called the Messiah. 1:17 So all the generations from Abraham to David are fourteen generations; and from David to the deportation to Babylon, fourteen generations; and from the deportation to Babylon to the Messiah, fourteen generations.

1:18 Now the birth of Jesus the Messiah took place in this way. When his mother Mary had been engaged to Joseph, but before they lived together, she was found to be with child from the Holy Spirit. 1:19 Her husband Joseph, being a righteous man and unwilling to expose her to public disgrace, planned to dismiss her quietly. 1:20 But just when he had resolved to do this, an angel of the Lord appeared to him in a dream and said, "Joseph, son of David, do not be afraid to take Mary as your wife, for the child conceived in her is from the Holy Spirit. 1:21 She will bear a son, and you are to name him Jesus, for he will save his people from their sins." 1:22 All this took place to fulfill what had been spoken by the Lord through the prophet: 1:23 "Look, the virgin shall conceive and bear a son, and they shall name him Emmanuel," which means, "God is with us." 1:24 When Joseph awoke from sleep, he did as the angel of the Lord commanded him; he took her as his wife, 1:25 but had no marital relations with her until she had borne a son; and he named him Jesus.

2:1 In the time of King Herod, after Jesus was born in Bethlehem of Judea, wise men from the East came to Jerusalem, 2:2 asking, "Where is the child who has been born king of the Jews? For we observed his star at its rising, and have come to pay him homage." 2:3 When King Herod heard this, he was frightened, and all Jerusalem with him; 2:4 and calling together all the chief priests and scribes of the people, he inquired of them where the Messiah was to be born. 2:5 They told him, "In Bethlehem of Judea; for so it has been written by the prophet: 2:6 'And you, Bethlehem, in the land of Judah, are by no means least among the rulers of Judah; for from you shall come a ruler who is to shepherd my people Israel.'" 2:7 Then Herod secretly called for the wise men and learned from them the exact time when the star had appeared. 2:8 Then he sent them to Bethlehem, saying, "Go and search diligently for the child; and when you have found him, bring me word so that I may also go and pay him homage." 2:9 When they had heard the king, they set out; and there, ahead of them, went the star that they had seen at its rising, until it stopped over the place where the child was. 2:10 When they saw that the star had stopped, they were overwhelmed with joy. 2:11 On entering the house, they saw the child with Mary his mother; and they knelt down and paid him homage. Then, opening their treasure chests, they offered him gifts of gold, frankincense, and myrrh. 2:12 And having been warned in a dream not to return to Herod, they left for their own country by another road.

2:13 Now after they had left, an angel of the Lord appeared to Joseph in a dream and said, "Get up, take the child and his mother, and flee to Egypt, and remain there until I tell you; for Herod is about to search for the child, to destroy him." 2:14 Then Joseph got up, took the child and his mother by night, and went to Egypt, 2:15 and remained there until the death of Herod. This was to fulfill what had been spoken by the Lord through the prophet, "Out of Egypt I have called my son." 2:16 When Herod saw that he had been tricked by the wise men, he was infuriated, and he sent and killed all the children in and around Bethlehem who were two years old or under, according to the time that he had learned from the wise men. 2:17 Then was fulfilled what had been spoken through the prophet Jeremiah: 2:18 "A voice was heard in Ramah, wailing and loud lamentation, Rachel weeping for her children; she refused to be consoled, because they are no more." 2:19 When Herod died, an angel of the Lord suddenly appeared in a dream to Joseph in Egypt and said, 2:20 "Get up, take the child and his mother, and go to the land of Israel, for those who were seeking the child's life are dead." 2:21 Then Joseph got up, took the child and his mother, and went to the land of Israel. 2:22 But when he heard that Archelaus was ruling over Judea in place of his father Herod, he was afraid to go there. And after being warned in a dream, he went away to the district of Galilee. 2:23 There he made his home in a town called Nazareth, so that what had been spoken through the prophets might be fulfilled, "He will be called a Nazorean."

3:1 In those days John the Baptist appeared in the wilderness of Judea, proclaiming, 3:2 "Repent, for the kingdom of heaven has come near." 3:3 This is the one of whom the prophet Isaiah spoke when he said, "The voice of one crying out in the wilderness: 'Prepare the way of the Lord, make his paths straight.'" 3:4 Now John wore clothing of camel's hair with a leather belt around his waist, and his food was locusts and wild honey. 3:5 Then the people of Jerusalem and all Judea were going out to him, and all the region along the Jordan, 3:6 and they were baptized by him in the river Jordan, confessing their sins. 3:7 But when he saw many Pharisees and Sadducees coming for baptism, he said to them, "You brood of vipers! Who warned you to flee from the wrath to come? 3:8 Bear fruit worthy of repentance. 3:9 Do not presume to say to yourselves, 'We have Abraham as our ancestor'; for I tell you, God is able from these stones to raise up children to Abraham. 3:10 Even now the ax is lying at the root of the trees; every tree therefore that does not bear good fruit is cut down and thrown into the fire. 3:11 I baptize you with water for repentance, but one who is more powerful than I is coming after me; I am not worthy to carry his sandals. He will baptize you with the Holy Spirit and fire. 3:12 His winnowing fork is in his hand, and he will clear his threshing floor and will gather his wheat into the granary; but the chaff he will burn with unquenchable fire."

3:13 Then Jesus came from Galilee to John at the Jordan, to be baptized by him. 3:14 John would have prevented him, saying, "I need to be baptized by you, and do you come to me?" 3:15 But Jesus answered him, "Let it be so now; for it is proper for us in this way to fulfill all righteousness." Then he consented. 3:16 And when Jesus had been baptized, just as he came up from the water, suddenly the heavens were opened to him and he saw the Spirit of God descending like a dove and alighting on him. 3:17 And a voice from heaven said, "This is my Son, the Beloved, with whom I am well pleased."

4:1 Then Jesus was led up by the Spirit into the wilderness to be tempted by the devil. 4:2 He fasted forty days and forty nights, and afterwards he was famished. 4:3 The tempter came and said to him, "If you are the Son of God, command these stones to become loaves of bread." 4:4 But he answered, "It is written, 'One does not live by bread alone, but by every word that comes from the mouth of God.'" 4:5 Then the devil took him to the holy city and placed him on the pinnacle of the temple, 4:6 saying to him, "If you are the Son of God, throw yourself down; for it is written, 'He will command his angels concerning you,' and 'On their hands they will bear you up, so that you will not dash your foot against a stone.'" 4:7 Jesus said to him, "Again it is written, 'Do not put the Lord your God to the test.'" 4:8 Again, the devil took him to a very high mountain and showed him all the kingdoms of the world and their splendor; 4:9 and he said to him, "All these I will give you, if you will fall down and worship me." 4:10 Jesus said to him, "Away with you, Satan! for it is written, 'Worship the Lord your God, and serve only him.'" 4:11 Then the devil left him, and suddenly angels came and waited on him.

4:12 Now when Jesus heard that John had been arrested, he withdrew to Galilee. 4:13 He left Nazareth and made his home in Capernaum by the sea, in the territory of Zebulun and Naphtali, 4:14 so that what had been spoken through the prophet Isaiah might be fulfilled: 4:15 "Land of Zebulun, land of Naphtali, on the road by the sea, across the Jordan, Galilee of the Gentiles—4:16 the people who sat in darkness have seen a great light, and for those who sat in the region and shadow of death light has dawned." 4:17 From that time Jesus began to proclaim, "Repent, for the kingdom of heaven has come near." 4:18 As he walked by the Sea of Galilee, he saw two brothers, Simon, who is called Peter, and Andrew his brother, casting a net into the sea—for they were fishermen. 4:19 And he said to them, "Follow me, and I will make you fish for people." 4:20 Immediately they left their nets and followed him. 4:21 As he went from there, he saw two other brothers, James son of Zebedee and his brother John, in the boat with their father Zebedee, mending their nets, and he called them. 4:22 Immediately they left the boat and their father, and followed him. 4:23 Jesus went throughout Galilee, teaching in their synagogues and proclaiming the good news of the kingdom and curing every disease and every sickness among the people. 4:24 So his fame spread throughout all Syria, and they brought to him all the sick, those who were afflicted with various diseases and pains, demoniacs, epileptics, and paralytics, and he cured them. 4:25 And great crowds followed him from Galilee, the Decapolis, Jerusalem, Judea, and from beyond the Jordan.

IGNATIUS, *LETTER TO THE MAGNESIANS*, INTRODUCTION

Ignatius was bishop of Antioch. He died around 107 CE. Ignatius was accused of being a Christian (which was certainly true) and he was taken to Rome to be martyred. On his journey through Asia Minor (modern-day Turkey) he wrote a series of letters to various Christian communities. The following letter, the Letter to the Magnesians, *was written after the bishop and several priests of Magnesia stopped to see Ignatius when he was being taken to Rome. The visitors told Ignatius that the Magnesians were having trouble accepting a young bishop. The advice of Ignatius was to ignore the age of the bishop, and he went so far as stating that the bishop should take the place of God in the church. His letter is an important witness to the rise of the power of bishops in early Christianity.*

Chapter I

Having been informed of your godly love, so well-ordered, I rejoiced greatly, and determined to commune with you in the faith of Jesus Christ. For as one who has been thought worthy of the most honorable of all names, in those bonds which I bear about, I commend the Churches, in which I pray for a union both of the flesh and spirit of Jesus Christ, the constant source of our life, and of faith and love, to which nothing is to be preferred, but especially of Jesus and the Father, in whom, if we endure all the assaults of the prince of this world, and escape them, we shall enjoy God.

Chapter II

Since, then, I have had the privilege of seeing you, through Damas your most worthy bishop, and through your worthy presbyters Bassus and Apollonius, and through my fellow-servant the deacon Sotio, whose friendship may I ever enjoy, inasmuch as he is subject to the bishop as to the grace of God, and to the presbytery as to the law of Jesus Christ, [I now write to you].

Chapter III

Now it becomes you also not to treat your bishop too familiarly on account of his youth, but to yield him all reverence, having respect to the power of God the Father, as I have known even holy presbyters do, not judging rashly, from the manifest youthful appearance [of their bishop], but as being themselves prudent in God, submitting to him, or rather not to him, but to the Father of Jesus Christ, the bishop of us all. It is therefore fitting that you should, after no hypocritical fashion, obey [your bishop], in honor of Him who has willed us [so to do], since he that does not so deceives not [by such conduct] the bishop that is visible, but seeks to mock Him that is invisible. And all such conduct has reference not to man, but to God, who knows all secrets.

Chapter IV

It is fitting, then, not only to be called Christians, but to be so in reality: as some indeed give one the title of bishop, but do all things without him. Now such persons seem to me to not be possessed of a good conscience, seeing they are not steadfastly gathered together according to the commandment.

Chapter V

Seeing, then, all things have an end, these two things are simultaneously set before us—death and life; and every one shall go unto his own place. For as there are two kinds of coins, the one of God, the other of the world, and each of these has its special character stamped upon it, [so is it also here.] The unbelieving are of this world; but the believing have, in love, the character of God the Father by Jesus Christ, by whom, if we are not in readiness to die into His passion, His life is not in us.

Chapter VI

Since therefore I have, in the persons before mentioned, seen the whole multitude of you in faith and love, I exhort you to study to do all things with a divine harmony, while your bishop presides in the place of God, and your presbyters in the place of the assembly of the apostles, along with your deacons, who are most dear to me, and are entrusted with the ministry of Jesus Christ, who was with the Father before the beginning of time, and in the end was revealed. Do all then, imitating the same divine conduct, pay respect to one another, and let no one look upon his neighbor after the flesh, but continually love each other in Jesus Christ. Let nothing exist among you that may divide you; but be united with your bishop, and those that preside over you, as a type and evidence of your immortality.

Chapter VII

As therefore the Lord did nothing without the Father, being united to Him, neither by Himself nor by the apostles, so neither do anything without the bishop and presbyters. Neither endeavor that anything appear reasonable and proper to yourselves apart; but come together into the same place, let there be one prayer, one supplication, one mind, one hope, in love and in joy undefiled. There is one Jesus Christ, than whom nothing is more excellent. Therefore all run together as into one temple of God, as to one altar, as to one Jesus Christ, who came forth from one Father, and is with and has gone to one.

Chapter VIII

Be not deceived with strange doctrines, nor with old fables, which are unprofitable. For if we still live according to the Jewish law, we acknowledge that we have not received grace. For the divinest prophets lived according to Christ Jesus. On this account also they were persecuted, being inspired by His grace to fully convince the unbelieving that there is one God, who has manifested Himself by Jesus Christ His Son, who is His eternal Word, not proceeding forth from silence, and who in all things pleased Him that sent Him.

Chapter IX

If, therefore, those who were brought up in the ancient order of things have come to the possession of a new hope, no longer observing the Sabbath, but living in the observance of the Lord's Day, on which also our life has sprung up again by Him and by His death—whom some deny, by which mystery we have obtained faith, and therefore endure, that we may be found the disciples of Jesus Christ, our only Master—how shall we be able to live apart from Him, whose disciples the prophets themselves in the Spirit did wait for Him as their Teacher? And therefore He whom they rightly waited for, being come, raised them from the dead.

Chapter X

Let us not, therefore, be insensible to His kindness. For were He to reward us according to our works, we should cease to be. Therefore, having become His disciples, let us learn to live according to the principles of Christianity. For whosoever is called by any other name besides this, is not of God. Lay aside, therefore, the evil, the old, the sour leaven, and be changed into the new leaven, which is Jesus Christ. Be salted in Him, unless anyone among you should be corrupted, since by your savior you shall be convicted. It is absurd to profess Christ Jesus, and to Judaize. For Christianity did not embrace Judaism, but Judaism Christianity, that so every tongue which believes might be gathered together to God.

Chapter XI

These things [I address to you], my beloved, not that I know any of you to be in such a state; but, as less than any of you, I desire to guard you beforehand, that you do not fall upon the hooks of vain doctrine, but that you attain to full assurance in regard to the birth, and passion, and resurrection which took place in the time of the government of Pontius Pilate, being truly and certainly accomplished by Jesus Christ, who is our hope, from which may none of you ever be turned aside.

Chapter XII

May I enjoy you in all respects, if indeed I be worthy! For though I am bound, I am not worthy to be compared to any of you that are at liberty. I know that you are not puffed up, for you have Jesus Christ in yourselves. And all the more when I commend you, I know that you cherish modesty of spirit; as it is written, "The righteous man is his own accuser."

Chapter XIII

Study, therefore, to be established in the doctrines of the Lord and the apostles, that so all things, whatsoever you do, may prosper both in the flesh and spirit; in faith and love; in the Son, and in the Father, and in the Spirit; in the beginning and in the end; with your most admirable bishop, and the well-compacted spiritual crown of your presbytery, and the deacons who are according to God. Be subject to the bishop, and to one another, as Jesus Christ to the Father, according to the flesh, and the apostles to Christ, and to the Father, and to the Spirit; that so there may be a union both fleshly and spiritual.

Chapter XIV

Knowing as I do that you are full of God, I have but briefly exhorted you. Be mindful of me in your prayers, that I may attain to God; and of the Church which is in Syria, whence I am not worthy to derive my name: for I stand in need of your united prayer in God, and your love, that the Church which is in Syria may be deemed worthy of being refreshed by your Church.

Chapter XV

The Ephesians from Smyrna (whence I also write to you), who are here for the glory of God, as you also are, who have in all things refreshed me, salute you, along with Polycarp, the bishop of the Smyrnaeans. The rest of the Churches, in honor of Jesus Christ, also salute you. Goodbye, in the harmony of God, you who have obtained the inseparable Spirit, who is Jesus Christ.

Source: Schaff, Philip. "Letter to the Magnesians." *The Apostolic Fathers with Justin Martyr and Irenaeus.* Edinburgh: T&T Clark, n.d. Available online at http://www.ccel.org/ccel/schaff /anf01.

IRENAEUS, *AGAINST HERESIES*, BOOK 3, CHAPTERS 1–3

Irenaeus was bishop of Lyon, France (then it was called Gaul), in the late second century. He probably died around 202 CE, and it isn't known exactly when he wrote this document. While a bishop, Irenaeus wrote Against Heresies, *which was a catalogue of people and groups who did not fit into Irenaeus's idea of Christianity. It is a very important source of information on these groups from the second century. In the passage below Irenaeus discusses the transmission of information from the original apostles down through the church. He also discusses the proper lineage of true bishops from those original disciples, which is something referred to as apostolic succession. Irenaeus does this because there are people who show up claiming to be bishops, but they cannot trace their lineage back to Christ and the disciples.*

Chapter 1

1. We have learned from none others the plan of our salvation, than from those through whom the Gospel has come down to us, which they did at one

time proclaim in public, and, at a later period, by the will of God, handed down to us in the Scriptures, to be the ground and pillar of our faith. For it is unlawful to assert that they preached before they possessed "perfect knowledge," as some do even venture to say, boasting themselves as improvers of the apostles. For, after our Lord rose from the dead, [the apostles] were invested with power from on high when the Holy Spirit came down [upon them], were filled from all [His gifts], and had perfect knowledge: they departed to the ends of the earth, preaching the glad tidings of the good things [sent] from God to us, and proclaiming the peace of heaven to men, who indeed do all equally and individually possess the Gospel of God. Matthew also issued a written Gospel among the Hebrews in their own dialect, while Peter and Paul were preaching at Rome, and laying the foundations of the Church. After their departure, Mark, the disciple and interpreter of Peter, did also hand down to us in writing what had been preached by Peter. Luke also, the companion of Paul, recorded in a book the Gospel preached by him. Afterwards, John, the disciple of the Lord, who also had leaned upon His breast, did himself publish a Gospel during his residence at Ephesus in Asia.

2. These have all declared to us that there is one God, Creator of heaven and earth, announced by the law and the prophets; and one Christ the Son of God. If anyone does not agree to these truths, he despises the companions of the Lord; and more, he despises Christ Himself the Lord; yes, he despises the Father also, and stands self-condemned, resisting and opposing his own salvation, as is the case with all heretics.

Chapter 2

1. When, however, they are denied from the Scriptures, they turn round and accuse these same Scriptures, as if they were not correct, nor of authority, and [assert] that they are ambiguous, and that the truth cannot be extracted from them by those who are ignorant of tradition. For [they allege] that the truth was not delivered by means of written documents, but by word of mouth: wherefore also Paul declared, "But we speak wisdom among those that are perfect, but not the wisdom of this world" (1 Corinthians 2:6). And in truth this wisdom each one of them alleges to be the fiction of his own inventing, so that, according to their idea, the truth properly resides at one time in Valentinus, at another in Marcion, at another in Cerinthus, then afterwards in Basilides, or has even been indifferently in any other opponent, who could speak nothing pertaining to salvation. For every one of these men, being altogether of a perverse disposition, depraving the system of truth, is not ashamed to preach himself.

2. But, again, when we refer them to that tradition which originates from the apostles, [and] which is preserved by means of the succession of presbyters in the Churches, they object to tradition, saying that they themselves are wiser not merely than the presbyters, but even than the apostles, because they have discovered the unadulterated truth. For [they maintain] that the apostles intermingled the things of the law with the words of the Savior; and that not the apostles alone, but even the Lord Himself, spoke as at one time from the Demiurge, at another from the intermediate place, and yet again from the Pleroma, but that they themselves, indubitably, cleanly, and purely, have knowledge of the hidden mystery: this is, indeed, to blaspheme their Creator after a most impudent manner! It comes to this, therefore, that these men do now consent neither to Scripture nor to tradition.

3. Such are the adversaries with whom we have to deal, my very dear friend, endeavoring like slippery serpents to escape at all points. Wherefore they must be opposed at all points, if per-chance, by cutting off their retreat, we may succeed in turning them back to the truth. For, though it is not an easy thing for a soul under the influence of error to repent, yet, on the other hand, it is not altogether impossible to escape from error when the truth is brought alongside it.

Chapter 3

1. It is within the power of all, therefore, in every Church, who may wish to see the truth, to contemplate clearly the tradition of the apostles manifested throughout the whole world; and we are in a position to count up those who were by the apostles instituted bishops in the Churches, and [to demonstrate] the succession of these men to our own times; those who neither taught nor knew of anything like what these [heretics] rave about. For if the apostles had known hidden mysteries, which they were in the habit of imparting to "the perfect" apart and privately from the rest, they would have delivered them especially to those to whom they were also committing the Churches themselves. For they were desirous that these men should be very perfect and blameless in all things, whom also they were leaving behind as their successors, delivering up their own place of government to these men; which men, if they discharged their functions honestly, would be a great boon [to the Church], but if they should fall away, the direst calamity. 2. Since, however, it would be very tedious, in such a volume as this, to count up the successions of all the Churches, we do put to confusion all those who, in whatever manner, whether by an evil self-pleasing, by vainglory, or by blindness and perverse opinion, assemble in unauthorized meetings; [we do

this, I say,] by indicating that tradition derived from the apostles, of the very great, the very ancient, and universally known Church founded and organized at Rome by the two most glorious apostles, Peter and Paul; as also [by pointing out] the faith preached to men, which comes down to our time by means of the successions of the bishops. For it is a matter of necessity that every Church should agree with this Church, on account of its preeminent authority, that is, the faithful everywhere, inasmuch as the apostolical tradition has been preserved continuously by those [faithful men] who exist everywhere.

Source: Schaff, Philip. "Against Heresies." *The Apostolic Fathers with Justin Martyr and Irenaeus.* Edinburgh: T&T Clark, n.d. Available online at http://www.ccel.org/ccel/schaff/anf01.

TERTULLIAN, *ON BAPTISM*, CHAPTERS 18, 19, AND 20

Tertullian was a priest in the North African city of Carthage who lived around 200 CE; he wrote On Baptism, *probably between 196 and 212 CE. He was very influential because he was one of the earliest Christians to write in both Latin and Greek. Many of the early Christian writers were writing only in Greek, and writing in Latin helped to spread Christianity even further. Tertullian was a theologian whose writing benefitted from the fact that he was previously a lawyer. In the following sections he discusses the decisions one makes before being baptized, when to be baptized, and then what people should do just before the ceremony.*

Chapter 18: But they whose office it is, know that baptism is not to be administered rashly. "Give to everyone who begs you" [Luke 6:30] has a reference of its own, appertaining especially to almsgiving. On the contrary, this precept is rather to be looked at carefully: "Do not give the holy thing to the dogs, nor cast your pearls before swine" [Matt. 7:6]; and, "Do not lay hands easily on any; do not share other men's sins" [1 Tim. 5:22]. If Philip so "easily" baptized the chamberlain, let us reflect that a manifest and conspicuous evidence that the Lord deemed him worthy had been interposed. The Spirit had enjoined Philip to proceed to that road: the eunuch himself, too, was not found idle, nor as one who was suddenly seized with an eager desire to be baptized; but, after going up to the temple for prayer's sake, being intently engaged on the divine Scripture, was thus suitably discovered—to whom God had, unasked, sent an apostle, which one, again, the Spirit adjoined himself to the chamberlain's chariot. The Scripture which he was reading falls in opportunely with his faith: Philip, being requested, is taken to sit beside him; the Lord is pointed out; faith does not linger, water needs no waiting for, the work is completed, and the apostle snatched away. "But Paul too was, in fact, 'speedily' baptized": for Simon, his host, speedily recognized him to be "an appointed vessel of election." God's approval sends sure prophetic signs before it; every "petition" may both deceive and be deceived. And so, according to the circumstances and disposition, and even age, of each individual, the delay of baptism is preferable; principally, however, in the case of little children. For why is it necessary—if (baptism itself) is not so necessary—that the sponsors likewise should be thrust into danger? Who both themselves, by reason of mortality, may fail to fulfil their promises, and may be disappointed by the development of an evil disposition, in those for whom they stood? The Lord does indeed say, "Do not forbid them to come to me" [Matt. 29:14]. Let them "come," then, while they are growing up; let them "come" while they are learning, while they are learning whether to come; let them become Christians when they are able to know Christ. Why does the innocent period of life hasten to the "remission of sins"? More caution will be exercised in worldly matters, so that one who is not trusted with earthly substance is trusted with divine! Let them know how to "ask" for salvation, that you may seem (at least) to have given "to him that asks" [Luke 6:30].

For no less cause the unmarried must also be deferred—in whom the ground of temptation is prepared, alike in such as never were married by means of their maturity, and in the widowed by means of their freedom—until they either marry, or else be more fully strengthened for continence. If any understand the weighty import of baptism, they will fear its reception more than its delay: sound faith is secure of salvation.

Chapter 19: The Passover affords a more than usually solemn day for baptism; when the Lord's passion, in which we are baptized, was completed. Nor will it be incongruous to interpret figuratively the fact that, when the Lord was about to celebrate the last Passover, He said to the disciples who were sent to make preparation, "You will meet a man bearing water" [Mk. 24:13]. He points out the place for celebrating the Passover by the sign of water. After that, Pentecost is a most joyous space for conferring baptisms; where too the resurrection of the Lord was repeatedly proved among the disciples, and the hope of the advent of the Lord indirectly pointed to, in that, at that time, when He had been received back into the heavens, the angels told the apostles that "He would so come, as He had ascended into the heavens" [Acts 1:10–11], at Pentecost, of course. But, moreover, when Jeremiah says, "And I will gather them together from the extremities of the land in the feast-day," he signifies the day of the Passover and of Pentecost, which is properly a "feast-day" [Jer. 31:8]. However, every day is the Lord's; every hour, every time, is apt for baptism: if there is a difference in the solemnity, distinction there is none in the grace.

Chapter 20: They who are about to enter baptism ought to pray with repeated prayers, fasts, and bending of the knee, and vigils all the night through, and with the confession of all previous sins, that they may express the meaning even of the baptism of John: "They were baptized," said (the Scripture), "confessing their own sins" [Matt. 3:6]. To us it is matter for thankfulness if we do now publicly confess our iniquities or our wickedness: for we do at the same time both make satisfaction for our former sins, by mortification of our flesh and spirit, and lay beforehand the foundation of defenses against the temptations which will closely follow. "Watch and pray," said (the Lord), "unless you fall into temptation" [Matt. 26:41]. And the reason, I believe, why they were tempted was that they fell asleep, so that they deserted the Lord when apprehended, and he who continued to stand by Him, and used the sword, even denied Him three times. Besides the word had gone before, that "no one untempted should attain the celestial kingdoms" [possibly Luke 22:28–29]. For the Lord Himself was surrounded by temptations immediately after baptism, when in forty days He had kept fast. "Then," someone will say, "it becomes us, too, to fast after baptism." Well, and who forbids you, unless it be the necessity for joy, and the thanksgiving for salvation? But so far as I, with my poor powers, understand, the Lord figuratively responded to Israel the reproach they had cast on the Lord. For the people, after crossing the sea, and being carried about in the desert during forty years, although they were there nourished with divine supplies, nevertheless were more mindful of their belly and their gullet than of God. Thereupon the Lord, driven apart into desert places after baptism, showed, by maintaining a fast of forty days, that the man of God lives "not by bread alone," but "by the word of God" [Matt. 4:1–4]; and that temptations related to fullness or immoderation of appetite are shattered by abstinence.

Therefore, blessed ones, whom the grace of God awaits, when you ascend from that most sacred font of your new birth, and spread your hands for the first time in the house of your mother, together with your brethren, ask from the Father, ask from the Lord, that His own specialties of grace and distributions of gifts may be supplied you. "Ask," He said, "and you shall receive" [Matt. 7:7]. Well, you have asked, and have received; you have knocked, and it has been opened to you. Only, I pray that, when you are asking, you be mindful likewise of Tertullian the sinner.

Source: Schaff, Philip. "On Baptism." *Latin Christianity: Its Founder, Tertullian.* Edinburgh: T&T Clark, n.d. Available online at http://www.ccel.org/ccel/schaff/anf03.

CYPRIAN, *ON THE UNITY OF THE CHURCH*

Cyprian was the bishop of Carthage, North Africa, from about 248 to 258 CE. He wrote a treatise titled On the Unity of the Church, *probably written in 251 CE. There were a few persecutions during the time that Cyprian was in Carthage. The most serious was the persecution by Emperor Decius, called the Decian Persecution, which ran from 250 to 251 CE. During this time Cyprian, who was certainly a target for persecution, fled Carthage and ruled the city in hiding. Many Christians lapsed out of Christianity during this period but when the persecution ended, wanted back into the church. Cyprian was adamant that these lapsed followers perform some type of penance before they were to be allowed back. During this conflict Cyprian wrote* On the Unity of the Church. *It was written to bring people together after the persecution had finished. Cyprian remained bishop until 258 when he himself was killed for his faith.*

5. And this unity we ought firmly to hold and assert, especially those of us that are bishops who preside in the Church, that we may also prove the episcopate itself to be one and undivided. Let no one deceive the brotherhood by a falsehood: let no one corrupt the truth of the faith by dishonest evasiveness. The episcopate is one, each part of which is held by each one for the whole. The Church also is one, which is spread abroad far and wide into a multitude by an increase of fruitfulness. As there are many rays of the sun, but one light; and many branches of a tree, but one strength based in its tenacious root; and since from one spring flow many streams, although the multiplicity seems diffused in the liberality of an overflowing abundance, yet the unity is still preserved in the source. Separate a ray of the sun from its body of light, its unity does not allow a division of light; break a branch from a tree,—when broken, it will not be able to bud; cut off the stream from its fountain, and that which is cut off dries up. Thus also the Church, shone over with the light of the Lord, sheds forth her rays over the whole world, yet it is one light which is everywhere diffused, nor is the unity of the body separated. Her fruitful abundance spreads her branches over the whole world. She broadly expands her rivers, liberally flowing, yet her head is one, her source one; and she is one mother, plentiful in the results of fruitfulness: from her womb we are born, by her milk we are nourished, by her spirit we are animated.

6. The spouse of Christ cannot be adulterous; she is uncorrupted and pure. She knows one home; she guards with chaste modesty the sanctity of one couch. She keeps us for God. She appoints the sons whom she has born for the kingdom. Whoever is separated from the Church and is joined to an adulteress, is separated from the promises of the Church; nor can he who forsakes the

Church of Christ attain to the rewards of Christ. He is a stranger; he is profane; he is an enemy. He can no longer have God for his Father, who has not the Church for his mother. If anyone could escape who was outside the ark of Noah, then he also may escape who shall be outside of the Church. The Lord warns, saying, "He who is not with me is against me, and he who is not gathered with me is scattered." He who breaks the peace and the concord of Christ, does so in opposition to Christ; he who gathers elsewhere than in the Church, scatters the Church of Christ. The Lord says, "I and the Father are one;" and again it is written of the Father, and of the Son, and of the Holy Spirit, "And these three are one." And does anyone believe that this unity which thus comes from the divine strength and coheres in celestial sacraments, can be divided in the Church, and can be separated by the parting asunder of opposing wills? He who does not hold this unity does not hold God's law, does not hold the faith of the Father and the Son, does not hold life and salvation.

7. This sacrament of unity, this bond of a concord inseparably cohering, is set forth where in the Gospel the coat of the Lord Jesus Christ is not at all divided nor cut, but is received as an entire garment, and is possessed as an uninjured and undivided robe by those who cast lots concerning Christ's garment, who should rather put on Christ. Holy Scripture speaks, saying, "But of the coat, because it was not sewed, but woven from the top throughout, they said one to another, Let us not rend it, but cast lots whose it shall be." That coat bore with it a unity that came down from the top, that is, that came from heaven and the Father, which was not to be at all rent by the receiver and the possessor, but without separation we obtain a whole and substantial entireness. He cannot possess the garment of Christ who parts and divides the Church of Christ. On the other hand, again, when at Solomon's death his kingdom and people were divided, Abijah the prophet, meeting Jeroboam the king in the field, divided his garment into twelve sections, saying, "Take your ten pieces; for thus says the Lord, Behold, I will rend the kingdom out of the hand of Solomon, and I will give ten scepters to you; and two scepters shall be unto him for my servant David's sake, and for Jerusalem, the city which I have chosen to place my name there." As the twelve tribes of Israel were divided, the prophet Abijah rent his garment. But because Christ's people cannot be rent, His robe, woven and united throughout, is not divided by those who possess it; undivided, united, connected, it shows the coherent concord of our people who put on Christ. By the sacrament and sign of His garment, He has declared the unity of the Church.

8. Who, then, is so wicked and faithless, who is so insane with the madness of discord, that either he should believe that the unity of God can be divided,

or should dare to rend it—the garment of the Lord—the Church of Christ? He Himself in His Gospel warns us, and teaches, saying, "And there shall be one flock and one shepherd." And does anyone believe that in one place there can be either many shepherds or many flocks? The Apostle Paul, moreover, urging upon us this same unity, beseeches and exhorts, saying, "I beseech you, brethren, by the name of our Lord Jesus Christ, that you all speak the same thing, and that there be no schisms among you; but that you be joined together in the same mind and in the same judgment." And again, he says, "Forbearing one another in love, endeavoring to keep the unity of the Spirit in the bond of peace." Do you think that you can stand and live if you withdraw from the Church, building for yourself other homes and a different dwelling, when it is said to Rahab, in whom was prefigured the Church, "Your father, and your mother, and your brethren, and all the house of your father, you shall gather into your house; and it shall come to pass, whosoever shall go abroad beyond the door of your house, his blood shall be upon his own head"? Also, the sacrament of the Passover contains nothing else in the law of the Exodus than that the lamb which is slain in the figure of Christ should be eaten in one house. God speaks, saying, "In one house you shall eat it; you shall not send its flesh abroad from the house." The flesh of Christ, and the holy of the Lord, cannot be sent abroad, nor is there any other home to believers but the one Church. This home, this household of unanimity, the Holy Spirit designates and points out in the Psalms, saying, "God, who makes men to dwell with one mind in a house." In the house of God, in the Church of Christ, men dwell with one mind, and continue in concord and simplicity.

9. Therefore also the Holy Spirit came as a dove, a simple and joyous creature, not bitter with gall, not cruel in its bite, not violent with the rending of its claws, loving human dwellings, knowing the association of one home; when they have young, bringing forth their young together; when they fly abroad, remaining in their flights by the side of one another, spending their life in mutual intercourse, acknowledging the concord of peace with the kiss of the beak, in all things fulfilling the law of unanimity. This is the simplicity that ought to be known in the Church, this is the charity that ought to be attained, that so the love of the brotherhood may imitate the doves, that their gentleness and meekness may be like the lambs and sheep. What does the fierceness of wolves do in the Christian breast? What the savageness of dogs, and the deadly venom of serpents, and the sanguinary cruelty of wild beasts? We are to be congratulated when such as these are separated from the Church, lest they should lay waste the doves and sheep of Christ with their cruel and envenomed contagion. Bitterness cannot consist and be associated with

sweetness, darkness with light, rain with clearness, battle with peace, barrenness with fertility, drought with springs, storm with tranquility. Let none think that the good can depart from the Church. The wind does not carry away the wheat, nor does the hurricane uproot the tree that is based on a solid root. The light straws are tossed about by the tempest, the feeble trees are overthrown by the onset of the whirlwind. The Apostle John execrates and severely assails these, when he says, "They went forth from us, but they were not of us; for if they had been of us, surely they would have continued with us."

Source: Schaff, Philip. "On the Unity of the Church." *Fathers of the Third Century: Hippolytus, Cyprian, Caius, Novatian, Appendix.* Edinburgh: T&T Clark, n.d. Available online at http://www.ccel.org/ccel/schaff/anf05.

EUSEBIUS, *ECCLESIASTICAL HISTORY*, BOOK 8, CHAPTERS 2–6 (ON THE PERSECUTION OF EMPEROR DIOCLETIAN)

Eusebius (died around 340) was the bishop of Caesarea, a very important city located in the eastern part of the Roman Empire. Eusebius is considered to be the first church historian. He wrote Ecclesiastical History, *a very influential book not only because it contains the first history of early Christianity, but he is also one of the first people to cite his sources. It was written between 300 and 320 CE. The passage below describes the persecution of the Christians that began in the early 300s CE by Emperor Diocletian. Eusebius is an important source for this since he lived through this persecution. He spends quite a bit of time in this passage talking about the various tortures that Christians were put through by the Roman authorities.*

Chapter 2

1. All these things were fulfilled in us, when we saw with our own eyes the houses of prayer thrown down to the very foundations, and the Divine and Sacred Scriptures committed to the flames in the midst of the market-places, and the shepherds of the churches basely hidden here and there, and some of them captured ignominiously, and mocked by their enemies. When also, according to another prophetic word, "Contempt was poured out upon rulers, and he caused them to wander in an untrodden and pathless way."

2. But it is not our place to describe the sad misfortunes which finally came upon them, as we do not think it proper, moreover, to record their divisions and unnatural conduct to each other before the persecution. Wherefore we

have decided to relate nothing concerning them except the things in which we can vindicate the Divine judgment.

3. Hence we shall not mention those who were shaken by the persecution, nor those who in everything pertaining to salvation were shipwrecked, and by their own will were sunk in the depths of the flood. But we shall introduce into this history in general only those events which may be useful first to ourselves and afterwards to posterity. Let us therefore proceed to describe briefly the sacred conflicts of the witnesses of the Divine Word.

4. It was in the nineteenth year of the reign of Diocletian, in the month Dystrus, called March by the Romans, when the feast of the Savior's passion was near at hand, that royal edicts were published everywhere, commanding that the churches be leveled to the ground and the Scriptures be destroyed by fire, and ordering that those who held places of honor be degraded, and that the household servants, if they persisted in the profession of Christianity, be deprived of freedom.

5. Such was the first edict against us. But not long after, other decrees were issued, commanding that all the rulers of the churches in every place be first thrown into prison, and afterwards by every artifice be compelled to sacrifice.

Chapter 3

1. Then truly a great many rulers of the churches eagerly endured terrible sufferings, and furnished examples of noble conflicts. But a multitude of others, numbed in spirit by fear, were easily weakened at the first onset. Of the rest each one endured different forms of torture. The body of one was scourged with rods. Another was punished with insupportable rackings and scrapings, in which some suffered a miserable death.

2. Others passed through different conflicts. Thus one, while those around pressed him on by force and dragged him to the abominable and impure sacrifices, was dismissed as if he had sacrificed, though he had not. Another, though he had not approached at all, nor touched any polluted thing, when others said that he had sacrificed, went away, bearing the accusation in silence. 3. Another being taken up half dead, was cast aside as if already dead, and again a certain one lying upon the ground was dragged a long distance by his feet and counted among those who had sacrificed. One cried out and with a loud voice testified his rejection of the sacrifice; another shouted that he was

a Christian, being resplendent in the confession of the saving Name. Another protested that he had not sacrificed and never would.

4. But they were struck in the mouth and silenced by a large band of soldiers who were drawn up for this purpose; and they were smitten on the face and cheeks and driven away by force; so important did the enemies of piety regard it, by any means, to seem to have accomplished their purpose. But these things did not avail them against the holy martyrs; for an accurate description of whom, what word of ours could suffice?

Chapter 4

1. For we might tell of many who showed admirable zeal for the religion of the God of the universe, not only from the beginning of the general persecution, but long before that time, while yet peace prevailed.

2. For though he who had received power was seemingly aroused now as from a deep sleep, yet from the time after Decius and Valerian, he had been plotting secretly and without notice against the churches. He did not wage war against all of us at once, but made trial at first only of those in the army. For he supposed that the others could be taken easily if he should first attack and subdue these. Thereupon many of the soldiers were seen most cheerfully embracing private life, so that they might not deny their piety toward the Creator of the universe.

3. For when the commander, whoever he was, began to persecute the soldiers, separating into tribes and purging those who were enrolled in the army, giving them the choice either by obeying to receive the honor which belonged to them, or on the other hand to be deprived of it if they disobeyed the command, a great many soldiers of Christ's kingdom, without hesitation, instantly preferred the confession of him to the seeming glory and prosperity which they were enjoying.

4. And one and another of them occasionally received in exchange, for their pious constancy, not only the loss of position, but death. But as yet the instigator of this plot proceeded with moderation, and ventured so far as blood only in some instances; for the multitude of believers, as it is likely, made him afraid, and deterred him from waging war at once against all.

5. But when he made the attack more boldly, it is impossible to relate how many and what sort of martyrs of God could be seen, among the inhabitants of all the cities and countries.

Chapter 5

1. Immediately on the publication of the decree against the churches in Nicomedia, a certain man, not obscure but very highly honored with distinguished temporal dignities, moved with zeal toward God, and incited with ardent faith, seized the edict as it was posted openly and publicly, and tore it to pieces as a profane and impious thing; and this was done while two of the sovereigns were in the same city,—the oldest of all, and the one who held the fourth place in the government after him.

2. But this man, first in that place, after distinguishing himself in such a manner suffered those things which were likely to follow such daring, and kept his spirit cheerful and undisturbed till death.

Chapter 6

1. This period produced divine and illustrious martyrs, above all whose praises have ever been sung and who have been celebrated for courage, whether among Greeks or barbarians, in the person of Dorotheus and the servants that were with him in the palace. Although they received the highest honors from their masters, and were treated by them as their own children, they esteemed reproaches and trials for religion, and the many forms of death that were invented against them, as, in truth, greater riches than the glory and luxury of this life.

2. We will describe the manner in which one of them ended his life, and leave our readers to infer from his case the sufferings of the others. A certain man was brought forward in the above-mentioned city, before the rulers of whom we have spoken. He was then commanded to sacrifice, but as he refused, he was ordered to be stripped and raised on high and beaten with rods over his entire body, until, being conquered, he should, even against his will, do what was commanded.

3. But as he was unmoved by these sufferings, and his bones were already appearing, they mixed vinegar with salt and poured it upon the mangled parts of his body. As he scorned these agonies, a gridiron and fire were brought forward. And the remnants of his body, like flesh intended for eating, were placed on the fire, not at once, lest he should expire instantly, but a little at a time. And those who placed him on the pyre were not permitted to desist until, after such sufferings, he should assent to the things commanded.

4. But he held his purpose firmly, and victoriously gave up his life while the tortures were still going on. Such was the martyrdom of one of the servants of the palace, who was indeed well worthy of his name, for he was called Peter.

5. The martyrdoms of the rest, though they were not inferior to his, we will pass by for the sake of brevity, recording only that Dorotheus and Gorgonius, with many others of the royal household, after varied sufferings, ended their lives by strangling, and bore away the trophies of God-given victory.

6. At this time Anthimus, who then presided over the church in Nicomedia, was beheaded for his testimony to Christ. A great multitude of martyrs were added to him, a conflagration having broken out in those very days in the palace at Nicomedia, I know not how, which through a false suspicion was laid to our people. Entire families of the pious in that place were put to death in masses at the royal command, some by the sword, and others by fire. It is reported that with a certain divine and indescribable eagerness men and women rushed into the fire. And the executioners bound a large number of others and put them on boats and threw them into the depths of the sea.

7. And those who had been esteemed their masters considered it necessary to dig up the bodies of the imperial servants, who had been committed to the earth with suitable burial and cast them into the sea, lest any, as they thought, regarding them as gods, might worship them lying in their sepulchers.

8. Such things occurred in Nicomedia at the beginning of the persecution. But not long after, as persons in the country called Melitene, and others throughout Syria, attempted to usurp the government, a royal edict directed that the rulers of the churches everywhere should be thrown into prison and bonds.

9. What was to be seen after this exceeds all description. A vast multitude were imprisoned in every place; and the prisons everywhere, which had long before been prepared for murderers and robbers of graves, were filled with bishops, presbyters and deacons, readers and exorcists, so that room was no longer left in them for those condemned for crimes.

10. And as other decrees followed the first, directing that those in prison if they would sacrifice should be permitted to depart in freedom, but that those who refused should be harassed with many tortures, how could anyone, again, number the multitude of martyrs in every province, and especially of

those in Africa, and Mauritania, and Thebais, and Egypt? From this last country many went into other cities and provinces, and became illustrious through martyrdom.

Source: Schaff, Philip. "Ecclesiastical History." *Eusebius Pamphilius: Church History, Life of Constantine, Oration in Praise of Constantine*. Edinburgh: T&T Clark, n.d. Available online at http://www.ccel.org/ccel/schaff/npnf201.

ORIGEN, *AGAINST CELCUS*, BOOK 1, CHAPTERS I–III

Origen was one of the most prolific early Christian writers. He lived between 185 and 251 CE. His father was a Christian who was killed for his belief in Christianity. Origen wrote a book titled Against Celcus, *but we don't know the exact date. Celcus was a philosopher who lived sometime in the 100s CE. Celcus wrote a book in which he attacked Christianity from a number of different angles. The book of Celcus did not seem to affect Christians too much until Origen found out about it decades after it was written. Origen then went through the book of Celcus and refuted it, point by point. The following passage from Origen highlights some of the main complaints that were given against Christians and Christianity.*

The first point which Celcus brings forward, in his desire to throw discredit upon Christianity, is, that the Christians entered into secret associations with each other contrary to law, saying, that "of associations some are public, and that these are in accordance with the laws; others, again, secret, and maintained in violation of the laws." And his wish is to bring into disrepute what are termed the "love-feasts" of the Christians, as if they had their origin in the common danger, and were more binding than any oaths. Since, then, he babbles about the public law, alleging that the associations of the Christians are in violation of it, we have to reply, that if a man were placed among Scythians, whose laws were unholy, and having no opportunity of escape, were compelled to live among them, such an one would with good reason, for the sake of the law of truth, which the Scythians would regard as wickedness, enter into associations contrary to their laws, with those like-minded with himself; so, if truth is to decide, the laws of the heathens which relate to images, and an atheistical polytheism, are "Scythian" laws, or more impious even than these, if there be any such. It is not irrational, then, to form associations in opposition to existing laws, if done for the sake of the truth. For as those persons would do well who should enter into a secret association in order to put to death a tyrant who had seized upon the liberties of a state, so Christians also, when tyrannized over by him who is called the devil, and by falsehood, form leagues contrary to the laws of the devil, against his power, and for the safety of those others whom they may succeed in persuading to revolt from a government which is, as it were, "Scythian," and despotic.

Chapter II.

Celcus next proceeds to say, that the system of doctrine, viz., Judaism, upon which Christianity depends, was barbarous in its origin. And with an appearance of fairness, he does not reproach Christianity because of its origin among barbarians, but gives the latter credit for their ability in discovering (such) doctrines. To this, however, he adds the statement, that the Greeks are more skillful than any others in judging, establishing, and reducing to practice the discoveries of barbarous nations. Now this is our answer to his allegations, and our defense of the truths contained in Christianity, that if any one were to come from the study of Grecian opinions and usages to the Gospel, he would not only decide that its doctrines were true, but would by practice establish their truth, and supply whatever seemed wanting, from a Grecian point of view, to their demonstration, and thus confirm the truth of Christianity. We have to say, moreover, that the Gospel has a demonstration of its own, more divine than any established by Grecian dialectics. And this diviner method is called by the apostle the "manifestation of the Spirit and of power": of "the Spirit," on account of the prophecies, which are sufficient to produce faith in anyone who reads them, especially in those things which relate to Christ; and of "power," because of the signs and wonders which we must believe to have been performed, both on many other grounds, and on this, that traces of them are still preserved among those who regulate their lives by the precepts of the Gospel.

Chapter III

After this, Celcus proceeding to speak of the Christians teaching and practicing their favorite doctrines in secret, and saying that they do this to some purpose, seeing they escape the penalty of death which is imminent, he compares their dangers with those which were encountered by such men as Socrates for the sake of philosophy; and here he might have mentioned Pythagoras as well, and other philosophers. But our answer to this is, that in the case of Socrates the Athenians immediately afterwards repented; and no feeling of bitterness remained in their minds regarding him, as also happened in the history of Pythagoras. The followers of the latter, indeed, for a considerable time established their schools in that part of Italy called Magna Graecia; but in the case of the Christians, the Roman Senate, and the princes of the time, and the soldiery, and the people, and the relatives of those who had become converts to the faith, made war upon their doctrine, and would have prevented (its progress), overcoming it by a confederacy of so powerful a nature, had it not, by the help of God, escaped the danger, and risen above it, so as (finally) to defeat the whole world in its conspiracy against it.

Source: Schaff, Philip. "Against Celcus." *Fathers of the Third Century: Tertullian, Part Fourth; Minucius Felix; Commodian; Origen, Parts First and Second.* Edinburgh: T&T Clark, n.d. Available online at http://www.ccel.org/ccel/schaff/anf04.

AMBROSE, *LETTER 17* TO EMPEROR VALENTINIAN II

Ambrose was the bishop of Milan, Italy, from 374 to 397 CE. Previous to this he was the civilian Roman governor of several provinces. Ambrose was a Catholic bishop and part of his duties (he felt) was to guide the emperor on religious matters. Before the Christians were allowed to openly practice their religion, the Roman Senate had a statue in the Senate House called Victory. When the emperors became Christian there was quite a bit of discussion on whether to allow the statue to remain in the Senate House. A pagan senator named Symmachus wanted the altar and statue to be set up once again. Symmachus wrote a letter to Emperor Valentinian II requesting this, probably in 384 CE. Bishop Ambrose found out about this and then sent his own letter to the emperor. The text below is the entire letter sent to Valentinian II telling the emperor that he would not allow the statue back into the Senate.

Ambrose, Bishop, to the most blessed Prince and most Christian Emperor Valentinian.

1. As all men who live under the Roman sway engage in military service under you, the Emperors and Princes of the world, so too do you yourselves owe service to Almighty God and our holy faith. For salvation is not sure unless everyone worship in truth the true God, that is the God of the Christians, under Whose sway are all things; for He alone is the true God, Who is to be worshipped from the bottom of the heart; for "the gods of the heathen," as Scripture says, "are devils."

2. Now everyone is a soldier of this true God, and he who receives and worships Him in his inmost spirit, does not bring to His service dishonesty, or pretense, but earnest faith and devotion. And if, in fine, he does not attain to this, at least he ought not to give any countenance to the worship of idols and to profane ceremonies. For no one deceives God, to whom all things, even the hidden things of the heart, are manifest.

3. Since, then, most Christian Emperor, there is due from you to the true God both faith and zeal, care and devotion for the faith, I wonder how the

hope has risen up to some, that you would feel it a duty to restore by your command altars to the gods of the heathen, and furnish the funds requisite for profane sacrifices; for whatsoever has long been claimed by either the imperial or the city treasury you will seem to give rather from your own funds, than to be restoring what is theirs.

4. And they are complaining of their losses, who never spared our blood, who destroyed the very buildings of the churches. And they petition you to grant them privileges, who by the last Julian law denied us the common right of speaking and teaching, and those privileges whereby Christians also have often been deceived; for by those privileges they endeavored to ensnare some, partly through inadvertence, partly in order to escape the burden of public requirements; and, because all are not found to be brave, even under Christian princes, many have lapsed.

5. Had these things not been abolished I could prove that they ought to be done away by your authority; but since they have been forbidden and prohibited by many princes throughout nearly the whole world, and were abolished at Rome by Gratian of august memory, the brother of your Clemency, in consideration of the true faith, and rendered void by a rescript; do not, I pray you, either pluck up what has been established in accordance with the faith, nor rescind your brother's precepts. In civil matters if he established anything, no one thinks that it ought to be treated lightly, while a precept about religion is trodden under foot.

6. Let no one take advantage of your youth; if he be a heathen who demands this, it is not right that he should bind your mind with the bonds of his own superstition; but by his zeal he ought to teach and admonish you how to be zealous for the true faith, since he defends vain things with all the passion of truth. I myself advise you to defer to the merits of illustrious men, but undoubtedly God must be preferred to all.

7. If we have to consult concerning military affairs, the opinion of a man experienced in warfare should be waited for, and his counsel be followed; when the question concerns religion, think upon God. No one is injured because God is set before him. He keeps his own opinion. You do not compel a man against his will to worship what he dislikes. Let the same liberty be given to you, O Emperor, and let everyone bear it with patience, if he cannot extort from the Emperor what he would take it ill if the Emperor desired to extort from him. A shuffling spirit is displeasing to the heathen themselves, for everyone ought freely to defend and maintain the faith and purpose of his own mind.

8. But if any, Christians in name, think that any such decree should be made, let not bare words mislead your mind, let not empty words deceive you. Whoever advises this, and whoever decrees it, sacrifices. But that one should sacrifice is more tolerable than that all should fall. Here the whole Senate of Christians is in danger.

9. If today any heathen Emperor should build an altar, which God forbid, to idols, and should compel Christians to come together to that place, in order to be among those who were sacrificing, so that the smoke and ashes from the altar, the sparks from the sacrilege, the smoke from the burning might choke the breath and throats of the faithful; and should give judgment in that court where members were compelled to vote after swearing at the altar of an idol (for they explain that an altar is so placed for this purpose, that every assembly should deliberate under its sanction, as they suppose, though the Senate is now made up with a majority of Christians), a Christian who was compelled with a choice such as this to come to the Senate, would consider it to be per-secution, which often happens, for they are compelled to come together even by violence. Are these Christians, when you are Emperor, compelled to swear at a heathen altar? What is an oath, but a confession of the divine power of Him Whom you invoke as watcher over your good faith? When you are Em-peror, this is sought and demanded, that you should command an altar to be built, and the cost of profane sacrifices to be granted.

10. But this cannot be decreed without sacrilege, wherefore I implore you not to decree or order it, nor to subscribe to any decrees of that sort. I, as a priest of Christ, call upon your faith, all of us bishops would have joined in calling upon you, were not the report so sudden and incredible, that any such thing had been either suggested in your council, or petitioned for by the Sen-ate. But far be it from the Senate to have petitioned this, a few heathen are making use of the common name. For, nearly two years ago, when the same attempt was being made, holy Damasus, Bishop of the Roman Church, elected by the judgment of God, sent to me a memorial, which the Christian senators in great numbers put forth, protesting that they had given no such authority, that they did not agree with such requests of the heathen, nor give consent to them, and they declared publicly and privately that they would not come to the Senate, if any such thing were decreed. Is it agreeable to the dignity of your, that is Christian, times, that Christian senators should be deprived of their dignity, in order that effect should be given to the profane will of the heathen? This memorial I sent to your Clemency's brother, and from it was plain that the Senate had made no order about the expenses of superstition.

11. But perhaps it may be said, why were they not before present in the Senate when those petitions were made? By not being present they sufficiently say what they wish, they said enough in what they said to the Emperor. And do we wonder if those persons deprive private persons at Rome of the liberty of resisting, who are unwilling that you should be free not to command what you do not approve, or to maintain your own opinion?

12. And so, remembering the legation lately entrusted to me, I call again upon your faith. I call upon your own feelings not to determine to answer according to this petition of the heathen, nor to attach to an answer of such a sort the sacrilege of your subscription. Refer to the father of your Piety, the Emperor Theodosius, whom you have been wont to consult in almost all matters of greater importance. Nothing is greater than religion, nothing more exalted than faith.

13. If it were a civil cause the right of reply would be reserved for the opposing party; it is a religious cause, and I the bishop make a claim. Let a copy of the memorial which has been sent be given me, that I may answer more fully, and then let your Clemency's father be consulted on the whole subject, and vouchsafe an answer. Certainly if anything else is decreed, we bishops cannot contentedly suffer it and take no notice; you indeed may come to the church, but will find either no priest there, or one who will resist you.

14. What will you answer a priest who says to you, "The church does not seek your gifts, because you have adorned the heathen temples with gifts. The Altar of Christ rejects your gifts, because you have made an altar for idols, for the voice is yours, the hand is yours, the subscription is yours, the deed is yours. The Lord Jesus refuses and rejects your service, because you have served idols, for He said to you: 'Ye cannot serve two masters.' The Virgins consecrated to God have no privileges from you, and do the Vestal Virgins claim them? Why do you ask for the priests of God, to whom you have preferred the profane petitions of the heathen? We cannot take up a share of the errors of others."

15. What will you answer to these words? That you who have fallen are but a boy? Every age is perfect in Christ, every age is full of God. No childhood is allowed in faith, for even children have confessed Christ against their persecutors with fearless mouth.

16. What will you answer your brother? Will he not say to you, "I did not feel that I was overcome, because I left you as Emperor; I did not grieve at dying,

because I had you as my heir; I did not mourn at leaving my imperial command, because I believed that my commands, especially those concerning divine religion, would endure through all ages. I had set up these memorials of piety and virtue, I offered up these spoils gained from the world, these trophies of victory over the devil, these I offered up as gained from the enemy of all, and in them is eternal victory. What more could my enemy take away from me? You have abrogated my decrees, which so far he who took up arms against me did not do. Now do I receive a more terrible wound in that my decrees are condemned by my brother. My better part is endangered by you, that was but the death of my body, this of my reputation. Now is my power annulled, and what is harder, annulled by my own family, and that is annulled, which even my enemies spoke well of in me. If you consented of your own free will, you have condemned the faith which was mine; if you yielded unwillingly, you have betrayed your own. So, too, which is more serious, I am in danger in your person."

17. What will you answer your father also, who with greater grief will address you, saying, "You judged very ill of me, my son, when you supposed that I could have connived at the heathen. No one ever told me that there was an altar in the Roman Senate House, I never believed such wickedness as that the heathen sacrificed in the common assembly of Christians and heathen, that is to say that the Gentiles should insult the Christians who were present, and that Christians should be compelled against their will to be present at the sacrifices. Many and various crimes were committed while I was Emperor. I punished such as were detected; if anyone then escaped notice, ought one to say that I approved of that of which no one informed me? You have judged very ill of me, if a foreign superstition and not my own faith preserved the empire."

18. Wherefore, O Emperor, since you see that if you decree anything of that kind, injury will be done, first to God, and then to your father and brother, I implore you to do that which you know will be profitable to your salvation before God.

Source: Schaff, Philip. "Letter 17." *Ambrose: Selected Works and Letters*. Edinburgh: T&T Clark, n.d. Available online at http://www.ccel.org/ccel/schaff/npnf210.

AUGUSTINE, *CONFESSIONS*, BOOK 1:9:14–1:11:18

Augustine, who was the bishop of Hippo in North Africa, is one of the most influential early church fathers. He lived from 354 to 430 CE. He was a Manichaean (a form of Christianity) before he converted to Catholicism. He was a prolific writer, both before and after his conversion. One of his most famous books is his Confessions, *written between 397 and 400 CE. The* Confessions *is an autobiography and a confession to God about his life and the choices he made. The following passage details the problems he had as a child in school where it was typical of teachers to beat their students if they did not learn. Augustine also wonders why he wasn't baptized when he was little and he thought he was on the verge of death.*

Chapter 9

14. O my God! What miseries and mockeries did I then experience, when obedience to my teachers was set before me as proper to my boyhood, that I might flourish in this world, and distinguish myself in the science of speech, which should get me honor among men, and deceitful riches! After that I was put to school to get learning, of which I (worthless as I was) knew not what use there was; and yet, if slow to learn, I was flogged! For this was deemed praiseworthy by our forefathers; and many before us, passing the same course, had appointed beforehand for us these troublesome ways by which we were compelled to pass, multiplying labor and sorrow upon the sons of Adam. But we found, O Lord, men praying to You, and we learned from them to conceive of You, according to our ability, to be some Great One, who was able (though not visible to our senses) to hear and help us. For as a boy I began to pray to You, my "help" and my "refuge," and in invoking You broke the bands of my tongue, and entreated You though little, with no little earnestness, that I might not be beaten at school. And when You did not hear me, giving me not over to folly thereby, my elders, yes, and my own parents too, who wished me no ill, laughed at my stripes, my then great and grievous ill.

15. Is there any one, Lord, with so high a spirit, cleaving to You with so strong an affection—for even a kind of obtuseness may do that much—but is there, I say, anyone who, by cleaving devoutly to You, is endowed with so great a courage that he can esteem lightly those racks and hooks, and varied tortures of the same sort, against which, throughout the whole world, men supplicate You with great fear, deriding those who most bitterly fear them, just as our parents derided the torments with which our masters punished us when we were boys? For we were no less afraid of our pains, nor did we pray less to You to avoid them; and yet we sinned, in writing, or reading, or reflecting upon our lessons less than was required of us. For we wanted not, O Lord, memory or capacity, of which, by Your will, we possessed enough for our age,—but we delighted only in play; and we were punished for this by those who were doing the same things themselves. But the idleness of our elders they call

business, while boys who do the like are punished by those same elders, and yet neither boys nor men find any pity. For will any one of good sense approve of my being whipped because, as a boy, I played ball, and so was hindered from learning quickly those lessons by means of which, as a man, I should play more unbecomingly? And did he by whom I was beaten do other than this, who, when he was overcome in any little controversy with a co-tutor, was more tormented by anger and envy than I when beaten by a playfellow in a match at ball?

Chapter 10

16. And yet I erred, O Lord God, the Creator and Disposer of all things in Nature,—but of sin the Disposer only,—I erred, O Lord my God, in doing contrary to the wishes of my parents and of those masters; for this learning which they (no matter for what motive) wished me to acquire, I might have put to good account afterwards. For I disobeyed them not because I had chosen a better way, but from a fondness for play, loving the honor of victory in the matches, and to have my ears tickled with lying fables, in order that they might itch the more furiously—the same curiosity beaming more and more in my eyes for the shows and sports of my elders. Yet those who give these entertainments are held in such high repute, that almost all desire the same for their children, whom they are still willing should be beaten, if so be these same games keep them from the studies by which they desire them to arrive at being the givers of them. Look down upon these things, O Lord, with compassion, and deliver us who now call upon You; deliver those also who do not call upon You, that they may call upon You, and that You may deliver them.

Chapter 11

17. Even as a boy I had heard of eternal life promised to us through the humility of the Lord our God condescending to our pride, and I was signed with the sign of the cross, and was seasoned with His salt even from the womb of my mother, who greatly trusted in You. You saw, O Lord, how at one time, while yet a boy, being suddenly seized with pains in the stomach, and being at the point of death—You saw, O my God, for even then You were my keeper, with what emotion of mind and with what faith I solicited from the piety of my mother, and of Your Church, the mother of us all, the baptism of Your Christ, my Lord and my God. On which, the mother of my flesh being much troubled,—since she, with a heart pure in Your faith, travailed in birth more lovingly for my eternal salvation,—would, had I not quickly recovered,

have without delay provided for my initiation and washing by Your life-giving sacraments, confessing You, O Lord Jesus, for the remission of sins. So my cleansing was deferred, as if I must needs, should I live, be further polluted; because, indeed, the guilt contracted by sin would, after baptism, be greater and more perilous. Thus I at that time believed with my mother and the whole house, except my father; yet he did not overcome the influence of my mother's piety in me so as to prevent my believing in Christ, as he had not yet believed in Him. For she was desirous that You, O my God, should be my Father rather than he; and in this You did aid her to overcome her husband, to whom, though the better of the two, she yielded obedience, because in this she yielded obedience to You, who so commands.

18. I beseech You, my God, I would gladly know, if it be Your will, to what end my baptism was then deferred? Was it for my good that the reins were slackened, as it were, upon me for me to sin? Or were they not slackened? If not, where does it come that it is still dinned into our ears on all sides, "Let him alone, let him act as he likes, for he is not yet baptized"? But as regards bodily health, no one exclaims, "Let him be more seriously wounded, for he is not yet cured!" How much better, then, had it been for me to have been cured at once; and then, by my own and my friends' diligence, my soul's restored health had been kept safe in Your keeping, who gave it! Better, in truth. But how numerous and great waves of temptation appeared to hang over me after my childhood! These were foreseen by my mother; and she preferred that the unformed clay should be exposed to them rather than the image itself.

Source: Schaff, Philip. "Confessions." *The Confessions and Letters of St. Augustine, with a Sketch of His Life and Work*. Edinburgh: T&T Clark, n.d. Available online at http://www.ccel.org /ccel/schaff/npnf101.

EUSEBIUS OF CAESAREA, *LIFE OF CONSTANTINE,* BOOK 1, CHAPTERS 1–7

As mentioned in the previous primary text written by Eusebius of Caesarea, Eusebius was the bishop of Caesarea. He was introduced to Emperor Constantine I early on in Constantine's imperial career. Constantine I ruled the Roman Empire from 306 to 337 CE. Constantine is famous in early Christianity because he was the first Roman emperor to be a Christian. Constantine allowed, for the very first time, Christians to practice their religion without fear of persecution. Eusebius lived through this persecution and, since he was a bishop, benefitted from the fact that Constantine made it illegal to persecute Christians. Eusebius's Life of Constantine *was a tribute to the Emperor and was written between 335 and 339 CE.*

Chapter 1: Already have all mankind united in celebrating with joyous festivities the completion of the second and third decennial period of this great emperor's reign; already have we ourselves received him as a triumphant conqueror in the assembly of God's ministers, and greeted him with the due reward of praise on the twentieth anniversary of his reign: and still more recently we have woven, as it were, garlands of words, wherewith we encircled his sacred head in his own palace on his thirtieth anniversary. But now, while I desire to give utterance to some of the customary sentiments, I stand perplexed and doubtful which way to turn, being wholly lost in wonder at the extraordinary spectacle before me. For to whatever quarter I direct my view, whether to the east, or to the west, or over the whole world, or toward heaven itself, everywhere and always I see the blessed one yet administering the selfsame empire. On earth I behold his sons, like some new reflectors of his brightness, diffusing everywhere the luster of their father's character, and himself still living and powerful, and governing all the affairs of men more completely than ever before, being multiplied in the succession of his children. They had indeed had previously the dignity of Caesars; but now, being invested with his very self, and graced by his accomplishments, for the excellence of their piety they are proclaimed by the titles of Sovereign, Augustus, Worshipful, and Emperor.

Chapter 2: And I am indeed amazed, when I consider that he who was but lately visible and present with us in his mortal body, is still, even after death, when the natural thought disclaims everything superfluous as unsuitable, most marvelously endowed with the same imperial dwellings, and honors, and praises as previously mentioned. But farther, when I raise my thoughts even to the arch of heaven, and there contemplate his three-times-blessed soul in communion with God himself, freed from every mortal and earthly vesture, and shining in a brilliant robe of light, and when I perceive that it is no more connected with the fleeting periods and occupations of mortal life, but honored with an ever-blooming crown, and an immortality of endless and blessed existence, I stand, as it were, without power of speech or thought and unable to utter a single phrase, but condemning my own weakness, and imposing silence on myself, I resign the task of speaking his praises worthily to one who is better able, even to him who, being the immortal God and veritable Word, alone has power to confirm his own sayings.

Chapter 3: Having given assurance that those who glorify and honor him will meet with an abundant reward at his hands, while those who set themselves against him as enemies and adversaries will compass the ruin of their own souls, he has already established the truth of these his own declarations, having shown on the one hand the fearful end of those tyrants who denied and opposed him, and at the same time having made it manifest that even the death of his servant, as well as his life, is worthy of admiration and praise, and justly claims the memorial, not merely of perishable, but of immortal monuments. Mankind, devising some consolation for the frail and precarious duration of human life, have thought by the erection of monuments to glorify the memories of their ancestors with immortal honors. Some have employed the vivid delineations and colors of painting; some have carved statues from lifeless blocks of wood; while others, by engraving their inscriptions deep on tablets and monuments, have thought to transmit the virtues of those whom they honored to perpetual remembrance. All these indeed are perishable, and consumed by the lapse of time, being representations of the corruptible body, and not expressing the image of the immortal soul. And yet these seemed sufficient to those who had no well-grounded hope of happiness after the termination of this mortal life. But God, that God, I say, who is the common Savior of all, having treasured up with himself, for those who love godliness, greater blessings than human thought has conceived, gives the earnest and first-fruits of future rewards even here, assuring in some sort immortal hopes to mortal eyes. The ancient oracles of the prophets, delivered to us in the Scripture, declare this; the lives of pious men, who shone in old time with every virtue, bear witness to posterity of the same; and our own days prove it to be true, wherein Constantine, who alone of all that ever wielded the Roman power was the friend of God the Sovereign of all, has appeared to all mankind so clear an example of a godly life.

Chapter 4: And God himself, whom Constantine worshiped, has confirmed this truth by the clearest manifestations of his will, being present to aid him at the commencement, during the course, and at the end of his reign, and holding him up to the human race as an instructive example of godliness. Accordingly, by the manifold blessings he has conferred on him, he has distinguished him alone of all the sovereigns of whom we have ever heard as at once a mighty luminary and most clear-voiced herald of genuine piety.

Chapter 5: With respect to the duration of his reign, God honored him with three complete periods of ten years, and something more, extending the whole term of his mortal life to twice this number of years. And being pleased to make him a representative of his own sovereign power, he displayed him as the conqueror of the whole race of tyrants, and the destroyer of those God-defying giants of the earth who madly raised their impious arms against him, the supreme King of all. They appeared, so to speak, for an instant, and then disappeared: while the one and only true God, when he had enabled his servant, clad in heavenly panoply, to stand singly against many foes, and by his means had relieved mankind from the multitude of the ungodly, constituted him a teacher of his worship to all nations, to testify with a loud voice in the hearing of all that he acknowledged the true God, and turned with abhorrence from the error of them that are no gods.

Chapter 6: Thus, like a faithful and good servant, did he act and testify, openly declaring and confessing himself the obedient minister of the supreme King. And God forthwith rewarded him, by making him ruler and sovereign, and victorious to such a degree that he alone of all rulers pursued a continual course of conquest, unsubdued and invincible, and through his trophies a greater ruler than tradition records ever to have been before. So dear was he to God, and so blessed, so pious, and so fortunate in all that he undertook, that with the greatest facility he obtained the authority over more nations than any who had preceded him, and yet retained his power, undisturbed, to the very close of his life.

Chapter 7: Ancient history describes Cyrus, king of the Persians, as by far the most illustrious of all kings up to his time. And yet if we regard the end of his days, we find it but little corresponded with his past prosperity, since he met with an inglorious and dishonorable death at the hands of a woman. Again, the sons of Greece celebrate Alexander the Macedonian as the conqueror of many and diverse nations; yet we find that he was removed by an early death, before he had reached maturity, being carried off by the effects of revelry and drunkenness. His whole life embraced but the space of thirty-two years, and his reign extended to no more than a third part of that period. Unsparing as the thunderbolt, he advanced through streams of blood and reduced entire nations and cities, young and old, to utter slavery. But when he had scarcely arrived at the maturity of life, and was lamenting the loss of youthful pleasures, death fell upon him with terrible stroke, and, that he might no longer outrage the human race, cut him off in a foreign and hostile land, childless, without successor, and homeless. His kingdom too was instantly dismembered, each of his officers taking away and appropriating a portion for himself. And yet this man is extolled for such deeds as these.

Chapter 8: But our emperor began his reign at the time of life at which the Macedonian died, yet doubled the length of his life, and trebled the length of his reign. And instructing his army in the mild and sober precepts of godliness, he carried his arms as far as the Britons, and the nations that dwell in the very bosom of the Western ocean. He subdued likewise all Scythia, though situated in the remotest North, and divided into numberless diverse and barbarous tribes. He even pushed his conquests to the Blemmyans and Ethiopians, on the very confines of the South; nor did he think the acquisition of the Eastern nations unworthy of his care. In short, diffusing the brilliance of his holy light to the ends of the whole world, even to the most distant Indians, the nations dwelling on the extreme circumference of the inhabited earth, he received the submission of all the rulers, governors, and satraps of barbarous nations, who cheerfully welcomed and saluted him, sending embassies and presents, and setting the highest value on his acquaintance and friendship, insomuch that they honored him with pictures and statues in their respective countries, and Constantine alone of all emperors was acknowledged and celebrated by all. Notwithstanding, even among these distant nations, he proclaimed the name of his God in his royal edicts with all boldness.

Source: Schaff, Philip. "Life of Constantine." *Eusebius Pamphilius: Church History, Life of Constantine, Oration in Praise of Constantine.* Edinburgh: T&T Clark, n.d. Available online at http://www.ccel.org/ccel/schaff/npnf201.

Key Questions

QUESTION 1: WHY WERE CHRISTIANS PERSECUTED?

Most people, when they learn about early Christianity, are fascinated and repelled when they learn about the persecution Christians faced in the first 300 years of its history. After learning about specific examples of it, their next thought is usually, "Why were they persecuted in the first place?" This is a very good question to ask since persecution, both by individuals and by the Roman state, played a dominant role in the formation of early Christianity. It shaped the way that Christians reacted to the larger world in which they lived.

Nearly every book written on the history of early Christianity covers the persecution of the Christians. It has been pointed out in numerous books that persecution of Christianity occurred early on in the history of the movement, as detailed in the New Testament. Part of the reason for the popularity on the topic of persecutions is that it shows up not only in the New Testament but in other texts that were either written about Christians or written by Christians. In the early second century we have an account by the Roman senator Tacitus of Emperor Nero. Nero severely persecuted some Christians in the city of Rome when a fire ravaged the districts. The emperor blamed the Christians. Justin Martyr, an early Christian writing in the middle of the second century CE, wrote two books titled *The First Apology* and *Second Apology*, and in them he discusses the various reasons why Christians were persecuted and explains how the charges against the Christians were not true. The first Christian historian, Eusebius of Caesarea, makes persecution a centerpiece of his *Ecclesiastical History*. Eusebius wrote this in the late 200s/early 300s CE and as mentioned, this was the first history of Christianity. There are also numerous accounts of persecution in other early Christian texts. From these few examples it is clear that persecution played an important part in the lives of early Christians, at least according to the primary accounts.

These persecutions led to a new kind of writing for Christians that focused on these martyrs, or people who died for their faith. Starting very early we see accounts of the trauma and killings that happened. The stories follow a similar pattern: they start off with the account of a Christian or Christians who were going about their daily business when someone in the Roman government decides to persecute them for their beliefs in Christ. The Christian refuses to recant and curse Christ, and this usually leads to a public execution, sometimes in a theater or sometimes in the middle of the town where the Christian lives. There is always a point to these writings: the persecuted Christian is held up as an example to all Christians who might be facing persecution. They are an example showing that if one stands up to the persecutors and is ultimately killed, the reward will be that they will meet Christ in heaven. This was a powerful motivator for people who were under the threat of torture and death. The message was so powerful that some Christian communities had to discourage Christians from wanting to be persecuted.

Because of its prevalence in early Christian texts we also see persecution discussed in modern books about early Christianity. Many of these books also focus, or at least discuss, the persecution and the effects the persecutions had on these early communities. A good example of this is W. H. C. Frend's book titled *Martyrdom and Persecution in the Early Church*. It is clear, at least in these books, that persecution had a profound effect on early Christian communities. But is that still the case? The answer is yes and no. Yes, in that most scholars still accept that persecution occurred and affected many Christian groups. The most current trend in modern books when discussing Christian persecution, however, is to now question, not the accounts of persecution, but the frequency and duration of the persecutions themselves. We see this in Morwenna Ludlow's book titled *The Early Church*, published in 2009. The current scholarship on the importance of persecution now is trying to make the point that although there was certainly persecutions, it was not as widespread as it used to be thought—in fact, it was sporadic. This is not to say that persecution was not important, but some current scholarship is suggesting that although persecution played an important part in the psychology of the early Christians, it was probably stressed too much by modern scholarship. Part of the reason for this also leads back to the ancient texts (discussed above). Persecution was commonly discussed in these books, and this led scholars to assume that persecution itself was common, especially when it was caused by the Roman state. Some scholars are even going beyond this to question how involved the Roman state actually was in its legislation to persecute various groups, including the Christians. Some are stating that there are no descriptions of Roman law that specifically state that Christians were to be persecuted. Because of these voices, scholars are beginning to examine persecution anew.

The two essays below discuss why Christians were persecuted in the early centuries of Christianity. Each essay was written independently of the other; both authors were given the question and were allowed to form any answer they felt appropriate. As you will soon read, this particular question leads to some very similar answers although each has a different approach to the problem.

Dr. Ethan Spanier's essay discusses the root problem that Romans had with the Christians—they believed that the Christians were essentially antisocial, especially to the Roman society of which they were part. This antisocial view led to the belief that Christians were not loyal to their government. As he points out, loyalty to the Roman government meant the payment of taxes (as Christians were commanded to do by Christ) and, more importantly, Romans were to support the Roman religious structure. Christians refused to do this since they believed that the Roman gods and goddesses were just idols, and, as Dr. Spanier states, the Christians believed that Roman culture was immoral. There were also many misperceptions of the Christians by the Romans, which also led to their persecution. One was very serious—that the Christians practiced human sacrifice, or at least ate human flesh and drank human blood. This misperception stems from the practice of the Eucharist where Christians are to believe they are drinking the blood of Christ and eating his flesh. Dr. Spanier also makes the excellent point that the Romans believed the health of their whole society was supported by a believing community, and when the Christians refused to take part in Roman religious practices, the Christians were blamed for natural disasters and any other problems that occurred in the Roman Empire. The results were numerous persecutions led by the state, ending with the Great Persecution led by Emperor Diocletian.

Dr. Bernard Doherty dissects the various reasons as to why the persecutions occurred and begins his article by focusing on two questions: "What was the usual legal basis and what were the general legal procedures surrounding the trials of Christian?" and "What were the main reasons for the popular dislike of Christians in the first place?" In answering his first question Dr. Doherty does an excellent job taking apart the letters that were exchanged in the early second century between Emperor Trajan and Pliny the Younger, a Roman governor. He points out that the letters state that Christians should not be hunted down, but if they admitted being Christians, they should receive the ultimate penalty—death. This leads him to ask what it was about Christians that they should be tortured and killed in the first place. Again, Dr. Doherty focuses on the letters of Trajan and Pliny. Like Spanier,

Dr. Doherty brings up the false charge that Christians were practicing cannibalism and even incest. These charges were brought against them because of misunderstanding about the basic religious practices of the Christians. He also points out that the most basic reason why the Christians were persecuted is because of their insistence on monotheism, or the belief in one God. Christian monotheism led to many problems for the Christians because, as also stated by Dr. Spanier, the health of the Roman Empire depended on worshipping the Roman gods and goddesses. The Christians refused to do this, and understanding early persecution is dependent on understanding the Roman institutions which the Christians rejected.

ANSWER: CHRISTIANS WERE PERSECUTED BECAUSE THEY WERE SEEN AS A THREAT TO ROMAN SOCIETY

Ethan Spanier

Roman authorities sanctioned popular violence and sponsored state persecutions because Christians were believed to be disloyal to Rome, a disruption of social unity, and that they carried out religious practices that traditional Romans considered "displeasing to the gods." This perception of Christians as "anti-Roman" had its origins in both the internal actions on the part of the Christians and the external prejudices of the Romans.

Christians distinguished themselves as separate from Roman society and publically chastised Roman culture as immoral. While Christians were amenable to paying general taxes, as Jesus instructed his followers in the synoptic gospels, "to render to Caesar that which was Caesar's" (Matthew 22:15; Mark 12:13–17; Luke 20:20–22), they refused to fund or partake in traditional Roman religious rituals, especially offering sacrifices to local deities or state-run cults. Indeed, many Christians saw themselves as a people separate from the "world," whose true allegiance was not to Rome but "the kingdom that was to come." Some Christians, especially leaders of religious communities, actively sought out their own arrest, imprisonment, and death. A person who was killed at the hands of the Roman state or mob violence because they identified as a Christian was called a martyr (μάρτυρ, Greek for "witness") while a person who was imprisoned, tortured, had his or her property confiscated by the state, but ultimately released was called a confessor (Latin for one who admitted to the *nomen christianum* or "Christian name"). Individuals who experienced a martyr's death were believed to be given "divine grace" by God and consequently were elevated as exemplars of pious Christian behavior. One such leader of the early church was Polycarp (69–155 CE), the bishop of Smyrna whose refusal to deny his Christian beliefs resulted in his torture and immolation. Polycarp's "death story" became the first of a new genre of Christian literature known as a martyrology. The heroic depiction of the way he faced death at the hands of Roman authorities gave Polycarp special spiritual status in the Christian community.

The persecutions of Christians by state authorities started slowly because Romans initially considered Christianity a sect of Judaism. Another factor that made persecutions a gradual process was the nature of localized power given to Roman magistrates. These representatives had complete authority to act on behalf of the emperor only in the territory they controlled. Occasionally, they would ask Rome for legal clarification. A good example of this occurred when a magistrate named Pliny, tasked with administering Roman law in the northern coastal region of Anatolia, wrote to Emperor Trajan (r. 98–117 CE) for guidance. Pliny began to receive complaints from the local population about the behavior of a religious sect unknown to Pliny, the Christians. Pliny and Trajan wrote a series of letters back and forth about what should be done. Pliny records that he asked those accused of bad behavior if they were Christians three times. If they persisted in admitting to the Christian faith, Pliny had them executed. Trajan responded that he approved of Pliny's methods, but that it was impossible for Rome to provide a general rule about this sect. The emperor further emphasized that "these people must not be sought out; if the charge against them is proved (that is to say, admitting to the Christian name) they should be punished" (Pliny, *Letters* 10.97). This rather lenient ruling indicates that the emperor was not actively hunting down Christians because of their faith in the early second century.

Part of the prejudice against Christianity has its origin in Roman misconceptions of Christian ritual practices. One ritual in particular, the Eucharist—the eating of bread and drinking of wine, symbolizing the body and blood of Jesus—was considered particularly abhorrent to Romans because of their social strictures against cannibalism. While historical sources may over-amplify the depth of this resentment, the theological concept of transubstantiation—that the bread and wine consumed during the ritual *literally* transformed into the body of blood of Jesus—was misinterpreted as a ritual involving the consumption of humans.

Christian attitudes of superiority and their enmity against Rome compounded with the misunderstanding of ritual practice made Christians targets of unorganized mob violence. One such incident occurred along the Rhône River valley in part because of an influx of Greek-speaking Christians from Anatolia, a people who were themselves refugees of religious violence. The increase of Eastern Christians in southeastern Gaul created resentment on the part of the local population. In 177 CE, local mobs attacked these Eastern Christians in towns like Lugdunum and Vienne. This disorganized persecution was so fierce that Roman troops were called in by the authorities to quell the violence.

Roman religious thinking also contributed to the persecution of the Christians. One key religious concept was *pax deorum* (Latin for "peace of the gods"). This belief held that Romans could only prosper on the earth in areas such as victory in battle, bountiful harvests, a growing economy, and there would be no natural disasters when proper religious rituals were observed in the correct way (known to modern scholars as orthopraxy). Conversely, unfortunate events such as defeat in battle, famine, poor tax revenues, and earthquakes or volcanos were believed to be signs from the divine that traditional Roman orthopraxy was not being followed. Thus, the political and economic health of the Roman Empire was closely associated to the orthopraxy of state-run cults, especially the Imperial Cult. This cult venerated deceased emperors and functioned as a civic outlet to demonstrate an individual's political loyalty to the state. It was funded by the imperial treasury and had centers in every corner of the empire. Advocates of traditional Roman religion theologically argued that only the correct prayer formulae and offerings to the spirits of the emperors in the Imperial Cult could ensure the favor of the gods. This cult grew in political significance during a turbulent period of Roman history, known to modern scholars as the "Crisis of the Third Century" (235–270 CE), when the Roman Empire experienced constant invasions, chronic civil war with numerous claimants for the throne, crop failures, and economic collapse. It is within this social context that the first state-coordinated, empire-wide persecution of Christians began during the reign of Emperor Decius in 250 CE. The emperor ordered that every person in the Roman Empire should participate in the Imperial Cult at least once a year to ascertain their loyalty to Rome. Those who offered a sacrifice of vows, incense, meat, or wine would receive a *libellus*, a certificate to corroborate their participation in the Imperial Cult, thereby establishing their *romanitas* (Latin for "Roman-ness"). As strict monotheists, early Christians had prohibitions against this ritual and thus were singled out.

Emperor Valerian (r. 253–259 CE) continued these persecutions by requiring all Christian clergy to perform sacrifices to the traditional Roman pantheon and denying Christians the right to assemble for religious services. Valerian seems to have targeted the upper class of Roman society. He ordered that all Christian bishops, usually of high social station, be executed. Valerian also ordered that any member of the senatorial and equestrian class who admitted to being a Christian would be stripped of their social rank and imprisoned. This resulted in the deaths of Bishop Cyprian of Carthage and two bishops of Rome, Stephen I and Sixtus II. These persecutions were only enforced for a few years early in Valerian's reign. A longer and farther-reaching period of persecution occurred during the reigns of co-emperors Diocletian (r. 285–305) and Galerius

(r. 293–311 CE). A famous story tells how these emperors decided to initiate what modern scholars call the "Great Persecutions" (303–313 CE). Diocletian and Galerius were at odds over the severity of laws against Christians. Diocletian merely wanted to exclude Christians from participating in the civil bureaucracy, while Galerius wanted to impose harsher penalties. Both co-emperors agreed to send messengers to the Oracle of Apollo at Didyma to ask for divine guidance. The story goes that the messengers returned to Rome without an answer because Christians had "prevented the gods from speaking." On hearing this news in 303 CE, Diocletian agreed with Galerius and ordered the confiscation and destruction of all Christian scriptures and buildings, banned church meetings, and stripped Christians of their legal rights. This sustained effort directed at Christians continued in various forms and in different places within the Roman Empire until the legal status of Christians was restored with the Edict of Milan in 313 CE. This imperial edict, formulated by Bishop Ambrose of Milan and passed into law by Emperor Constantine I (r. 312–337 CE), effectively decriminalized Christianity by granting toleration to all religions in the Empire, "to grant both to the Christians and to all the free choice of following whatever form of worship they pleased" (Eusebius, *Ecclesiastical History* 10.5). With the Edict of Milan, not only was Christianity legally protected, but the faith was favored by Emperor Constantine and his sons.

ANSWER: CHRISTIANS WERE PERSECUTED BECAUSE THEIR BELIEFS AND PRACTICES WERE MISUNDERSTOOD AND THEIR MONOTHEISM WAS SEEN AS DETRIMENTAL TO THE ROMAN SOCIAL ORDER

Bernard Doherty

In his *Apology*, written in the late second century, the Christian writer Tertullian of Carthage made a memorable statement:

> If the Tiber rises as high as the city walls, if the Nile does not rise to the fields, if the weather will not change, if there is an earthquake, a famine, a plague— straightway the cry is heard: "Toss the Christians to the lion!"[1]

By the time Tertullian was writing, the Christians had endured over a century of sporadic persecution in the form of legal trials, torture, execution, and mob violence in cities across the Roman Empire. As such, it is important to ask the specific question: why were the early Christians persecuted? In answering this question historians often separate their inquiry into two subsidiary questions: What was the usual legal basis and what were the general legal procedures surrounding the trials of Christian? And, what were the main reasons for the popular dislike of Christians in the first place?

While as early as the first century the followers of Jesus had been hauled before magistrates for disturbing the peace, it was during the reign of the Emperor Nero (54–68 CE) that the Christians were scapegoated for the fire at Rome that raged in July 64 CE. They were singled out as a particularly threatening group, distinct for what the Roman historian Tacitus called their "hatred of the human race" (*odium humani generis*).[2] Nero had the Christians arrested and then executed. From this time until the mid-third century Christians were to experience a series of localized outbreaks of persecutions in various regions for the mere fact that they were Christians, regardless of any other offence. In order to understand this situation one particular document from the second century is invaluable. What follows will analyze some of its content in order to shed light on the question of persecution. Writing to Emperor Trajan (r. 98–117 CE) in the early second century (c. 112/113 CE), the Roman governor of Bithynia-Pontus, Pliny (the Younger), requested clarification regarding the procedure for cases brought against Christians. This document gives an insight into the Roman perspective on why they felt the need to persecute the Christians.

While it is highly probable that by this time the crime of professing the "name of Christian" (*nomen Christianum*) had become sufficient grounds to warrant a death sentence, in terms of explicit evidence for the legal basis of this charge it remains unclear whether it was enunciated by a specific decree of an emperor or the Senate, or the exact legal form in which the crime was understood. It was not until the rescript (*rescripta*) from the Emperor Trajan in reply to Pliny's letter that a general pattern emerges that was to serve as a general legal precedent (*exemplum*) for future persecutions, and this allows us to illuminate both the procedure and the reasons for the persecutions prior to the mid-third century. For Trajan Pliny's actions (discussed below) had been exemplary; however, he added the cautionary note:

> These people must not be hunted out; if they are brought before you and a charge against them is proved, they must be punished, but in the case of anyone who denies that he is a Christian, and makes it clear that he is not by offering prayers to our gods, he is to be pardoned . . . but pamphlets circulated anonymously must play no part in any accusations.[3]

The evidence of Pliny's prosecution of Christians from Bithynia-Pontus indicates that prosecution of Christians took place according to the process usually referred to as *cognitio extra ordinem*, a form of court proceeding where a judge, usually a provincial governor, had sole authority in adjudicating a legal matter as he saw fit. The *cognitio* process accorded to the magistrate wide discretionary powers including ignoring accusations altogether. The usual procedure followed in such proceedings, which Pliny's letter attests, was that during a governor's annual assize (a tour of the province for the purposes of administration) an accuser (*delator*) would bring an accusation (*accusatio*) of Christianity before a tribunal. The governor would then decide whether to commit a Christian to stand trial or dismiss the matter.

Such trials could take a variety of legal forms but usually followed a standard formula set out in Pliny's letter in which a Christian was questioned a number of times as to whether they were a Christian, accompanied by warnings that an affirmative answer would result in punishment. Those who confessed, and subsequently refused to recant in the face of punishment, were usually summarily executed; those who denied they were Christians were required to perform a token pagan religious gesture such as offering incense, pouring a libation, or swearing an oath in order to prove their innocence, the understanding being that no Christian could perform such actions because they were tantamount to idolatry (see below).

Bringing a charge against a Christian, however, was not a simple business. Aside from the often prohibitive amount of judicial business a governor was required to adjudicate during an assize, any accusation that could not be proven left a *delator* open to an accusation of *calumnia* (i.e., vexatious litigation), a charge that carried with it significant legal penalties. This raises the second question as to why were the Christians so despised that willing accusers could be found? Pliny's letter provides a number of clues here. First, Pliny inquires whether Christians are to be punished for the name alone, or rather for the "crimes associated with the name" (*flagitia cohaerentia nomini*).[4] The Latin term utilized here (*flagitia*) is indicative of a series of rumors about Christians that circulated during the first and second centuries in which they were accused of secret crimes ranging from incest to cannibalism. While these stories most likely originated from a combination of Christian secretiveness and a misunderstanding of early Christian liturgical practices, they were widely believed, and while, as Pliny soon discovered by torturing a number of Christian slaves, they lacked any foundation, they continued to circulate widely over the course of the second century, fueling suspicion toward the already unpopular Christians.

Second, Pliny notes that those who denied they were Christians were required to "[repeat] after me a formula of invocation to the gods and had made offerings of wine and incense to your statue" on the understanding that "none of which things, I understand, any genuine Christian can be induced to do."[5] This alerts us to the major reason for Christianity's unpopularity: its exclusive monotheism and subsequent refusal to partake in the worship of the pagan gods.

In Roman religion the practices of religion were intertwined, if not coextensive, with those of civic and indeed imperial identity, and Christian refusal to participate in public ceremonies resulted in suspicions of misanthropy and atheism. As the governor Saturninus told a group of accused Christians in North Africa in 180 CE, "our religion is a simple one: we swear by the genius of our lord emperor and we offer prayers for his health—as you also ought to do."[6] For the committed Christian this was not possible. In their eyes the pagan gods were not gods but, in the words of Justin Martyr, "wicked and impious demons"[7] unworthy of worship, and to perform these rites violated their monotheistic beliefs. In this sense the accusation of atheism was true, as Justin Martyr himself admitted, "we confess that we are atheists, so far as gods of this sort are concerned."[8]

Such a stance, however, had wider ramifications. In Roman understanding the well-being of the city and the empire were only guaranteed by the maintenance of a correct relationship of deference and respect (exhibited by the Latin term *pietas*) towards the Roman gods; a concept sometimes referred to as the "peace of the gods" (*pax deorum*). Thus, the Christians' refusal to participate in public ceremonies that sought to honor the gods was viewed as a threat to the wider social fabric of the cities in which they lived. Pliny's letter again alludes to this when he notes that having dealt with the Christians, the "people have begun to throng the temples which had been almost entirely deserted for a long time; the sacred rites which had been allowed to lapse are being performed again, and flesh of sacrificial victims is on sale everywhere."[9]

In sum, the persecution of Christians took place under the auspices of Roman law and the civic life of the Roman Empire and cannot be properly understood without reference to these institutions. Christians' separate identity, understood by their pagan neighbors as indicative of atheism and misanthropy, gave birth to rumors about this secretive groups that further fueled suspicions and led to judicial actions. When, as happened in the case of the early Christian bishop Polycarp around 160 CE the populace cried out, "Away with the atheists!"[10] it became incumbent on a governor to acquiesce to the wishes of the mob in order to preserve civic concord.

CLOSING

The question of why the Christians were persecuted is an important one, and the authors have taken different approaches in their answers. Despite these differences, they come to similar conclusions in answering the question. Both wrote that the Christians were monotheistic, or believed in only one God, and because of this they were seen as being subversive and separate from the Roman society of which they were a part. These perceived differences led to persecution of the Christians.

Dr. Spanier takes a more global (or better, empire-wide) approach to the problem and examines the question by looking at the specifics of why the Christians were persecuted, starting with an investigation of why the Christians were seen as being separated from Roman society. This separation led the Roman authorities to persecute the Christians because they believed the health of the empire demanded that its citizens worship their ancestral gods and goddesses. Dr. Spanier looks at the specific charges and then gives a very good overview of persecutions led by the Roman government up through the time of Emperor Diocletian (the Great Persecution). Dr. Spanier also approaches the problem by also looking at what people had to do to not be persecuted—they had to offer sacrifices and then they would receive a statement that said they had performed the sacrifices and thus were not Christian.

Dr. Doherty takes a mostly text-specific approach to answer the same question. His approach to the problem is to examine the letters exchanged between Emperor Trajan and one of his governors, Pliny the Younger (which were also mentioned by Dr. Spanier). These letters, written in the first decades of the second century, give one of the first examples we have of the problem of the Christians as seen by Roman authorities. They are extremely important letters in the study of early Christianity for just that reason. Doherty looks at the Latin words (which is the language of these particular letters) to show the nuances that can occur with studying texts in a different language. He points out that the Latin word *flagitia,* meaning "crimes," refers to the rumors of cannibalism and incest that dogged the Christian communities long after this particular period. Dr. Doherty also gives a summary of Roman law and how things were supposed to work when someone was accused of a crime—he proves that the letters by Governor Pliny the Younger follow Roman law.

DOING MORE

There are many resources that can be easily accessed on the topic of persecution of the Christians. It is a popular topic for scholars and for people interested in early Christianity. Below you will find a list of books, journal articles, Web sites, videos, and podcasts that discuss this topic in detail. I do want to specifically point out one book that is made up of the actual texts regarding the persecution of Christians. This book is: Herbert Musurillo, *Acts of the Christian Martyrs* (Oxford: Clarendon Press, 1972). Professor Musurillo has given many of the primary sources scholars use when writing histories of Christian persecution. You can also find some of these texts online. Ideally these primary sources should be read first to understand the Christian mindset, and then the secondary material should be read in order to give a bit more understanding of the issues surrounding persecution.

NOTES

1. Tertullian, *Apology* XL.2, in Sider, *Christian and Pagan in the Roman Empire.*
2. Tacitus, *Annals* XV.44.6, in Stevenson, *A New Eusebius.*
3. Pliny, *Ep.* XCVII.2, in Radice, *Letters of the Younger Pliny.*
4. Ibid.
5. Pliny, *Ep.* XCVI.5, in Radice, *Letters of the Younger Pliny.*
6. *The Acts of the Scillitan Martyrs* III, in Musurillo, *Acts of the Christian Martyrs.*
7. Justin, *First Apology* V, in Stevenson, *A New Eusebius.*
8. Justin, *First Apology* VI, in Stevenson, *A New Eusebius.*
9. Pliny, Ep. XCVI. 10, in Radice, *Letters of the Younger Pliny.*
10. *The Martyrdom of Polycarp* III, in Musurillo, *Acts of the Christian Martyrs.*

BOOKS AND JOURNAL ARTICLES

Barnes, T. D. "Legislation against the Christians." *Journal of Roman Studies* 51, nos. 1 and 2 (1968): 32–50.

Beard, Mary, John North, and Simon Price. *Religions of Rome Volume 1: A History.* Cambridge: Cambridge University Press, 1998.

Bowersock, G. W. *Martyrdom and Rome.* Cambridge: Cambridge University Press, 1995.

Frend, W. H. C. *Martyrdom and Persecution in the Early Church.* Oxford: Basil Blackwell, 1965.

Ludlow, Morwenna. *The Early Church.* New York: I. B. Tauris, 2009.

Moss, Candida R. *Ancient Christian Martyrdom: Diverse Practices, Theologies, and Traditions.* New Haven, CT: Yale University Press, 2012.

Musurillo, Herbert. *Acts of the Christian Martyrs.* Oxford: Clarendon Press, 1972.

Radice, Betty. *The Letters of the Younger Pliny.* London: Penguin Books, 1963.

Sherwin-White, A. N. *The Letters of Pliny: A Historical and Social Commentary.* Oxford: Clarendon Press, 1966.

Sider, Robert D. *Christian and Pagan in the Roman Empire: The Witness of Tertullian.* Washington, DC: Catholic University of America Press, 2001.

de Ste. Croix, G. E. M. "Why Were the Early Christians Persecuted?" *Past and Present* 26 (1963): 6–26.

Stevenson, J. *A New Eusebius: Documents Illustrating the History of the Church to AD 337.* London: SPCK, 1987.

WEB RESOURCES

"The Diversity of Christianity," *Frontline.* http://www.pbs.org/wgbh/pages/frontline/shows/religion/first/diversity.html.

"Early Christianity and the Church." *USU 1320: History and Civilization.* http://www.usu.edu/markdamen/1320hist&civ/chapters/13xity.htm.

"From Jesus to Christ." *Frontline*. http://www.pbs.org/wgbh/pages/frontline/shows
    /religion/.
"From Jesus to Christ: Chronology." *Frontline*. http://www.pbs.org/wgbh/pages
    /frontline/shows/religion/maps/cron.html.
"Guide to Early Church Documents: Creeds and Canons." *Internet Christian Li-
    brary*. http://www.iclnet.org/pub/resources/christian-history.html#creeds.
"The Nag Hammadi Library." *Gnostic Society Library*. http://www.gnosis.org
    /naghamm/nhl.html.

VIDEOS

"The First Christian Art and Its Symbolism." https://www.youtube.com/watch?v
    =dcQ9NB3D_ho#t=141.
"From Jesus to Christ: The First Christians" https://www.youtube.com/watch
    ?v=OhJUDhitYlc

QUESTION 2: HOW DID CHRISTIANITY SPREAD?

By all accounts Christianity spread very quickly, from a few people in the
early part of the first century CE to becoming the major religious movement
in the Roman Empire by the early 300s. An important question to ask is
"How did Christianity spread?" If indeed it gathered a large number of
followers over the first three centuries, it makes sense to figure out the reasons
for this. There were certainly other new religious movements during this period, but they did not have rapid growth like Christianity. Unlike many other
new religious movements, Christianity experienced sporadic persecution as
well, but this did not inhibit its growth and in fact might have spurred it on
because some people felt sorry for them.

Many ancient writers mention the rapid growth of Christianity. We can
see this directly in the New Testament, where descriptions of numbers of
people joining the new religious movement and mass conversions are described. Paul's description of his journeys, even though he was going around
the eastern Mediterranean to convert Jewish and Gentile populations, show
that there were already Christian communities in existence before Paul arrived to do his own converting—so Paul wasn't the first, but he was certainly
the most influential. Morwenna Ludlow, in her book *The Early Church* (p.
23) points out that other early Christian writers who discuss the rapid growth
were Eusebius and especially Irenaeus (who died around the year
200 CE). Irenaeus wrote (in his *Against Heresies*, Book 1, Chapter 10):

The Church, though dispersed through our the whole world, even to the ends
of the earth, has received from the apostles and their disciples this faith: [She
believes] in one God, the Father Almighty, Maker of heaven, and earth, and the

sea, and all things that are in them; and in one Christ Jesus, the Son of God, who became incarnate for our salvation . . .

He wrote this sometime in the late 100s CE. Other writers like Irenaeus stated the same thing. As Ludlow further points out, Christians were found throughout the Roman Empire and found outside of the Roman boundaries, including north and east into the Persian Empire. Modern historians, using these ancient sources, add to them by finding specific examples of this growth. They also go beyond these to explain why Christianity expanded like it did.

One method that has been used to investigate why Christianity spread like it did was to examine the culture in which Christianity existed—Greco-Roman society. Early Christians soon realized that they had to adapt their language so that educated individuals would take the message of Christianity seriously. The way they did this was to adopt some Greek philosophical terms. Many scholars investigate the use of philosophical language (both written and oral) by early Christians. They usually focus on writers like Justin Martyr (died in the 160s) and Tertullian (died in the 220s). Both of these writers were educated and therefore knew Greek philosophy, and both of these men (and many other early Christians) realized that they could use philosophical terms to describe some of the ideas of Christianity. Other scholars also looked at the role that persecution played in getting people to join Christianity. It may seem counterintuitive that the torture and killing of Christians would actually attract more people to the religion, but the public spectacles of torture in the arenas led many to wonder what it was about Christianity that made people choose to die rather than leave their religious beliefs. Scholars also realized that the stories of persecution were also used by early Christians as examples of what it was to be a perfect Christian who did not waver when persecuted.

Important changes in the way this question is approached started to appear in the late 1960s, 1970s, and 1980s when historians began to examine the social conditions, both in the Roman Empire and within Christian communities, that led to this growth. One highly influential book that addressed this very problem was Wayne Meeks's *The First Urban Christians*. While Meeks is mostly concerned with who was becoming a Christian, a side benefit of his study was to discuss the growth of early Christianity in terms of which social classes were joining. As discussed in Professor Thompson's essay (below), getting the urban upper classes (those living in the cities) to believe in Christ was an important part in getting the population of Christianity to grow. Without the support of the upper classes, Christianity would have had a more difficult time spreading. Another important change which took place at this time (in the 1960s, 1970s, and 1980s) was to begin examining the role that women played in these early Christian groups. Before this period scholars did not always investigate what women were doing, but when more and more women were able to get into universities and become historians, they (and men too) began to focus on the roles of women. It was shown that women played a vital part in the growth of Christianity—from public teaching to the financing of many of the early male Christians who were teaching about Christianity.

The spreading of Christianity is one of the most important topics in the study of early Christianity. As mentioned above, early Christians mention the growth of their own religion and make the point that their religion had spread throughout the entire world (which wasn't really the entire world, but the world that the early Christians knew about). It is likely that they were exaggerating, but most scholars agree that there is no doubt Christianity spread very quickly. They also, not surprisingly, differ on the reasons why it grew like it did. Some believe that it was the adoption of Greek ideas and philosophy that helped Christianity to adapt to its environment; others believed that the actual message of Christ was the reason it grew; yet others believe that the adoption of the religion by the upper-class Romans pushed Christianity to be the most dominant religion in the Roman Empire by the 300s CE.

Prof. Nancy Thompson's essay focuses primarily on the society in which Christianity grew up, namely, Greek culture. Although the territory was Roman by the time Christianity got its start, it had been under the control of Greeks for nearly three centuries. People (in general) spoke Greek, dressed like Greeks, and followed Greek ideas when it came to philosophy and religion. For their religion to grow and flourish in this Greek atmosphere, Christians had to adapt their religious ideas in order to convince the population that Christianity was the religion to join. Prof. Thompson points out that Christians did this in a number of ways, including using Greek philosophical terms and designing their religious structures much like Greek structures. The melding of Greek ideas with Christian ones, coupled with the fact that some early Christians like Paul wanted Christians to leave behind some Jewish religious practices such as circumcision, helped Christianity to grow among non-Jewish people. Prof. Thompson also makes the excellent point that Christians needed to convince the upper classes that their religion was a reasonable one by once again adapting Greek ideas into their Christian beliefs.

Traci Boozer's essay focuses not on the message of Christianity but on the actual methods used in its dispersion from Palestine to all areas of Europe and beyond. Ms. Boozer points out that public preaching played an important role in the first century or two. People like Paul were very influential in gathering new Christian converts because they actively traveled around the Mediterranean spreading their message of Christ. Other later Christians like Justin Martyr did the same thing, except through writing instead of travel. When persecutions became more prevalent, Ms. Boozer makes the argument that Christianity then spread not by traveling Christians (because it was too dangerous) but by word of mouth and through public spectacles like persecution.

ANSWER: CHRISTIANITY WAS ABLE TO SPREAD BY ADOPTING GREEK IDEAS AND LANGUAGE, AND IT THUS APPEALED TO THE GREEK CULTURE OF THE ROMAN TERRITORIES

Nancy Thompson

Jesus was a Jew. The message he preached, repentance and reform, was directed toward his fellow Jews (Matthew 10.6, 15.24). It is therefore remarkable that he inspired a faith that came to dominate the Roman Empire. For most people of his day, Jesus' native religion must have seemed rather strange, with its strict monotheism and unusual practices, such as male circumcision, Sabbath laws, and dietary restrictions. To spread, Christianity had to shake off some of its Jewish trappings and conform to the expectations of the diverse peoples living around the Mediterranean. Ultimately its success depended on capturing the allegiance of two very different groups of people, the urban lower classes and the educated elite. The Christianization of the Roman Empire was a long and complicated process, but several factors were particularly important: the early incorporation of Greek ideas, the adoption of Greco-Roman forms of organization, and the role of Christian converts from less-privileged segments of society: the urban poor, slaves, and especially women. Christianity spread by adapting to the wider Greco-Roman world, offering a message that spoke to high and low.

Jesus' followers, at least initially, continued as practicing Jews (Acts 2.46), and a significant number of them thought that any new converts to the budding Christian movement should be likewise bound by Jewish law, including circumcision for men. Others disagreed: Peter, who according to the Book of Acts was moved by a vision, baptized a noncircumcised Roman (Acts 10:1–48), and Paul argued strongly for releasing non-Jews from the law's strict requirements (Acts 15:1–21, and cf. 21.20–30; Galatians 2.7–14). His view ultimately won the day, and the new religion began to spread among Jews residing in Greek cities and among non-Jewish proselytes (i.e., those who were sympathetic to Judaism, but may or may not have been circumcised) (Acts 10.22, 13.16–26, 43).

The relaxation of Jewish law removed a significant impediment to the growth of Christianity, and it could be widely disseminated once its key teachings were translated into Greek, which was commonly spoken throughout the ancient Mediterranean. Paul deserves much (though not all) of the credit for the first expansion of the new religion. He preached to audiences of Jews and proselytes in synagogues (a Greek term for an assembly) in Greek cities throughout the eastern Mediterranean (e.g., Acts 13.14, 14.1, 17.1, 19.8), before finally traveling to Rome. He wrote in Greek, as did the authors of the Gospels and the other books of the New Testament. The principal rites of the early church received Greek names: *eucharistia*, "thanksgiving" (the Eucharist or Communion), and *baptisma*, "ritual washing" (baptism). Early Christian communities met in an *ecclesia*, another Greek word for an assembly (hence *iglesia* in Spanish, *église* in French, and the English adjective *ecclesiastical*). (The English word *church* is derived from another Greek word, *kyriakos* or "belonging to the Lord.") Even the title used for Jesus, *Christos* or Christ, comes from the Greek word meaning "anointed." Greek gave Christianity access to both the elite and lower classes. It was the language of educated people, but it was also the everyday language of millions of the empire's inhabitants.

Paul also began to give Christianity a philosophical foundation—that is, a theology. Jesus had spoken of repentance and the forgiveness of sin, but said little about how it was accomplished. What did it mean to be saved? How did Christ's death contribute to redemption? Why was redemption even necessary? Paul pondered these questions and began to work out answers for his followers (see, e.g., Romans 3.23–26, 5.12–21). His successors, the group of Christian writers known collectively as the Fathers of the Church, continued the process. Many of these writers were trained in classical philosophy. They used arguments based in reason to deal with controversies within the church, to plead for tolerance from those outside the Christian community, and to gain converts.

The infusion of Greek philosophy was a vital step in answering the objections that educated people had toward Christianity. While upper-class Romans participated in traditional religious rites as part of their civic duty, when they wanted metaphysical truths, the answers to life's big questions, they turned, not to the old gods, but to Greek philosophy. Many believed in a divine force, or *Logos*, animating the universe, but found Christian notions of Jesus' divinity repugnant. The idea that an all-powerful God could be born a weak and helpless baby, that God might suffer and die by crucifixion, the agonizing and shameful penalty meted out to rebellious slaves—these ideas were inconsistent with the philosopher's concept of divinity (cf. Augustine, *Confessions* 5.10.19). The Fathers of the Church had to convince their challengers that Christianity was intellectually respectable. Justin Martyr (d. ca. 165) drew comparisons between Christian teachings and pagan ideas. Clement of Alexandria (d. ca. 215) identified Christ with the *Logos*. Origen (d. 254) incorporated in his theology ideas derived from his study of Neoplatonic philosophy. The intellectual arguments of Ambrose of Milan convinced the as-yet-unconverted Augustine of Hippo that truth might be found in the Christian church (*Confessions* 5.14.24).

In general, however, the educated upper classes were slow to adopt Christianity. They were reluctant to associate with what they considered the dregs of society: credulous women, unskilled laborers, and slaves (Minucius Felix, *Octavius* 8). Their characterization of the Christian community had some validity. Christianity did indeed spread more quickly among the urban poor, and women played a prominent role. The church offered these disenfranchised groups a close-knit fellowship with other believers, as well as material assistance in times of need.

In this respect, the early church resembled other associations of the time. Mutual self-help groups, called *collegia* (singular: *collegium*), were common in the bustling cities of the Roman Empire. They served as social clubs, trade guilds, or burial associations providing deceased members with a respectable funeral. The Roman *collegia*, like Christian churches, were socially heterogeneous: they included slaves and former slaves along with freeborn people of modest means. They often had religious functions as well. When outsiders saw Christians eating together, gathering to honor their god, and looking after the widows and orphans of their members, they naturally thought in terms of a *collegium*.

Christianity also resembled the mystery cults, which supplemented traditional polytheism for many people of the empire. The mystery cults honored a particular god or goddess, often a deity associated with death and rebirth because of his or her connection with the cycle of fertility or the yearly course of the sun, which seems to wane in winter and grow again in spring. In many cases, the gods were originally from the east: the Greek Demeter and Persephone, the Egyptian Isis, the Phrygian Attis, or the Persian Mithras, for example. Members underwent an initiation rite, and their rituals were secret, open only to initiates. Christians too worshiped a dying and reborn god from the east. They did not speak of their rites to outsiders, keeping secret even their creed, which was revealed to them just before their initiation into the church by baptism. There were some differences: Jesus was a historical figure, while the gods of the mysteries originated in the mystic past, and Christianity was rigorously monotheistic, while adherents of the mysteries acknowledged many gods. But again, from the perspective of outsiders, Christianity looked familiar, one cult of many in the Roman empire.

Most converts entered the Christian church the same way they joined the *collegia* or mysteries, through person-to-person contact. Unfortunately, we do not have conversion accounts for ordinary people, but we know of prominent figures (Justin Martyr, Clement of Alexandria) who were persuaded to convert by encounters with individual Christians. Others were influenced by family members who were already Christian (Augustine, Ambrose, and Jerome).

In this regard, women were especially important, and often bridged the gap between the lower classes and the elite. Well-born women had been among the Jewish proselytes who adhered to (and opposed) the preaching of Paul (Acts 13.50, 17.4, 12). They continued to play a significant role in the early church, providing one of the means by which Christianity reached the upper classes. The life of Perpetua is a case in point. A young matron of good family and the mother of an infant son, she was arrested with several of her fellow Christians, some of whom were slaves. Although her father begged her to renounce her faith for her child's sake, she refused. She died in the arena in 202. As a high-ranking woman communing with slaves, Perpetua shows the social mixing in the early church. She also shows one way Christianity moved up the social ladder: had she survived, Perpetua would have undoubtedly raised her son as a Christian.

By Perpetua's day, Christianity had traveled far from its Judean beginnings. The church had adapted to its environment, not from any conscious design, but because organizations are shaped by the needs and expectations of their members. It provided community and a support system for the socially disenfranchised, but to really be viable, it had to take hold in the classes with political and social power. An intellectually satisfying theology and the support of high-ranking women enabled it to do so. Upper-class support sealed Christianity's success.

ANSWER: CHRISTIANITY WAS ABLE TO SPREAD THROUGH PUBLIC PREACHING AND THE TRAVEL OF CHRISTIAN CONVERTS TO OTHER LANDS

Traci Boozer

> And he said to them, "Go into all the world and proclaim the gospel to the whole creation."
>
> —Mark 16:15

Unlike the rapid transmission of information in the 21st century, the dissemination of ideas and information took years to span the developing world. One such idea—Christianity—was in no way different. By word of mouth and the tenacity of its followers, Christianity quickly grew into one of the world's most influential and powerfully organized religious groups. By the fourth century CE, the nascent religion of the first century had become the dominant religion of the ancient world with the religious conversion of Constantine I (c. 272–337).

Regarded as heretics, early Christians were persecuted by Romans and followers of Judaism. Romans believed Christianity was a subversive religion intent on overthrowing the government while Judean leaders, such as Herod Agrippa (c. 10 BCE–44 CE) believed Christianity to be subversive to Judaism. Christian martyrs, executed for their beliefs and their attempts to convert others, were used as examples to discourage the spread of the new religion. While punishment and death may have created obstacles for Christians, history has shown us the threat of such actions did not deter or stop the spread of Christianity.

An important component in the spread of Christianity during the first century CE was the use of public preaching and philosophical argument. Used by the leaders of the movement, public displays of rhetoric and open-air preaching were a means to gain attention for Christian teachings. Early leaders and followers of Christianity traveled throughout the Mediterranean, gathering in open-air markets, Jewish synagogues, and village centers to preach their specific brand of religion. Perhaps one of the most well-known leaders of the Christian movement, and considered by many historians to be the second founder of Christianity, was Paul of Tarsus (c. 5–c. 67). A Roman Pharisee by birth, Paul had been a strong opponent of Christianity, but following his own conversion to Christianity (c. 31–36) he would eventually use his knowledge to spread the religion across the Mediterranean world.

Paul's first mission (c. 46–49) took him to Galatia (modern-day Turkey), the second mission (c. 50–52) was to Greece, and the third mission (c. 53–58) found him returning to previous sites in Asia and Greece. It is in the New Testament books attributed to Paul that he describes his missions to teach all people—Jews, Romans, Greeks, anyone who would listen—about the religious teachings of a man named Jesus from Nazareth. What made the places Paul traveled to important was not only the number of people potentially exposed to Paul's teachings but also the nature of those places being located on trading routes, ensuring a large cross-section of people. Traders and artisans from Egypt, Greece, Italy, and beyond would be exposed to Paul's preaching of Christianity and in turn provide an opportunity for Paul's messages to be carried back to those places.

The use of rhetoric, or persuasive argument to spread the message of Christianity, is seen in such instances as the *First Apology* (c. 155–157) of Justin Martyr (c. 100–165) to the Roman Emperor Antoninus Pius (86–161). In the

Apology, Justin argues and defends the merits of Christianity by explaining its rituals and meanings in an attempt to change the way Pius reacts to Christians. By using intellectual and reasoned discourse rather than emotional reaction, Justin clarifies the methodology of Christianity and addresses criticisms of the religion. In his argument, Justin reveals there are those who say they are Christians and are capable of misdeeds, but not all Christians are capable of misdeeds; therefore punishment should be meted out based on the individual and not their religious affiliation.

While both public preaching and use of philosophical arguments proved to be useful methods, the use of the public sphere as a way of reaching larger audiences would eventually begin to fall out of favor as Roman rulers began to create restrictions for preaching and escalate the persecution of Christians. With the growing threat of persecution hovering, many Christians found themselves pushed into or voluntarily receding into the background. Without admitting defeat or ceasing their activities, Christians found new ways to practice and demonstrate their religion.

Personal witnessing or evangelism was a powerful yet subtle tool used by Christians to convert others. Simply talking to a nonbeliever and extolling the benefits of Christianity was, at times, enough to change minds. Justin Martyr was one such person, as was Cyprian who converted later in life but who would become the bishop of Carthage not long after his conversion. Each of these men, and countless others, converted to Christianity through casual interactions with believers, and in turn they would become part of the cycle of interaction and conversion.

The socioeconomic character of the ancient world was also an element of the personal evangelism of Christianity. With its message of everlasting salvation and the rewards of an unburdened afterlife, Christianity was appealing to the lower and slave classes, especially women. Early Christian gatherings did not separate women and men but rather allowed for the intermingling of all, creating a more equal environment that those immersed in would share with others.

Another component of personal witnessing was in the way Christians were perceived by others following certain activities or events. A climactic event such as the martyrdom of Perpetua (c. 202), a Christian woman in Carthage who was put to death for her beliefs, or the account of Dionysius, the Bishop of Alexandria, and the Christians he witnesses caring for plague victims without consideration for themselves (c. 252), had a strong impact on bystanders. After witnessing martyrdom or acts of kindness towards believers and nonbelievers alike, observers of Christian behavior were strongly influenced by those actions and sought to gain a more comprehensive understanding of a religion that created bravery in the face of danger and acts of compassion to all.

Later influences in the spread of Christianity would be found in the literature of Christian leaders and their associates. As the number of educated men and women converting to Christianity began to rise there was also an increase in the production of scholarly works in defense of and praising the Christian faith. Theologians in the early centuries of Christianity sought to define Christianity, not by the simple actions of common men and women but rather in a more complex and philosophical manner. The writings of these early Christian thinkers continue to leave their mark on and contribute to Christian doctrine today.

Paul's time spent on his three missions allowed for the creation of new churches in the areas where traveled. Each new church, in turn, gained a stronger following with the continuing spread of Christianity. Those following in Paul's footsteps and using his missions as an example would find cities with large populations offered a greater opportunity to reach large numbers of people than did sparsely populated rural areas.

Each method of the transmission of Christianity had a particular audience to influence. One cannot be said to be more important, but rather some were more effective than others.

From traveling adherents to the eventual establishment of churches throughout the Mediterranean, Christianity gained a foothold that would last until the present.

CLOSING

The methods and reasons for why Christianity spread as it did in the first three centuries is an important topic for scholars of ancient Christianity. It is very rare in the ancient world to have a religious idea begin within a persecuted group and grow into the dominant religion of an empire. Scholars have spent quite a bit of effort in trying to understand how and why this happened, leading to many theories. Some of these focus on the culture of the Christians and how that might have helped spread its message. Others examine the actual message of Christ in trying to explain its popularity.

Prof. Thompson focuses on the culture in which Christianity grew. She notes that in the first century the Christians were being influenced by the Greeks, the Romans, and their own Jewish roots. This is an important point to concentrate on since, as was stated at the beginning of this volume, Christianity grew up in a multicultural context. Prof. Thompson approaches the problem through this lens. The Christians had to adapt their message using the language of the majority of the people in the east, which was Greek. They also had to use Greek philosophical terms to help non-Jewish people understand the basic message of Christ. The Christians also had similar structures like the *ecclesia* (the church), which would have been very familiar to the Greek and Roman population, especially when they compared it to their *collegia*, or the self-help societies. Christianity then did not appear so strange when viewed like this. Prof. Thompson ends her article by examining the important role that women played in terms of helping to spread Christianity.

Ms. Boozer tackles the same problem but in a different way. She examines the methods that Christians used to spread their message. As she rightly points out, preaching in public was one of the more successful ways to convert people to Christianity. Public teaching/preaching was very common in the Roman and Greek world, so when a Christian like Paul taught in the public square, it would have been accepted as a normal way of broadcasting a message. She also makes the argument that this method of teaching then spread outwards to other areas, and, just as important, people began to also help Christianity become popular through the written word. As Ms. Boozer points out, persecution became the way that the Roman government attempted to stop the growth of popularity. This made it very difficult for preachers to stand in the middle of a city or village and talk about Christ. The public message then was spread in a more private way by word of mouth.

DOING MORE

There are many sources available on the topic of how and why early Christianity spread. Below you will find a list of books, journal articles, Web sites, videos, and other online materials.

BOOKS AND JOURNAL ARTICLES

Arlandson, James M. *Women, Class, and Society in Early Christianity: Models from Luke-Acts.* Grand Rapids, MI: Baker Academic, 1994.

Barnett, Paul. *Jesus & the Rise of Early Christianity: A History of New Testament Times.* Downer's Grove, IL: IVP Academic, 2002.

Barnett, Paul. *The Birth of Christianity: The First Twenty Years.* Grand Rapids, MI: William B. Eerdmans, 2005.

Cameron, A. *The Mediterranean World in Late Antiquity: A.D. 395–600.* London: Routledge, 1993.

Cameron, A. *Christianity and the Rhetoric of Empire: The Development of Christian Discourse* (Sather Classical Lectures). Berkeley: University of California Press, 1994.

Dowley, Tim. *Introduction to the History of Christianity*, 2nd ed. Minneapolis: Fortress Press, 2014.

Esler, P. F. *The Early Christian World.* London: Routledge 2001.

Fox, R. L. *Pagans and Christians.* New York: HarperSanFrancisco, 1986.

Jeffers, J. S. *The Greco-Roman World of the New Testament Era: Exploring the Background of Early Christianity.* Downer's Grove, IL: IVP Academic, 1999.

Klauck, H. J. *The Religious Context of Early Christianity: A Guide to Graeco-Roman Religions* (Studies of the New Testament and Its World). Minneapolis: Fortress Press, 2003.

Kraemer, R. S., and M. R. D'Angelo, eds. *Women and Christian Origins.* Oxford: Oxford University Press. 1999.

Markus, R. A. *Christianity in the Roman World.* New York: Charles Scribner's Sons, 1974.

Matthews, Shelly. *First Converts: Rich Pagan Women and the Rhetoric of Mission in Early Judaism and Christianity.* Stanford, CA: Stanford University Press, 2002.

Meyers, E. M. "The Challenge of Hellenism for Early Judaism and Christianity." *Biblical Archaeologist* 55, no. 2 (June 1992): 84–91.

Pelikan, J. *Christianity and Classical Culture: The Metamorphosis of Natural Theology in the Christian Encounter with Hellenism.* New Haven, CT: Yale University Press, 1993.

Pernot, Laurent. "The Rhetoric of Religion." *Rhetorica: A Journal of the History of Rhetoric* 24, no. 3 (Summer 2006): 235–54.

Schmuch, Enid. "Exploring the Mediterranean Background of Early Christianity." *Biblical Archaeologist* 46, no. 1 (Winter 1983): 43–48.

Torjesen, K. J. *When Women Were Priests: Women's Leadership in the Early Church and the Scandal of Their Subordination in the Rise of Christianity.* New York: Harper-SanFrancisco, 1995.

VIDEOS

"Christianity from Judaism to Constantine." *Crash Course World History* #11. https://www.youtube.com/watch?v=TG55ErfdaeY.

"From Jesus to Christ: The First Christians." https://www.youtube.com/watch?v=kZPKCDOeyMg.

"Early Christianity : Documentary on the Spread of Christianity in Rome's Reign (Full Documentary)." https://www.youtube.com/watch?v=ZYCsfJdajgQ.

"The Early Christianity (From a Cult to a Religion)—How the First Christians Changed the World." https://www.youtube.com/watch?v=vHqxmgdZP68.

"The Life of Paul the Apostle." https://www.youtube.com/watch?v=3jXGPS7P4cs.

WEB RESOURCES

"In the Fullness of Time: Christianity in the Roman Empire." http://mason.gmu.edu/~ddonald/typeassignment/index3.htm.

"When Did Christianity Begin to Spread?" http://www.biblicalarchaeology.org/daily/biblical-sites-places/biblical-archaeology-sites/when-did-christianity-begin-to-spread/.

PODCASTS

"Religions of the Ancient Mediterranean." http://www.philipharland.com/Blog/2009/08/31/podcast-series-3-diversity-in-early-christianity-heresies-and-struggles/.

"The History of the Early Church Podcast." https://historyoftheearlychurch
.wordpress.com/.

QUESTION 3: WHY WAS CHRISTIANITY POPULAR?

Since the beginning of Christianity people have often wondered why
Christianity was so popular. After all, it is founded on the teachings of a person the Roman government considered to be a criminal and who was put to
death because of these very teachings. Jesus and the early disciples were not
influential in terms of their social status: Jesus, as far as we can tell, was
brought up in a fairly poor household, and all of the disciples were poor as
well. Christianity began in the town of Nazareth, which was considered to be
small even at the time of Jesus. Despite these drawbacks, Christianity thrived
in the later centuries. Why? That is the question this section will attempt to
answer.

Scholars have long questioned why Christianity was as popular as it was. It
is an interesting question because today Christianity is the most popular religion on the planet with billions of believers. All of this started out in the first
couple of decades of the first century CE and grew from there. Early Christian writers certainly commented on its growth. Paul, the earliest writer of
what we call the New Testament, believed that it was purely the message of
Christ and the other disciples that led to its popularity. Another early example
was written by Polycarp, the bishop of Smyrna (died in the 150s CE) in a
letter to the Christian community in Philippi, which begins:

> I have greatly rejoiced with you in our Lord Jesus Christ, because you have fol-
> lowed the example of true love [as displayed by God], and have accompanied,
> as became you, those who were bound in chains, the fitting ornaments of
> saints, and which are indeed the diadems of the true elect of God and our Lord;
> and because the strong root of your faith, spoken of in days long gone by, en-
> dures even until now, and brings forth fruit to our Lord Jesus Christ, who for
> our sins suffered even unto death, [but] "whom God raised from the dead,
> having loosed the bands of the grave." "In whom, though now you see Him
> not, you believe, and believing, rejoice with joy unspeakable and full of glory";
> into which joy many desire to enter, knowing that "by grace you are saved, not
> of works," but by the will of God through Jesus Christ.

The message of Christianity that made it popular was about love,
about Jesus who died for humanity's sins, and about being saved. The answer
given as to why Christianity was popular was repeated over and over again
by most Christian writers in the first four centuries (and in many respects
still continues today). For many of them the answer to this question was

self-evident—if you wanted to have eternal life, then you should believe in Jesus. But scholars today look for more concrete reasons to explain its popularity.

One early very influential book, written in 1949 by Rudolf Bultmann and titled *Primitive Christianity in Its Contemporary Setting*, examines this question and concentrates on the message of Jesus (especially the teachings on the end of time). He also looks at the mixing of different ideas that led to its popularity. Bultmann's ideas were also used as a base for books that came later. R. A. Markus, in his book titled *Christianity in the Roman World* (published in 1974), looks at the adaption of Greek philosophy to the Christian message as a cause for Christianity's popularity. He also looks at the reasons for why it became a "respectable" religion—primarily because there were Christians in high-level positions in Roman society. Some scholars also pointed out that Christianity grew in popularity because the native Roman and Greek religions were on the decline (these are usually called "pagan" religions). Another clear reason for the popularity of Christianity, at least starting in the 300s CE, was that the Roman emperor became Christian: Emperor Constantine I. His policies were directed at making Christianity legal and at making the so-called pagan religions more difficult to practice. Constantine gave legitimacy to Christians and made it possible for many others to join without fear of persecution.

Other scholars still answer the question of why Christianity was popular with these very same answers from the earlier scholars, but they have also begun to ask if there were other reasons for its popularity. Some have discussed the idea that early Christian communities opened their doors to many different kinds of people—rich and poor, slave and free, men and women. This was fairly unusual in that time and certainly went a long way in getting people to join. Related to this, more and more scholars are focusing on women in early Christianity—what they were doing, why they joined, and why they stayed. The study of women in early Christianity has grown tremendously in the last 50 years. While the inclusion of women into Christianity cannot totally explain its popularity, it goes a long way in explaining why Christianity grew and expanded as it did.

Why Christianity was popular is an important question to ask, especially considering that Christians were a persecuted group during its first three centuries of existence. What would make people join a group where there was a possibility you would be thrown to the lions or thrown out of your community (or synagogue in the case of Jewish converts)? What could explain the attractiveness of the teachings of an obscure preacher from a backwater town like Nazareth? There are many answers to this question, and usually books on the history of early Christianity have to tackle it.

Dr. Gonzales and Dr. Kim answer this question in the following essays. Dr. Gonzales begins by pointing out the reasons Christianity would not have been so attractive to people: that they were persecuted by the Roman state for being antisocial and that their founder, Jesus, was killed in a typically Roman way, crucifixion. These should have been reasons why people *would not* have joined. Dr. Gonzales points out that despite these obstacles, Christianity grew in popularity because it allowed a number of different types of people to join. This included, as Paul stated in Galatians 3:28, Jewish and Greek people, male and female, slave and free. Paul's message in Galatians actually states that when people join Christianity, they are no longer considered parts of these groups—they are all Christian. As Dr. Gonzales states, this was revolutionary for any early religious group. And this was particularly radical in terms of allowing women to take part in the religion, including having positions in the official hierarchy.

Dr. Kim also examines this question, but comes at it from a different angle. He answers it by looking at five different causes, which he identifies as "Socio-Political." The first was due to the personalities of the leaders of the early Christian groups. The second related to the joining of the new religion by people who first belonged to the native Greek and Roman religions. These people were tired of their own religion and looked for something easier to believe in. He finishes his essay by looking at the role that women played, the training that Christians had to go through, and finally, the conversion of Emperor Constantine to Christianity.

ANSWER: CHRISTIANITY WAS POPULAR BECAUSE IT ALLOWED PEOPLE FROM DIFFERENT BACKGROUNDS TO BECOME MEMBERS OF THE FAITH

Eliezer Gonzales

There is no question that Christianity grew rapidly. Rodney Stark has calculated that by 350 CE, Christianity would have represented just over half the population of the Roman Empire. In a time when mass media did not exist, that rate of growth was unprecedented in the ancient world. So just why was Christianity so popular?

Old Ideas

There have been some common ideas in the past about why Christianity was so popular. These ideas are no longer considered valid, because they are not supported by the evidence, and they appear to have too much Christian bias. One of these ideas is that Christianity was successful because of its superior religious doctrines. The difficulty with this idea is that it is very difficult to evaluate the superiority of any religious doctrine in and of itself. For this reason it is better to focus on the impacts of particular religious doctrines for individuals, organizations, and for society. Another view about why Christianity succeeded is that the conditions in the world were ideally suited for the emergence of Christianity. This view was presented by Adolf von Harnack in the early 20th century, and the view is referred to, in Latin, as the *praeparatio evangelica* ("preparation for the gospel"). The flaw with this argument is that Christianity did not arise in a vacuum, but rather in an environment where many alternatives competed for the attention of society. The general social conditions were equally favorable for the emergence of those movements, yet it was Christianity that rose to become widely popular. Another view about why Christianity became popular is that paganism was in decay. People in the first-century Mediterranean world worshipped many gods, and this view says that people didn't believe in those gods anymore and that they were no longer worshipping in the temples as much. However, the evidence points to the reality that paganism was as strong as ever during the time in which Christianity emerged.

Obstacles to Christianity

We have seen that it is not true that Christianity become popular because the conditions were ideal, or because its doctrines were superior, or because paganism was weak. Actually, the opposite was true. Christianity had to face many serious obstacles in its path to becoming popular. First, before the coming of Christianity, the concept of conversion as we understand it was at most exceptionally rare, and essentially unknown, in the ancient world. You could almost say that Christianity "invented" the idea of conversion. If that sounds strange to us, it is because we are not thinking like people in the first-century Mediterranean world. For them, it was unthinkable to totally renounce the religion of your ancestors and to give your exclusive allegiance to a completely different religion. And although Judaism was similar to Christianity in its understanding of conversion, Christianity was much more radical in its idea of conversion.

Second, Christianity directly challenged key aspects of the worldviews of society at the time. That is why Christianity was considered by the Roman Empire as supporting antisocial and criminal behavior. For that reason Christians were viewed with suspicion, and at times severely persecuted. Third, the doctrines of Christianity should have themselves been a deterrent for people in the first-century Mediterranean world, rather than an attractant. The idea that God would come to earth and allow himself to be crucified was totally ridiculous, as was the idea of the resurrection. What made all of this even worse was that Christianity then claimed that salvation was through Jesus alone. That sort of strict religious exclusivity was unknown in the first-century Mediterranean world. All of these things were huge obstacles to Christianity being popular.

All of this brings us back to the question of why it was that Christianity succeeded and became popular. Larry Hurtado uses a business model to talk about the rise of Christianity, so that Christianity had to compete for attention in a religious market, and its products and services had to be perceived favorably in relation to whatever else was on offer. I want to focus especially on Pauline Christianity, by which I mean the churches that were founded by or that were in the tradition of the apostle Paul. The reason for this is that the Western Christian tradition derives significantly from that tradition. What I write here was specifically true for Pauline Christianity, and more generally for the rest of Christianity as well. But it was the apostle Paul who specially championed the ideas that I am going to mention.

What Did Christianity Offer That Was New?

If we put aside specific religious doctrines, the new element that Christianity offered was what we might call "moral universalism." Benhabib defines moral universalism as the idea that "all human beings, regardless of race, gender, sexual preference, ethnic, cultural, linguistic, and religious background, are to be considered moral equals and are therefore to be treated as equally entitled to moral respect." To see how radical the inclusiveness of Christianity was, we must understand that for people in the ancient world, it was self-evident that people were not created equal. The great philosophers Plato and Aristotle saw the social hierarchy as absolutely necessary. For someone to leave his or her allotted station in life was a threat to the very fabric of society. Aristotle, for example, taught that it was natural for human beings to rule over animals, and in the same way, for masters to rule over slaves, and for men to rule over women.

Paul's thinking does not start with the distinctions that divide people from one another, but from what is common to all. The point held in common by all humanity is its distance from God and its failure to respond to him. All people had the same problem, and everyone needed the same solution. This kept early Christianity from becoming elitist, so it could keep growing. Paul famously wrote, "There is neither Jew nor Greek, there is neither slave nor free man, there is neither male nor female; for you are all one in Christ Jesus" (Galatians 3:28). The apostle Paul took this position because he believed that the death of Jesus Christ on the cross had changed everything about the reality of this world. He taught that the people in the Christian communities had to be part of a "new creation" (2 Corinthians 5:17) that lived by very different rules than those of the society of his day.

In the first-century Mediterranean world, religion was essentially racially and ethnically based. This meant that particular religions were closely identified with particular racial and ethnic groups, so that people followed the religious preferences of their parents. Early Christianity claimed to be a truly universal religion, in which there was no distinction of culture or race. Within the Christian community, differences of race and ethnicity no longer counted. People in the Roman Empire were very rigidly divided according to social status as well. It is true that there were some other cults and societies apart from Christianity where people of different social status could associate together, but Christian communities allowed a breadth of participation for people of all classes that could not be found elsewhere. Society was also divided very strictly according to gender lines, although in the centuries before Christianity, there had been a gradual liberation of women in the Greco-Roman world, at least in theory if not really much in practice. The reality was that Roman and Greek culture traditionally totally excluded women from all public or political roles.

The letters of the apostle Paul make it clear that his churches accepted women into full participation in their communities, and even in key leadership roles. They prayed and prophesied, and they taught and led in the various functions of the Pauline communities. Pagans such as Celsus and Porphyry mocked the Christians for allowing women to lead in such roles. While it is true that Paul places some restrictions on women, it was for the protection of the communities within the culture of that time. Paul is particularly concerned with issues of immortality—both in relation to women and to men. Of course, "moral universalism" is a modern term. This means that we cannot expect Paul, for example, to understand it or to have put it in practice in the same way that we would try to do as people living in the 21st century. And so some people have accused Paul of actually repressing women, which was not the case at all.

Conclusion

What Christianity did was to allow people to enter a new kind of community. It is obvious that the early Christian communities were sufficiently attractive to grow rapidly. Their universalism would have appealed to the disenfranchised of society, whether they were disenfranchised on the basis of race, social status, or gender. Similarly, the cogent universalism of the Pauline communities would have appealed to the elite classes on philosophical grounds. The creation of such communities was unquestionably difficult, and the letters of Paul demonstrate just how difficult it was. They are full of bitter conflicts over his ideas and methods. However, they succeeded. We know that they succeeded because the Christian church survived and became popular. It is true that the Christian church retreated from its origins and became more organized and hierarchical over time. As it did that, some of the emphasis on moral universalism disappeared, and at times the Christian religion has been a repressive force in society. However, in the ancient world, Christianity was a tremendously liberating force. This has to be considered as an important reason why Christianity became popular. We are still feeling the impact of that today in our 21st-century Western culture.

ANSWER: CHRISTIANITY BECAME POPULAR BECAUSE OF SOCIAL AND POLITICAL FACTORS

David W. Kim

The beginning of the practice of Christianity was problematic because early Christians were regarded as a sectarian group of Judaism among Jews, Romans, and Greeks. The followers of Jesus had to endure repression and persecution under the authority and power of the Roman emperors. However, Christianity did not lose its trace in history. The people of the fourth century witnessed the Christianization of the Greco-Roman world and beyond. Why was Christianity still popular among the ancient Mediterranean people after long suffering? The answer to this issue cannot be easily gained from general statistics, but by a sociopolitical approach one may be able to understand the survival of this marginal belief and religious efforts in that multiple factors of "leadership," "new teaching of afterlife," "gender," "catechumenate," and "legitimation by Constantine" reversed the social status of early Christians in the first four centuries. The narratives of various ancient texts support this perspective, including 1 Corinthians 15, Galatians 1, Acts 6–8, Pliny the Younger's *Letters* 10. 96–97, *Didache*, *Epistle to Diognetus*, Athenagoras's *Plea*, and *Mystagogue*.

The Sociopolitical Endeavors in the Greco-Roman Empire

The work of earliest Christianity was primarily performed to "the indigenous Jews who spoke Aramaic and the Greek-speaking, bilingual Jews who had lived abroad in the Hellenistic cultures in the Jewish diaspora."[1] The early church of the first two decades after the death of Jesus and the second half of the first century was not individually operated, but the sacrificial efforts of the apostolic leadership led the new Christian movement at first. Their direct and indirect experiences with Jesus were the key sources for passion and compassion over different regions and ethnic groups. The apostolic leadership was divided into four different groups.[2] The 12 disciples were led by Peter (Cephas) in Galilee and the surrounding regions (1 Corinthians 15: 3–8). James, the brother of Jesus, took care of Hebrews, called "the Brethren group," who used Hebrew in the synagogues, spoke Aramaic in their homes, and who tended to separate themselves from Greek society (Galatians 1: 18–19). Meanwhile, Stephen and Philip worked among Hellenists, members of Greek communities (Acts 6–8). They were the descendants of Jewish culture, but the Jewish diaspora adopted the Greek language and culture in the home and in the synagogues. The group of "God-fearers" (Greeks) was the concern of Paul and Barnabas (Acts 4: 34–37). The leaders for Gentiles did not meet Jesus personally. They knew him only through the resurrection vision and the testimonies of the disciples. The last leadership regarded those who were interested in Judaism but who were not proselytes. Although the apostolic leadership was under religious pressure, the courage and boldness of each leader became the invisible impetus to carry on the new faith. The crowds observed the public preaching and miracles, and they marveled and were saved (Acts 2: 41).

Second, the boredom and exhaustion of the Roman citizens with Greek and Roman religions was energized when Christianity began to circulate, because the polytheistic Greek and Roman gods did not concern themselves about the perspective of eternal salvation. Instead, the imperial religions required enormous demands of worship and offering. Each god had his or her set of rules to follow. It was difficult for the people to remember. On the other hand, Christianity demanded less sacrifice in ritual and promised "a well-defined, promulgated afterlife."[3] The essential teaching of Christianity attracted the pagan people who had been disappointed by their native beliefs. The Christian vision of the afterlife, with a simplified monotheism, progressively affected those people and transformed them. As Christians refused to worship the Roman gods and make offerings to them, Christian persecution increased. Nevertheless, the willingness to keep their faith despite death became a witness to potential members. The Christian ideal of redemption intellectually challenged outsiders with the message of salvation.

Third, gender in society was another significant factor in that women performed a crucial role in the spread of the early Christian movement, for the position of women was presumed higher within the Christian community than it was in Greco-Roman societies. The local religions of the era including Judaism comprised an androcentric culture, and females were disrespected even from the time of their birth.[4] On the other hand, Christian doctrine prohibited infanticide, with the condemnation of divorce, incest, marital infidelity, and polygamy. The participation of females in early Christianity is seen in the view that "women were more likely than men to become Christians."[5] There were the middle- and lower-class women, but Brown particularly argues that many of those women were from the upper class in the second and third centuries and that they were able to persuade their husbands to keep the new faith.[6] The proselytization of husband and children were dominantly preceded by the household of wife, mother, aunt, sister, or niece. It is theorized that the pattern of conversion was often that the females of the house were "primary converts" and that their spouses and family members including servants and slaves were "secondary converts" (1 Corinthians 7: 13–14). The feminist influence was also strong in egalitarian house churches, if one considers the case where Pliny the Younger reported to Emperor Trajan that he had tortured two young Christian women "who were called deaconesses (of the early church)" (*Letters* 10. 96–97).

Fourth, the study of the Christian doctrine systematically supported newcomers to understand the primary belief of the new religion. When each Christian brought an unbeliever to the church, the catechumenate (meaning "to instruct someone, especially in the rudiments of a subject and a skill") offered an opportunity to idealize this unique worldview,[7] for there were theological differences between paganism and Christianity.[8] Justin, with the apologists Tertullian, Clement of Alexandria, and Origen, mentioned the publication of *Didache* (*The Teaching of the Twelve Apostles*). There were also the so-called *Epistle to Diognetus*, Athenagoras's *Plea*, and *Mystagogue*. The rigorous training programs reflected the process of conversion and its relation to discipleship.[9] The pattern of the catechumenate became the basic curriculum of the church to convert seekers or converts from paganism to Christianity. The *Apostolic Tradition* of Hippolytus outlines the system of the catechumenate, with three features of "enrolment with sponsorship," "instruction in scripture, doctrine and ethics," and "rites of initiation (baptism, confirmation, and Eucharist)." The practice of the catechumenate promoted the qualitative development of the Church.

Finally, the conversion of Emperor Constantine the Great (306–337 CE) was the official turning point after which Christianity was able to establish its public foundation after 300 years of struggle. Christianity progressively began to affect regional society and culture, but imperial Christianization was ultimately determined by the political efforts of the first Christian emperor who ceased the persecution. The reason Constantine became a Christian in about 312 CE is not certain, whether due to the influence of his mother Helena or whether he adopted it gradually over the course of his life.[10] However, he called the Council of Nicea in 325, at which the Nicene Creed was created by Christians. Constantine also supported the church to build basilicas (including the Church of the Holy Sepulchre and Old Saint Peter's Basilica) and granted privileges to clergy.[11] The investment of Christians to high office was another action due to his faith. Although there is evidence that Constantine did not patronize Christianity alone, the first Christian emperor made laws that forbade Jews to own Christian slaves. The Christian church eventually was declared the state religion in 380 CE. The transformative shift of imperial policy changed the social world of the fourth century remarkably.

Conclusion

Christianity survived and spread all over the world, person to person, family to family, town to town, nation to nation, and empire to beyond. Stark's arithmetic indicates that there were approximately 34 million Christians out of 60 million people (56.5 percent) by the end of the third century.[12] The early church communities were usual in the Mediterranean cities. They not only grew in number, but also in geographic spread. Christians advanced socially as well. The success of the new movement did not happen by a single factor, but rather the multiple environments of the era together induced its achievement.[13] The apostolic sacrifice through martyrdom initially propagated belief in the new religion, while the teachings of Jesus based on salvation within the assurance of the afterlife attracted practitioners of Greek religions who had already been exhausted by heavy obligations. The voluntary and substantial engagement of women played a major role in a personal level of community life. The training programs of the catechumenate subsequently functioned as the professional system that the Church used to guide the proselytes. The legalization of Christianity by Constantine accelerated the social domination of the Jesus movement even beyond the Roman world. Such a historical process, with those five factors, sufficiently demonstrates why Christianity was so popular while the situation of Greco-Roman religions and Judaism degenerated.

CLOSING

Knowing why an ancient religion (or any group for that matter) was appealing to people is an important part of understanding ancient cultures. The study of early Christianity is no different. Christianity started in the first century CE in a small town and today is the largest religion on the planet, with billions of members. There must be reasons to explain why it grew the way it did. The essays above attempt to answer the question of what made Christianity so popular.

For Dr. Gonzales, the openness of Christianity to all people is the key to understanding its popularity in the Roman Empire. Roman society was very hierarchical, and in many cases it was difficult and sometimes socially unacceptable to interact with other social classes, let alone move up from one class to another. Christianity, however, allowed all social classes to join its ranks. It also allowed women to join, regardless of their social position. As Dr. Gonzales states, this openness to all people gave them the freedom to escape their social bonds.

Dr. Kim looks at what he terms "sociopolitical" reasons to explain the popularity of Christianity, and he answers the question by looking deeply into six general categories. Like Dr. Gonzales, Dr. Kim believes that allowing women into Christianity helped to increase its appeal factor. He also examines the structures of Christianity, especially in terms of its leadership. Having an active leadership and preaching to all the different people greatly expanded the broadcasting of the Christian message. Dr. Kim also points out that Christians had a structure in place to help support the new members, and this undoubtedly helped the new members to learn about their religion and encouraged others to join.

DOING MORE

There are many, many sources, both in print and online, on the topic of the popularity of early Christianity. Following the notes there are lists of books used by the scholars above to put their essays together, and I have also included some Web sites, videos, and other online materials that will help you to explore this topic.

NOTES

1. Brox, *History of the Early Church*, 5.
2. Eberts, "Plurality and Ethnicity in Early Christian Mission," 305–21.
3. Ekelund and Tollison, *Economic Origins of Roman Christianity*, 56.
4. Stark, "Reconstructing the Rise of Christianity," 231–39.
5. Stark, "Reconstructing the Rise of Christianity," 233.
6. Brown, *Body and Society*, 151.
7. Sittser, "The Catechumenate and the Rise of Christianity," 181.
8. Esler, *Early Christian World Volume I*, 307.
9. Esler, *Early Christian World Volume I*, 300.
10. Brown, *Rise of Christianity*, 60.
11. Brox, *History of the Early Church*, 46–51.
12. Stark, *Rise of Christianity*.
13. Frend, *Rise of Christianity*.

BOOKS AND JOURNAL ARTICLES

Avalos, Hector. *Health Care and the Rise of Christianity*. Peabody, MA: Hendrickson Publishers, 1999.

Barnett, Paul. *Jesus and the Rise of Early Christianity: A History of New Testament Times*. Downers Grove, IL: InterVarsity, 1999.

Brown, Peter. *The Body and Society: Men, Women, and Sexual Renunciation in Early Christianity*. New York: Columbia University Press, 1988.

Brown, Peter. *The Rise of Christianity*, 2nd ed. Oxford: Blackwell, 2003.

Brox, Norbert. *A History of the Early Church*. London: SCM Press, 1994.

Bultmann, Rudolf. *Primitive Christianity in its Contemporary Setting*. London: Thames and Hudson, 1983.

Eberts, Harry W., Jr. "Plurality and Ethnicity in Early Christian Mission." *Sociology of Religion* 58, no. 4 (1997): 305–21.

Ekelund, Robert B. Jr., and Robert D. Tollison. *Economic Origins of Roman Christianity*. Chicago: University of Chicago Press, 2011.

Esler, Philip F. *The Early Christian World, Volume I*. London: Routledge, 2000.

Finneran, Niall. "Hermits, Saints, and Snakes: The Archaeology of the Early Ethiopian Monastery in Wider Context." *International Journal of African Historical Studies* 45, no. 2 (2012): 247–71.

Frend, W. H. C. *The Rise of Christianity*. Minneapolis: Fortress Press, 1984.

Hazlett, Ian, ed. *Early Christianity: Origins and Evolution to AD 600*. London: SPCK, 1991.

Hurtado, Larry W. *How on Earth Did Jesus Become God? Historical Questions about earliest Devotion to Christ*. Grand Rapids, MI: Wm. B. Eerdmans Publishing Company, 2005.

Shiel, James. *Greek Thought and the Rise of Christianity*. London: Longmans, 1968.

Sittser, Gerald L. "The Catechumenate and the Rise of Christianity." *Journal of Spiritual Formation & Soul Care* 6, no. 2 (2013): 179–203.

Stark, Rodney. "Reconstructing the Rise of Christianity: The Role of Women." *Sociology of Religion* 56, no. 3 (1995): 229–44.

Stark, Rodney. *The Rise of Christianity: A Sociologist Reconsiders History*. Princeton, NJ: Princeton University Press, 1997.

Torjesen, Karen Jo. *When Women Were Priests: Women's Leadership in the Early Church and the Scandal of Their Subordination in the Rise of Christianity*. New York: HarperSanFrancisco, 1993.

Von Harnack, Adolf. *What is Christianity?* Reprint. Eastford, CT, Martino Fine Books, 2011.

WEB RESOURCES

"Christianity and the 'Mystery Religions'." *Early Christian History*. http://www.earlychristianhistory.info/mystrel.html.

"The Rise of Christianity: A Sociologist Reconsiders History." "From Jesus to Christ," *Frontline*. http://www.pbs.org/wgbh/pages/frontline/shows/religion/why/starksociology.html.

"Roman Religion." *Illustrated History of the Roman Empire*. http://www.roman-empire.net/religion/religion.html.

VIDEOS

"The First Christians." *Lost Worlds*. https://www.youtube.com/watch?v=KPsZe5z35Zk&index=6&list=PLybnITJm6U-t_mggbjLgvAQsxEvZJfIN_.

"From Jesus to Christ: The First Christians." *Frontline*. https://www.youtube.com/watch?v=OhJUDhitYlc&index=25&list=PLybnITJm6U-t_mggbjLgvAQsxEvZJfIN_.

"Rise of Christianity." *When Rome Ruled*. https://www.youtube.com/watch?v=jdyJTdf-0CA&index=4&list=PLybnITJm6U-t_mggbjLgvAQsxEvZJfIN_.

"The Bible's Buried Secrets." *National Geographic*. https://www.youtube.com/watch?v=awnFgTNIHEM.

PODCASTS

"Diversity in Ancient Christianity: 'Heresies' and Struggles." *Religions of the Ancient Mediterranean*. http://www.philipharland.com/Blog/2009/08/31/podcast-series-3-diversity-in-early-christianity-heresies-and-struggles/.

Sects and Violence in the Ancient World. https://sawiggins.wordpress.com/podcasts/.

Select Annotated Bibliography

BOOKS AND JOURNAL ARTICLES

Armstrong, Gregory T. "Constantine's Churches." *Gesta* 6 (January 1967): 1–9. This journal article lists and discusses the churches that Emperor Constantine I built, both in and outside of Rome. Armstrong lays out what the problems are for people studying these early churches: inscriptions, which don't cover all of the churches; the lack of written evidence as to who built a specific church and when it was built; and how to figure out if a specific church belongs in the Constantinian period. Although the article consists mainly of listing the churches, the analysis of the problems associated with determining the history of these churches is very important. Armstrong then gives an extensive list of these churches.

Barnes, T. D. "Legislation against the Christians." *Journal of Roman Studies* 51, nos. 1 and 2 (1968): 32–50. Barnes, who is an expert in early Christianity, examines the various laws that were possibly passed by the Roman government and that led to persecution. Barnes is very careful to note that his article does not include modern interpretation of these laws and that he will only focus on laws passed before 250 CE. Barnes then looks at the various laws that might have been passed, starting with Emperor Tiberius, and a possible mention of the divinity of Jesus all the way up to the trials of Christians. The article does contain some Greek and Latin, but Barnes translates some of these for the readers. He comes to the conclusion that it is difficult to find official laws of persecutions of Christians by the Roman authorities.

Barrett, C. K. *The New Testament Background: Selected Documents*, revised and expanded edition. San Francisco: Harper and Row Publishers, 1987. This is a collection of primary texts that does not look at early Christ texts themselves, but at texts that reveal the society in which Christianity was growing (the Roman

Empire) and had come out of (the Greeks). It is a very important collection of texts to read because it helps to make sense of the Christian environment of the early period. Barrett also does a very good job with giving an introduction to each section.

Bettenson, H. ed. *Documents of the Christian Church*, 2nd ed. Oxford: Oxford University Press, 1963. This volume is an excellent collection of primary texts from early Christianity, dating from the beginning up through the current period. It is especially useful for the first part, which focuses on early Christianity. The book contains primary texts from both sides of the issue—those considered to be orthodox and those considered to be heretical.

Bradbury, Scott. "Constantine and the Problem of Anti-Pagan Legislation in the Fourth Century." *Classical Philology* 89, no. 2 (April 1994): 120–39. One problem that surfaces with studying Emperor Constantine I is when exactly did he become a Christian and what type of legislation did he pass to help Christianity. One particular question is whether Constantine banned blood sacrifice, which was used by those who practiced some of the Roman religions. Bradbury argues that it was Constantine himself who started the antipagan legislation that banned blood sacrifice, and he does this by first examining the primary texts, in particular those of Eusebius of Nicomedia, and a body of Roman law titled the Theodosian Laws. After examining the various ancient writers, Bradbury convincingly states that Constantine was very active in suppressing pagan religious practices, especially those involving sacrifices.

Chadwick, H. *The Early Church*, rev. ed. London: Penguin, 1993. Henry Chadwick is another famous early Christian scholar, and this book is a very good introduction to the history of early Christianity. The language is very approachable. Chadwick starts off with a discussion on the Jewish background of Christianity. His book is a bit different from other early Christian histories in that he looks at what is happening on a larger scale. For example, his chapter 7 is titled "Church, State and Society in the Third Century." It is an excellent overview of the problems the church had during this tumultuous period. There are 18 chapters in this book. Chapter 17 is an important chapter titled "The Church and the Barbarians," and the book ends with a chapter on early Christian art and liturgy. The book has an extensive "Further Reading" section.

Frend, W. H. C. *The Early Church*. Minneapolis: Fortress Press, 1991. This is an excellent history of early Christianity by one of the foremost scholars. It is well written and covers the period from the beginnings up through the time of Pope Leo in the fifth century. The first chapter is titled "Rome and the Mediterranean" and covers the background history of early Christianity. It is very helpful in terms of the discussion on both what Roman society was like and how early Christianity came out of Judaism. The second chapter is about Rome and Judaism and is a very good introduction to the background of the early Christians. This book is also a good source of information about other books on Christianity with its "Further Reading" section at the end of every chapter. The book is fully footnoted and these footnotes are very useful for learning more about this topic.

Frend W. H. C. *The Rise of Christianity*. Minneapolis: Fortress Press, 1984. This is really the "go-to" book for learning about early Christianity. It is rather large (1,022 pages, including the bibliography and the indices). Frend, as in his earlier *The Early Church*, starts the book off with an excellent discussion on Jewish history and how the early Christian community came out of Judaism. The book begins in 587 BCE and goes up to the Byzantine Empire in the early 600s CE. This book contains much more detail than *The Early Church*, and it should also be noted that it is a totally different book. The one bonus of *The Rise of Christianity* is a very detailed timeline towards the end of the volume.

Fritsch, Charles T. *The Qumran Community: Its History and Scrolls*. New York: Macmillan, 1956. Although this is an older book, Fritsch includes a very good breakdown of the history of the community at Qumran and, in particular, does a good job describing the archaeology of the area. There are certainly newer books detailing newer archaeological finds, but *The Qumran Community* sets the stage for the other books. He spends quite a bit of time discussing the texts found in the caves at Qumran.

Gray-Fow, Michael J. G. "Why the Christians? Nero and the Great Fire." *Latomus* 57, no. 3 (July–September 1998): 595–616. In this article Gray-Fow examines why Nero would have been interested in persecuting Christians and how and when Nero would have heard about this group. He does a great job looking at the historical background of Nero, from when he was growing up until he was emperor, for evidence on how Nero would have known about the Christians. Gray-Fow makes the argument that some of Nero's early contacts were anti-Jewish and that at this stage Roman officials may not have known about the differences between the Jewish and Christian religions. He also spends quite a bit of time arguing that there were probably Christian slaves in Nero's household, which would have helped to inform Nero.

Kaatz, K. W. *Early Controversies and the Growth of Christianity*. Santa Barbara, CA: ABC CLIO, 2012. This book is an examination of the various problems that plagued early Christians, starting with Paul. Paul had many problems with getting people to listen to his message including the main difficulty of not being an original apostle of Jesus, yet still calling himself an apostle. The book ends with an examination of the rise of the bishop in the fourth century and in particular some of the problems various bishops like Ambrose and Augustine had when they were trying to spread their faith.

Kaatz, K. W., ed. *Voices of Early Christianity: Documents from the Origins of Christianity*. Santa Barbara, CA: Greenwood, 2013. This book is a collection of primary texts that help readers to understand early Christianity. The collection starts with a section titled "Early Christian Life" and then examines a number of different topics such as "Early Christian Women," "Persecution," and "Church and Politics." The volume was created as a workbook for students, so it contains a historical background to each text, how it was received by Christians, various questions students can think about after reading the primary texts, and a section titled "Topics to Consider." Each chapter contains a "Further Reading" section.

MacMullen, Ramsay. *Christianizing the Roman Empire: AD 100–400*. New Haven, CT: Yale University Press, 1984. The growth of Christianity throughout the Roman Empire has always been a topic interesting to historians. Why did it grow so quickly? What were the factors that helped that growth? MacMullen tackles these very questions. His first chapter is very useful in terms of understanding where he is going with the book: it will be a work of history and not theology. This first chapter sets out, in detail, to explain the differences. Of course, if you are going to study the growth of Christianity, you must first understand the Roman world, and MacMullen's second chapter discusses what the non-Christian Romans believed in their own religions. The very important chapter 6, titled "Nonreligious Factors in Conversion," in particular looks at the issue of money. The book ends with a discussion on people who were converted by force, which is a timely topic in today's world.

McCane, Byron R. "Simply Irresistible: Augustus, Herod, and the Empire." *Journal of Biblical Literature* 127, no. 4 (Winter 2008): 725–35. McCane's article is a very good example of how historians view some topics. McCane argues that modern scholarship on King Herod is now viewing him differently than older scholarship. Some modern scholars see Herod as a king who did the best he could under the circumstances, while older scholars saw him as a horrible person. He was seen as being terrible primarily because of the story found in the New Testament that Herod had killed all Jewish children under the age of two to prevent Jesus from becoming the future king of the Jews. Part of the reason for this change is that there have been more archaeological sites discovered, which helps to round out the picture of King Herod. Another reason for this change of heart was that Herod is now seen as being more Roman than he was viewed earlier.

Moule, C. F. D. *The Birth of the New Testament*, 3rd ed. London: Adam and Charles Black, 1981. This book focuses primarily on the first century when the Christians were just getting organized. In particular Moule examines the creation of Christian scripture, or the New Testament. He does this by looking at various subjects such as the impact of the Jewish scriptures (the Old Testament) on early Christians and how persecution of the church affected the writings. The last chapter (before the Conclusion) is extremely important in that it examines how all of the various early Christian writings were collected and put into a usable collection that we now call the New Testament.

Musurillo, Herbert. *Acts of the Christian Martyrs*, Volume 2. Oxford: Clarendon Press, 1972. This is the book to read if you are interested in learning about Christian martyrs. Musurillo has collected many primary texts on this particular subject, giving both the original language and a translation. He put the 28 texts in chronological order, starting with *The Martyrdom of Polycarp* and finishing with *The Testament of the Forty Martyrs or Sebaste*. The book also begins with a detailed look at the manuscript history. This is the second volume—the first volume is titled *Acts of the Pagan Martyrs* and is another excellent volume of primary texts.

Quasten, J. ed. *Patrology*, Volumes 1–4. Allen, TX: Christian Classics, 1983. While there are many books that are made up of primary texts, there are very few books that detail the authors and the contents of early Christian primary texts. Quasten's book is the best introduction to nearly every early Christian writer. He gives a very detailed account of the history of the manuscripts, the history of the author, the texts that a particular author has written, and then breaks down each text by category (such as ecclesiology and Christology). His books cover four volumes, stretching from the beginnings of Christianity up through the fourth century.

Stark, Rodney. "Reconstructing the Rise of Christianity: The Role of Women." *Sociology of Religion* 56, no. 3 (1995): 229–44. Stark's article argues that women were extremely important in the spread of Christianity. He questions why Christian women were afforded higher status in their communities, especially when you compare the status of pagan women in their own communities. He argues that more women would have joined Christianity in the first place and their sheer numbers would have helped them in their social status within Christian groups. Their social status was increased in part because the Christians rejected abortion and infanticide (the killing of children); widows were highly respected and were not expected to remarry as in the pagan culture; and Christian women married at a later age and had more of a choice in their spouses than their pagan counterparts.

Stevenson, J., ed., revised by W. H. C. Frend. *Creeds, Councils and Controversies: Documents Illustrating the History of the Church, AD 337–461*. Grand Rapids, MI: Baker Academic, 2012. Primary texts are extremely important to read since these are the writings from the ancient Christians. They are also important because these are the texts that historians use in order to write their histories. This book contains 264 texts, starting with a text about Athanasius (the bishop of Alexandria) and ending with a letter written by St. Patrick. Like many primary source books, it is sometimes the case that the entire text is not included. This is unfortunate, but necessary to keep the size of the book down. There are, however, excellent notes included for all of the texts, and these are very useful to read in order to understand the backgrounds of some the works. The book ends with a description of the authors of these writings, along with a "Further Reading" section and a very good timeline.

Tabbernee, W., ed. *Early Christianity in Contexts: An Exploration across Cultures and Continents*. Grand Rapids, MI: Baker Academic, 2014. This book contains a number of essays written by various early Christian scholars. It is a book about the material remains of early Christians: mosaics, tombs, churches, and so on. The book's main goal is to examine these artifacts in the contexts in which they were created, which includes looking at the society, the economy, and the various other religions that existed side-by-side with Christianity. The geographical range of the book spreads from Asia to Britain.

Thompson, J. W. *The Church According to Paul: Rediscovering the Community Conformed to Christ*. Grand Rapids, MI: Baker Academic, 2014. This new book is a great addition to the discussion around Paul and his work to bring as many people to Christ as possible. His book looks in great detail at the writings of Paul and recreates the churches that Paul had a hand in making. It is a very good book for taking apart these letters in the New Testament and seeing how a historian/ theologian puts together a history of the early Christian communities. His focus is to look at the various passages in the Pauline epistles that discuss the church itself, or ecclesiology (the study of the church). His book also ties in what happened in ancient Christianity with how this information can affect the modern church.

Wallace, R., and W. Williams. *The Three Worlds of Paul of Tarsus*. New York: Routledge, 1988. This book is an excellence source for material on the cities that the apostle Paul visited on his journeys. The book begins by looking at the geography of where Paul traveled, and then has an excellent section on how people traveled during this period. The authors examine each city in terms of its history and the history of its population. It is a great source for background information on early Christianity.

VIDEOS

"History of St. Peter's Basilica." http://www.history.com/videos/history-of-saint -peters-basilica#history-of-saint-peters-basilica.

    This History Channel Web site contains a few short videos on the history of St. Peter's Basilica, along with videos on the history of the Vatican and on the Vatican Archives.

"Rise of Christianity." https://www.youtube.com/watch?v=jdyJTdf-0CA&index=4&list =PLybnITJm6U-t_mggbjLgvAQsxEvZJfIN_.

    This is an episode of National Geographic's *When Rome Ruled*. It is a very good video that explains how Christianity spread from a small area in Palestine to conquer the Roman Empire in the 300s CE. The video begins by explaining that Roman authorities would have known little about Jesus and his crucifixion. It does a good job explaining the Roman religion and how different it was from Christianity. The video examines the trials and tribulations that the Christians suffered and ends by looking at the rise of Emperor Constantine I, the first Christian emperor.

"The First Christians." https://www.youtube.com/watch?v=KPsZe5z35Zk&index =6&list=PLybnITJm6U-t_mggbjLgvAQsxEvZJfIN_.

    This episode of *Lost Worlds* does a good job examining Christians and Christianity in the first century CE. It tries to recreate the Roman society from which Christianity sprang and then explain how Christianity could have spread as it did. The video primarily concentrates on Paul and his journeys through Asia Minor. It was on these trips that Paul attempted to create new Christian groups from either the Jewish population or from the Roman pagan community.

"The Jesus Mysteries." https://www.youtube.com/watch?v=cG7jAOxpC8g.

This is a video put together by National Geographic. It tries to explain the history of Jesus. This should be easy since he is the most famous person in early Christianity, but in reality he is still a mystery. The video uses primary texts (especially the New Testament) to put together the timeline of Jesus, from his birth to his crucifixion. The video contains many scholars of Christianity.

WEB SITES

Early Christian Writings. http://earlychristianwritings.com/.
   This is an excellent Web site that is full of primary texts. These start with the New Testament and go up to the middle of the 300s. When you click on one of the texts you also get a wealth of information about the text including a chronology, various translations of the text, a list of books and articles if you want to read more, and a short historical breakdown of each text.
From Jesus to Christ: The First Christians. http://www.pbs.org/wgbh/pages/frontline /shows/religion/.
   This PBS video and Web site is probably one of the best resources on early Christianity. You can watch the entire PBS show, *From Jesus to Christ*, online. There are maps, articles written by scholars in the area of early Christianity, and articles on Christian archaeology. You can also listen to the audio of the shows. You can see the episodes at YouTube as well: https://www.youtube.com/watch?v =OhJUDhitYlc&index=25&list=PLybnITJm6U-t_mggbjLgvAQsxEvZJfIN_.

Index

Boldface page numbers indicate main entries in the encyclopedia.

About the Author and Contributors

KEVIN W. KAATZ is an assistant professor in the Department of History at California State University, East Bay Campus, Hayward, CA. He edited *Voices of Early Christianity: Documents from the Origins of Christianity* (2013), authored *Early Controversies and the Growth of Christianity: From Paul to Augustine* (2012), co-edited *Hegemonius, Acta Archelai ("The Acts of Archelaus")*, *Manichaean Studies* 4 (2001), and has written a number of book chapters on early church history and articles in the field of neurology.

TRACI BOOZER is a graduate student at California State University, East Bay, pursuing her degree in History with an emphasis on teaching. Traci's area of research interest is the Elizabethan Age of England, specifically Queen Elizabeth I and religious reform. Traci currently resides in the Pacific Northwest.

BERNARD DOHERTY is a graduate of Macquarie University. Following his PhD, Doherty was a Postdoctoral Fellow at the Institute for Studies of Religion at Baylor University, where he worked on a series of projects on New Religious Movements in Australia and abroad and on applying social science methodologies to the study of early Christianity. He has published in a number of academic journals including *Journal of Religious History*, *Nova Religio*, *International Journal for the Study of New Religions*, *Alternative Spirituality and Religions Review*, *Phronema*, and *Journal of the Australian Catholic Historical Society*. His research interests are wide ranging and include new religious movements, patristics, Australian religious history, church and state issues, and religion and the media.

ELIEZER GONZALES has a BA(Hons) Dip Ed, a master's degree in Theology, a master's degree in Early Christian History, and a PhD in Early Christian History from Macquarie University in Sydney, Australia. He has authored many articles in popular Christian magazines and peer-reviewed academic theological and historical journals. His doctoral dissertation was also published in 2014, titled *The Fate of the Dead in Early Third Century North African Christianity*.

DAVID W. KIM is a Research Fellow at the School of Culture, History, and Language, Australian National University. He previously did postdoctoral research at New College, University of Edinburgh, and the Institute for Humanities, Seoul National University, South Korea, and lectured at Charles Stuart University in Australia after receiving a PhD (History of Christianity) from the University of Sydney. His research and teaching cover the subjects of the history of Christianity, early Christian texts, New Testament studies, Coptic literature, Gnosticism, Asian history, Korean Christianity, and Diaspora studies. He has written four books and over 15 articles including *The Thomasine Logia: The Genesis of a Jesus Tradition* (Equinox Publishing, 2015), *Religious Transformation in Modern Asia: A Transnational Movement* (Brill, 2015), *Intercultural Transmission in the Medieval Mediterranean* (Continuum, 2012), *Revivals Awaken Generations: A History of Church Revivals* (Sydney, 2007), and several book reviews for the *Journal of Religious History* and *Theology in Scotland*.

ETHAN SPANIER received his PhD at the University of Washington, where he focused on social and cultural changes brought about by the dissolution of the Roman Republic and the advent of the position of emperor during the Principate. He teaches on a wide variety of subjects including the historical religious developments of Judaism, Christianity (both east and west), Zoroastrianism, and Islam. He is currently writing an article on the intersection of Roman militarism with attitudes of elite identity. He teaches at California State University, East Bay; San Francisco State University; and Menlo College.

NANCY THOMPSON is Professor of History at California State University, East Bay, where she teaches classes in the history of Rome, Christianity, and the Middle Ages. Her current research focuses on the religious education of lay Christians in late antique and early medieval Europe.